It's rare to come across a book that gives as much value and insight to the person studying marketing as it does to the practitioner. Whether your career is in digital marketing, growth hacking or business development, this book is for you. If you are an entrepreneur or business owner and your bottom line depends on understanding and embracing digital marketing, this book is for you. In fact, Dawn has a wonderfully easy writing style that makes it easy to both read and absorb, and to me that is really important. There is no point buying a book just for it to sit on the shelf. I wouldn't really call it a book, I'd call it a handbook - and the more you use it, the more impact you'll have; on your customers and your bottom line.

Shaa Wasmund MBE Best Selling Author, Entrepreneur & Speaker

If you want to keep ahead of your competitors in the digital age, then Dawn McGruer's book lays the steps to market your business and revolutionise your online presence - perfect for any age at any stage!

Andy Harrington Sunday Times Best Selling Author of Passion Into Profit *& Founder of The Professional Speakers Academy.*

DYNAMIC DIGITAL MARKETING

DYNAMIC DIGITAL MARKETING

MASTER THE WORLD OF ONLINE AND SOCIAL MEDIA
MARKETING TO GROW YOUR BUSINESS

DAWN MCGRUER FRSA FCIM

WILEY

This edition first published 2020

© 2020 Dawn McGruer.

Registered office
John Wiley & Sons Ltd, The Atrium, Southern Gate, Chichester, West Sussex, PO19 8SQ, United
Kingdom

For details of our global editorial offices, for customer services and for information about how
to apply for permission to reuse the copyright material in this book please see our website at
www.wiley.com.

Wiley publishes in a variety of print and electronic formats and by print-on-demand. Some
material included with standard print versions of this book may not be included in e-books or
in print-on-demand. If this book refers to media such as a CD or DVD that is not included in the
version you purchased, you may download this material at http://booksupport.wiley.com. For
more information about Wiley products, visit www.wiley.com.

Designations used by companies to distinguish their products are often claimed as trademarks.
All brand names and product names used in this book are trade names, service marks,
trademarks or registered trademarks of their respective owners. The publisher is not associated
with any product or vendor mentioned in this book.

Limit of Liability/Disclaimer of Warranty: While the publisher and author have used their best
efforts in preparing this book, they make no representations or warranties with respect to the
accuracy or completeness of the contents of this book and specifically disclaim any implied
warranties of merchantability or fitness for a particular purpose. It is sold on the understanding
that the publisher is not engaged in rendering professional services and neither the publisher
nor the author shall be liable for damages arising herefrom. If professional advice or other
expert assistance is required, the services of a competent professional should be sought.

Library of Congress Cataloging-in-Publication Data is Available

ISBN 978-1-119-63588-8 (hardback)
ISBN 978-1-119-63593-2 (ePDF)
ISBN 978-1-119-63589-5 (epub)

Cover Design: Wiley

Set in 10/14.5pts Palatino LT Std by SPi Global, Chennai, India

Printed in Great Britain by TJ International Ltd, Padstow, Cornwall, UK

10 9 8 7 6 5 4 3 2 1

CONTENTS

ACKNOWLEDGEMENTS

I'd like to acknowledge all of the incredibly inspiring people I have met throughout my life; from people I have shared a journey of professional development, to those in my business network.

My first book was published nearly 20 years ago – *Character Building* – which seems a distant memory. Although it focused on overcoming adversity and seeing the negatives of life as a building block to push through, it is oddly closely connected to the inception of this book.

This book stemmed from working with over 25,000 customers who have been trained and certified through my digital marketing academy – Business Consort – and it wouldn't be possible for me to share my knowledge without the help of my team too.

I'd like to make an extra special acknowledgement to the support of my family because, as any entrepreneur or business owner will know, growing and scaling a business does take effort and determination.

The good news is that I was determined to succeed, and I have successfully grown my business year on year with a team of 17 to support me. Yes, I followed my dreams – and yes, achieving my goals has resulted in some pretty amazing accolades and opportunities – but this has come at a cost and has meant a lot of travelling and time away from loved ones.

Having peers to inspire and bounce ideas off has been crucial to researching and developing unique digital strategies. In particular, professional networks of like-minded professionals at The Royal Society of

Art, Manufacture and Commerce, Chartered Institute of Marketing, and Professional Speakers Academy has been invaluable to my continuous professional development.

I have always felt that the key to success is to learn from those who are successful. Over the years, I have followed many people in a range of disciplines and watched what they do and strived to emulate their successes in my own field. I feel that I am constantly evolving and every single day I am growing as a person. Running a business isn't just about the money, it is crucial to achieve a work–life balance too and understand what it is that makes you happy and what constitutes as success to you. Finding a mentor and inspirational figure is great place to start, and Dr Chery Chapman who runs Find My Why Foundation has been my mentor for the past year; she must have done a pretty good job because I won **Female Speaker of the Year at The Professional Speaker Awards**!

Sunday Times Best Seller, Andy Harrington, has been my sell from stage guru, and after investing a week in Dubai to learn direct from him I am proud to say I have not only successfully mastered this art, but I love this new aspect of my skillset.

Continuous professional development is the most empowering area of any successful business along with having the ability to be dynamic in your approach. I feel I am a really pragmatic person who could also be deemed impatient, but you need to harness every part of your personality and use it as a strength. If you wake every day loving what you do and how you do it then this lays a great foundation for you to build on.

I think the biggest epiphany I ever had about marketing my business online was that it is all about visibility. I know this sounds obvious and perhaps a little clichéd, but I don't just mean seeing a brand, products or services, but seeing consistent, frequent content from a person – and by content, I mean video.

I work with many clients who market their business, but when you look at purchase behaviour, it always comes down to the people – people buy based on emotion and people buy people.

I feel that ever since embracing the world of social selling and bringing me and my personality as brand to the forefront of the business as a figurehead, our brand visibility and buy-in has grown exponentially.

I challenge you to find anyone online who is an influencer in their industry who doesn't create video.

Video will make up 82% of all internet traffic in 2021, according to forecasts released by Cisco (Figure 1).[1]

FIGURE 1   The future of video marketing.

There will be people who read this book who have never heard of me, but that doesn't matter as my mission is to develop digital skills each and every day to maximise digital marketing profits to scale and grow a business. My aim is to empower people to be the best at what they do and reap the rewards they deserve, and in particular to also reach today's youth

[1]*Source:* https://www.cisco.com/c/en/us/solutions/collateral/service-provider/visual-networking-index-vni/complete-white-paper-c11-481360.html.

who will be tomorrow's digital marketers, and help them grow and sustain our valuable worldwide economy through driving digital experience.

I may have founded an academy and an agency (among other businesses), but they are only the vehicles to reach my end goal and not what I do: helping businesses increase their online visibility and, ultimately, profits.

'Maximising digital marketing profits to scale and grow YOUR business.'

INTRODUCTION

'If your business is not on the internet, then your business will be out of business.'

Bill Gates, Microsoft founder

The easiest way to describe **digital marketing, is the promotion of a business, product, service, or a brand online.**

Digital marketing harnesses digital technologies, such as the internet and digital channels – as well as devices such as mobile phones, digital display advertising, and other digital platforms.

This book covers **eight powerful ways to market your business online** which focuses on proven strategies that you need to be successful in business today.

So, if you would like to generate more leads and convert more customers, then you will 100% benefit from reading this book.

However, if you not only want to generate more leads and convert more customers, but you also want to **spend less time, less effort, and money reaping those results,** then this book will help you take what you learn and implement, manage, and measure successful digital marketing campaigns.

There has never ever been a more exciting time for digital marketers. **Why?**

Well, the opportunities are literally endless. The great news for digital marketers is that you can generate a lead in a matter of minutes. You can convert customers in a far shorter sale cycle. Results can be almost instant and so can PROFITS!

You can **maximise your digital marketing profits to scale and grow your business** and ultimately be the best digital marketer possible because there is no monopoly online. It doesn't matter what size, shape, or sector you are in: the opportunity exists for all, whether you are new to digital or are an experienced practitioner, because I am going to share proven strategies, tools, technologies, and tips that will revolutionise your digital marketing.

If your marketing is not a revenue generator, then your marketing is not performing.

Digital marketing is ever evolving. But instead of being phased by the fast pace of digital, I encourage you to embrace it because – honestly – when you can take advantage of a trend before your competitor it will give you a massive advantage.

Some people say marketing has changed more in the past 2 years than in the past 50 . . . and I agree!

Now, I think that for us digital marketers, we've got all of this lovely technology; but when people start talking about the latest trends, like Artificial Intelligence and the internet of things, this scares a lot of people.

And your competitors are probably very scared.

So, what's the biggest opportunity for you?

It is when you embrace these new technologies. My aim is to demystify digital marketing and simplify new technologies and show you easy ways that you can start implementing them in your digital campaigns.

Have you ever felt you could achieve more?. . .
Well if the answer is YES then I think YOU are in the right place!

Answer these questions to see if YOU are ready to take action and benefit from what you'll learn in this book.

- Are YOU an entrepreneur, marketer, business owner, or professional who wants to save time, money, or effort when trying to promote your business?

- Fancy hearing about some amazing strategies YOU can use to generate leads quickly?

- Want to be empowered with the knowledge YOU need to get a steady flow of leads every single day?

- Are YOU interested in proven strategies that are 100% guaranteed to deliver success for YOU?

- I spent thousands on learning, researching, and testing but I can SAVE you time, effort, and money. Would YOU like me to take you on a short-cut to success?

- If you want to reap the profits you deserve, reach the pinnacle of your career and become an influencer in your industry – are YOU prepared to invest some of your time with me? I promise you won't regret it.

- This book is not for people who don't want results – and big results – fast. This book is for any marketer, entrepreneur, or business professional ready to make their mark on this world. Is that YOU?

- The people who will remember me will be the people who I shared my knowledge with; the people who were burnt out, frustrated, stressed, and those who wanted to reap the results they deserved – and did; the people who accelerated their careers and landed their ideal job. These are the types of people I want to join me and meet me, to take the next step by reading this book – Is this YOU?

- What are you waiting for? Get reading . . . Are you ready to BECOME THE BEST YOU?

- I think you ARE. So, let's do this – I am going to take you on a non-nonsense journey like no other: It's going to be **Digital Marketing Made Easy!**

The key to digital marketing is matching content to demand at every stage of the sales cycle to nurture leads through to profitable customers.

Who I am and why you should read this book

'Momentum, motivation, and mindset are essential to be successful in the ever-evolving world of Digital Marketing.'
Dawn McGruer FRSA MCIM, Business
Consort founder

I was born during a nursing strike in Glasgow and lived in Scotland until I was 7. Then, due to my Dad's job, we moved to England – and I have lived in Cheshire ever since. Our Business Consort Head Office is based there too, in Wilmslow (Figure 1).

If I am honest, I really wasn't someone who enjoyed school. The regimented approach of private school didn't sit well with me and I felt lessons and the pace of learning were painfully slow.

I never did homework or assignments on time and submitted my GCSE art project on the day of marking (but pulled off a respectable Grade A).

FIGURE 1 Dawn McGruer, multi-award-winning digital marketing speaker, author, and trainer.

I guess I didn't see the purpose of many of the projects and knew I could get by with little work outside class.

I was 'asked to leave' school after attaining 9 GCSEs: 1 A, 5 Bs, and 3 Cs, mainly (I would say), for having an opinion; but probably more likely for not achieving what I was very capable of. I had three days to find a place in college and with waiting lists of 50 plus, I began to panic. But after meeting the principal, I managed to secure a place.

College and I only lasted a year, as I took my exams a year early and only managed 32% attendance. If I thought the learning pace was slow at my previous school, this took it to another level. It wasn't that my school or college was no good, it was my own impatience that prevented me from excelling and reaching my full potential. In short, I was very bored; and although I had many friends at school, much of the politics exhausted me.

My family, friends, and colleagues never call me serious, but perhaps they would say I have always been older than my years. By the time I was in college, I already knew that I would thrive in a work environment, because since the age of 14 I'd had a paper round, worked in a sandwich shop, done breakfast shifts and banqueting at a local hotel, and worked nights in a silver service restaurant.

I loved how you could make the job your own, which you may think sounds odd when talking about a paper round, but I realised I loved control – and the harder I worked, the better the benefits.

This type of effort-based logic definitely appealed to me, because after a job as an audiology telephone appointment maker, I landed a job that was way above others of my age at Volvo.

I got promoted in my first month and continued from showroom reception to marketing coordinator. Literally a year later, I got an opportunity to work for a global multinational in the construction industry, and at the ripe old age of 18 fell into pretty much anything that crossed the realms of running a business, as it was their first UK division and an amazing learning curve.

My job role evolved into a strange mix of IT and Marketing, and after doing all my Microsoft Engineering and Developer exams, I had learned to code – and my career launched as a programmer/tech geek. I was even wiring patch panels and organising category 5 cabling.

I am still not entirely sure how that even came about, but it wasn't long until I decided that IT and programming weren't really my lifelong ambition, and so I embarked on a journey of discovery into the world of psychology and marketing.

In 1996, I took my CIM exams and learnt from an array of businesses like Marks and Spencer. who were on my course. It was a whole new world, but a world that definitely sparked a passion.

My job then took me to exhibitions around Europe and found me promoted to UK Marketing Manager. I also managed to gain a scholarship with Newcastle College and study around 12 diplomas across marketing, business performance, coaching, and NLP (neuro linguistic programming).

Then, four years later in 2000 I took a giant leap; probably clouded by my own ambition, arrogance, and eagerness, to set up my own agency – Aurora Marketing. At just 21, I am not sure this was ever going to be the easiest path, but as hard as it was, I still feel that it was worth the pain.

It was a slow slog and required getting £5000 worth of funding from the Princes Trust. I turned up for that initial interview wearing odd coloured tights (I thought they were black, but it turns out in daylight they were red . . .) but nevertheless I got my place on the Enterprise programme.

I rented my first office on the second floor of the old cinema, 'The Rex', overlooking the centre of Wilmslow in Cheshire – which has gone full circle and has actually re-opened as a cinema! The rates were higher than the rent and my landlord was an extremely endearing old man whose eccentric ways were simply intriguing, but I think he saw my drive and worked with me to make the rental agreement work. The type of people I met along my way were all part of the journey and just added to the experience, and helped form the rich tapestry of life I feel I have been part of.

If I died tomorrow, I really would feel I had packed in as much as possible; but this isn't to say it was all easy, because I also feel I have lived the hardest, and sometimes most lonely life. Not because I have ever been alone, but because an entrepreneur's journey is lonely.

You are the heart and soul of your business, and when you take a blank sheet of paper and start your own business it's never going to be easy. I can honestly say that at times I felt like giving up, but for me the option of getting a 'real job' didn't appeal and, let's be honest, after my experience at school it would be highly likely that it wouldn't be long before I was handed my P45.

So, in the beginning I attended numerous networking events, and experienced a bit of ageism at first when certain members in the older generation wouldn't even honour my presence or shake my hand, but I forged on. I wouldn't be 21 forever!

My biggest breakthrough was setting up the **'Virtual Business Partner Programme'** which was for businesses who neither had their own dedicated marketing resource nor had a budget for agency fees. At a time when the internet was still so new and marketing online was only in its infancy, this provided a huge opportunity – especially with my programming background, because building websites was something I could do and do well.

You see, the thing was that I knew websites didn't just need to look pretty, they also needed to be structured right to appeal to search engines to drive traffic.

I really do think this was when I fully understood that promoting my business day in day out was the wrong approach, and I started working smarter and actually spent a fair bit of time researching who my ideal customer was – rather than looking at what I had to offer and marketing it to 'businesses like SMEs. I really honed in on my target customers' immediate problem that was their burning concern and key focus. This was revolutionary to the success of my business, simple as it was, but I can assure you many business owners and marketers don't put in this time at the beginning.

So, what was the big shift? It was the way I marketed and how I explained what I did. I started to attract my market because I was presenting the problem they had, and showing them a way of overcoming it through demonstrating the step-by-step process of the Virtual Business Partner Programme. I felt like the meetings I was now attending were with well-qualified leads, who were actually my ideal customer, who I didn't have to spend time convincing that the price was worth it. The way I was presenting the solution was with a clear process, timeline, and methodology they could relate to and visualise in their own business, and this made it very easy to convert because we both came out winning!

So, clarity in my mind actually gave clarity and evoked trust in theirs. My clients started referring and I was never spending time endlessly promoting and trying to sell, I was now positioning myself through case studies, writing helpful guides, and sharing my own story because this exact process was how I achieved success.

Then I was approached to **build a social network forum** where my programming background definitely came in handy – it was for a large north west exhibition to connect exhibitors to delegates. It wasn't quite Facebook, more like an online rolodex, but it did the job.

The exhibition ended and then we had 50,000 people ready and waiting to network some more, and eagerly wanting to know what was next.

It was then that I formed **Business Consort in 2005.** I chose the name in irony, thinking about consorting with the enemy, and reviewing synonyms of the word – such as associate, keep company, mix, mingle, go around, spend time, socialise, fraternise, have dealings, rub shoulders.

I felt it lent itself well to our mission, which was to bring professionals together through networking both online and at events across the UK – which was a fantastic in-road to expand our digital agency.

After the extreme success of the **Virtual Business Partner Programme** which was for SMEs and **growth businesses,** we then launched the **platinum club for businesses over 10 million,** sponsored by brands like Coutts, and a business growth club sponsored by HSBC for those trading up to 10 million. We hosted all of our events in car showrooms like Aston Martin, Ferrari, Bentley, etc.

They were styled as business networking with a twist and had a social element, with our flagship cocktail parties attracting around 150 attendees. We had bars, chocolate fountains, driving simulators, and even had our logos spinning around and a toastmaster, with a red carpet welcoming guests. We had business speakers sharing tips and an expert panel to support our Business Consort Community.

Our online portal offered a great route of connecting and referring; it was like an early, less sophisticated version of LinkedIn.

As digital evolved, so did we, as more and more clients wanted us to train their teams to implement the strategies we'd created – hence the organic formation of our **award winning and CIM (Chartered Institute of Marketing) academy of excellence**.

We host courses in London and Manchester and online – worldwide supported by our team of 17 – and have achieved numerous commendations for sustaining a 99% pass rate for digital marketing qualifications. We train about 5000 students a year, and I spend my time training, working with clients' digital strategy, and speaking on stages around the world.

I decided to write this book when I attended the Professional Speaker Awards in 2018 and won an award for Best Female Speaker and Solution Framework of the Year. It just felt like the natural next step to share my **passion to help others profit.**

Key accolades

- Founder and Head Trainer at Business Consort – Digital & Social Media Academy & Agency (Trained & Certified 20K students – 5 million subscribers).

- Speaker – won Best Female Speaker at The Professional Speaker Awards (Figure 2).

- The Dynamic Digital Marketing Model – won Solution Framework of the Year, which is our methodology to maximise digital marketing profits. This is the formula we teach at the digital academy.

 PROFESSIONAL SPEAKER AWARDS 2018
BEST FEMALE SPEAKER

 MARKETING EXCELLENCE AWARDS 2018   FINALIST MARKETER OF THE YEAR

FIGURE 2 Dawn with her awards for Best Female Speaker and Solution Framework of the Year.

- Author of *Character Building* available on Amazon to raise money for charity – the Cancer Research Campaign. (Also the only publication I know that was given the rights to publish Rudyard Kipling's 'If'. It includes stories from 30 + authors, including celebrities like Philip Schofield; it was endorsed by Sir Nigel Hawthorne before he sadly died of cancer.) Those who contributed to it left an accolade in the British Library for their family to remember them by.

- Ranked top 1% by LinkedIn in the digital industry with a network of 45,000.

- Invited to be Lifetime Fellow of The Royal Society for the Encouragement of Arts, Manufactures & Commerce as recognition of expertise in the field of social media marketing.

- Awarded Fellowship of The Chartered Institute of Marketing for extensive experience and expertise in digital marketing over the past 20 years.

The time is now and if you don't act immediately, be fully prepared to see your competitors shine online.

The 90-day plan

Recent research shows that many organisations are doing digital marketing, but they **don't have a strategy or plan.** The reality is that digital marketing is ever evolving, so many businesses haven't responded adequately and are losing out (Figure 3).

This is where the magic happens. Our proven methods shown throughout the book, help structure how to prioritise and approach your marketing.

We have created this **90-day plan** to give you a quick view of your priorities. The rest of the book is structured around this approach. Part I covers Days 1–30. These are key pieces of research and decisions you need to take before moving on to Part II. Don't skip any of the stages – and don't rush through them. Some chapters might look quite short – but this is because they require YOUR input and effort to make them work. So, think hard, research deeply, and carry out the TAKE ACTION NOW tasks that you'll find at the end of each chapter.

Days 1–30

1. Create avatars for your ideal customer

2. Map out your customer journey

3. Carry out market and competitor analysis

4. Develop your proposition

5. Decide on key digital channels for presence

6. Review your internal processes

7. Calculate your ideal sales revenue and profit target per day

8. Review your skills gaps and bridge with training

9. Implement time management and mindset practices

10. Safeguard against digital pitfalls

Once you have done this basic groundwork, you'll be ready to move onto Part II: **Eight Powerful Ways to Market Your Business Online.** Chapters 11 to 18 focus in on our key topic areas: **Search; Social; Send; Substance; Sell; Sponsor; Strategy; and Score.** This is where you'll find all the tools and information you need to complete days 31–90 of the 90-day plan.

Days 31–60

1. **SEARCH:** SEO is a priority – fix web visibility issues and use PPC Ads to plug any gaps.

2. **SOCIAL:** Implement a daily media strategy and develop weekly.

3. **SEND:** Develop one lead magnet for one audience segment. Create an email marketing campaign to market to customers and prospects.

4. **SUBSTANCE:** Create your brand storyboard. Review your website visitor content consumption behaviour for conversion optimisation.

5. **SELL:** Consider a Customer Relationship Management database.

6. **SPONSOR:** Create an advertising campaign for your lead magnet.

7. **STRATEGY:** Start blogging – use snippets to construct social media posts.

8. **SCORE:** set up basic analytics and measurement processes.

Days 61–90

1. **SEARCH:** Research content marketing opportunities. Create a blog and articles to enhance visibility and ranking.

2. **SOCIAL:** Share blogs and articles on social media, create snippets using the key points and create social media posts over the 30 days; theme your days.

3. **SEND:** Review automation tools and set up a nurture series – give your prospects value!

4. **SUSBTANCE:** Start using video and animation, infographics, etc. on your website.

5. **SELL:** Create a 'reach and retain' campaign.

6. **SPONSOR:** Identify alliance opportunities with key influencers.

7. **STRATEGY:** Map out your digital marketing plan.

8. **SCORE:** Review results and ways to improve – using Google Analytics and reports through software like Facebook, MailChimp etc. Start A/B testing.

Summary: maximise digital marketing

- Optimise your content.

- Create and share content on a blog.

- Connect with influencers.

- Run a campaign, contest, or giveaway.

- Create a lead magnet and sales funnel.

- Deliver real value through email marketing.

- Advertise, i.e. through Google PPC or social media etc.

- Develop joint ventures and partnerships.

- Learn from successful brands and competitors who've scaled.

- Focus on what you want to be – not what you are!

Make sure you're ready and fully prepared to scale – Protect your business values – Build a great team of likeminded people – Identify your barriers to growth – Forecast for the future.

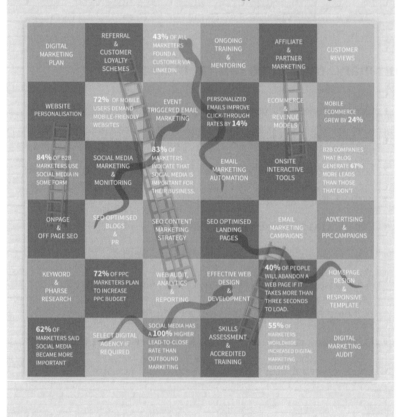

FIGURE 3 Digital strategy snakes and ladders.

Part I

Getting started

Chapter 1

Create your customer avatar

'Get closer than ever to your customers. So close that
you tell them what they need well before they realize it
themselves.'
Steve Jobs, Apple co-founder

A crucial digital marketing fact to remember is that it is all about matching demand with content. If you know who your ideal customer is and what problem they want to solve, then you can create content based on demand which will always get engagement.

Successful digital marketing is about using digital channels to reach your audience and generate leads; but don't lose sight of the end game. There is only one goal for a business and that's conversion. This can take different forms for different companies – it could be profitable customers or, for other organisations who don't sell traditional products or services, it could be utilising online marketing to share content to educate or promote awareness etc. **But regardless of what your organisation does, there is always an objective. And whatever that objective is, is where your conversion success lies.**

Your conversion success

So, you need to find out who you are marketing to, where your target audience hang out, and the best channels to use to reach them.

The first step is to create a **'customer avatar', which is your ideal customer.** This activity will help you identify what their aims are, their sources of information (and channels they use), the problem they want to solve, and any objections to purchasing your solution. This is one of the most valuable activities you can do because it will really help you identify what type of content they will be looking for online and this will be fundamental to helping you craft the kind of information you will use to attract, nurture, and convert them.

Consider:

- demographic

- shopping habits

- location

- job role/description

- interest in product

- need for product.

Customer surveys and testimonials and reviews often reveal lots of great information to help create an avatar, plus you will find out how they found you, why they chose you, what their need or specific problem or pain is, and what their motivation was for purchase – as well as identifying cross-sell/upsell opportunities and case studies and success stories.

I would suggest looking at your current customer base, if you have one, and interviewing any clients you can or potential clients who have expressed an interest, or anyone who you think is your target market.

I would research online and search keywords on social channels and in Google Search to collect all the information that you can; also look out for any consumer behaviour reports for your market that you can read.

Developing your customer profile and knowing who your ideal customer is will be critical in reaching, attracting, and converting profitable customers.

YOUR TURN – TAKE ACTION NOW

Create your customer avatar

Here are 12 key questions to ask yourself and research when developing your customer avatar. Take your time thinking about these and make sure you do your research thoroughly. Figure 1.1 is a template you can use to organise your research.

1. Where do my customers hang out – both online and in the physical world?

2. What websites do they visit?

3. What do they read?

4. What do they watch, types of videos etc. (what YouTube Channels do they subscribe to)?

5. What are their interests?

6. What are their goals?

7. Who are their influencers?

8. Who are your competitors that they may buy from or work with?

9. Who do they want to please – is it themselves, or a boss or a team etc.?

10. Who are they responsible for?

11. Who might they let down or fail; consider their working environment and issues such as safety etc.?

12. What worries them?

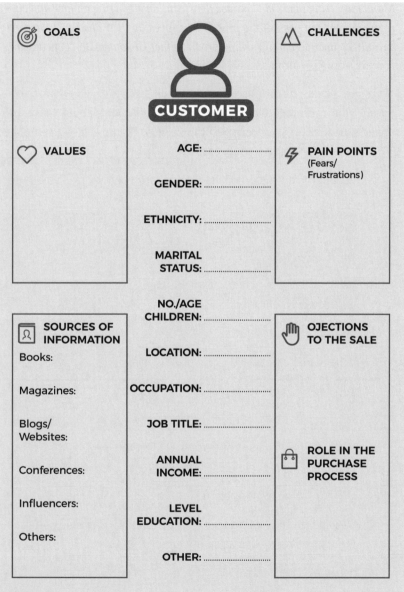

FIGURE 1.1 Customer avatar creation template.

Many marketing plans fail because they focus on attracting anyone and everyone rather than positioning products to appeal to their ideal customer. As a result, companies end up selling products that customers don't even want.

Chapter 2

Map your customer journey

'We see our customers as invited guests to a party, and we are the hosts. It's our job every day to make every important aspect of the customer experience a little bit better.'

Jeff Bezos, founder of Amazon

Now you have your ideal customer avatar created in Chapter 1, it is time to map out your customer journey.

Figure 2.1 is simple way to help you visualise this journey: from your customer as a complete stranger, to one who is so delighted with their customer experience that they become a valuable promoter. This is the ideal customer journey and one that is a huge win–win both for the customer – who has exactly what they want and is delighted with the result; and for you – as you now have a customer who has purchased AND the huge asset of someone who will tell other people about their experience and recommend you to others.

Questions to help you map your customer journey:

- Think about the stages from the viewpoint of your biggest audience: the 'unaware'. How would they find out about you?

- If they searched for you, how would they find you?

- What would make them choose you in a search result and visit your website?

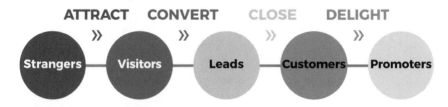

FIGURE 2.1 The customer journey.

- Do you appear in Google for searches about the advice, solutions, and problems that your ideal customer has?

- Do you just appear for your brand, products, and services?

- How would they see your competitors on their journey?

- Where does your audience hang out and are you visible?

- What's the top converting touchpoint of their journey for generating leads or gaining a profitable customer?

- Can they research and evaluate your products and services easily?

YOUR TURN – TAKE ACTION NOW

How to create a customer journey map

- Set clear objectives for the map – think about one clear goal.

- Use your customer avatar to define their goals.

- List all the touchpoints you think they will have, from attracting to them in the first place to them becoming a repeat customer.

- Take the customer journey yourself and judge what content they would or could engage with from unaware to aware, to evaluation, to lead or enquiry, and ultimately conversion; all the way through to purchase and repeat purchase.

Review the user experience from your customer's point of view (Figure 2.2), focusing on:

- motivation

- action

- touchpoints

(continued)

- questions

- pain points

- customer experience/satisfaction

- ideas for improvement/recommendations.

Review the User Experience from your customer point of view:

	STRANGERS	VISITORS	LEADS	CUSTOMERS	PROMOTERS
Motiv-ation					
Action					
Touch-points					
Quest-ions					
Pain points					
Customer experience / Satisfaction					
Ideas for improvement / Recommen-dations					

FIGURE 2.2 Review user experience template.

Gaining insight into customer pain points through mapping out your customer journey helps improve customer experience and interaction and aids development of propositions that are perfectly positioned to satisfy their needs.

Chapter 3

Carry out market and competitor analysis

'Insanity: doing the same thing over and over again and expecting different results.'

Albert Einstein, physicist

Every business measures its success against its competitors, so you must aim to keep ahead of what they are doing and monitor to see how you compare. It is wise to look at the good, the bad, and the ugly because some competitors may perform better on specific elements – don't neglect the newer or smaller competitors.

Remember that in the world of digital marketing there is no monopoly online, so the new kid on the block could be tomorrow's market leader.

Competitor analysis and benchmarking success factors

Choose a few competitors and create a grid (Figure 3.1 can be used as a template) to record your findings. The best way to carry out research is to look at the motivation you have identified for your own customer avatars and then for each persona carry out a customer journey in their shoes. Look at your competitors and where you appear and rank versus them and evaluate their offering objectively and honestly, considering their branding, tone, messaging, and propositions as well as how the customer experience feels.

Key questions to consider:

1. It is important to look at all channels: how do they appear within social networks and how do they communicate with their audience?

2. Is their email and content marketing tailored to each specific customer journey?

3. Do they have good presence in search engines?

4. Are they using advertising to generate leads?

5. Are they using any industry reports or themes to position the need for their product or service?

6. Do they use a lower value product or service to recruit customers?

7. How do they position themselves as unique versus their competitors?

8. Is there anything particularly memorable when evaluating their brand and consumer awareness?

Tools for competitor research:

- https://www.spyfu.com – Identify your competitors' **keywords** and **ads** for paid and organic searches.

- https://www.owletter.com – Captures, stores and analyses your **competitors' emails.**

- https://www.rivaliq.com – Free tools to see how your social media profiles, metrics, hashtags, and content measure up against thousands of social profiles in your industry.

You are only as good as the competition and the share you hold in your own market.

Detailed competitor research

Throughout your research, try and nail down answers to the following, more detailed questions.

- Communication – How are they engaging their audiences and getting interactivity? Are they using groups, pages, forums?

- Branding – What is their tag line, brand look and feel, messaging, tone?

- Proposition – What are they offering to solve their customers' pain or problem?

- Strategy – What is their strategy/business model? What is their key objective? What tactics are they using?

- Content – How are they using content to attract, nurture, convert, and get repeat customers? Video, blogs, whitepapers, case studies, posts, articles etc.?

- Channels – Where are they promoting their business? Where are they generating leads from?

- USP – What is their 'unique selling point'?

- Advertising – Where are they advertising and what is their traffic and spend for this channel?

- Social – What networks are they using and how big is their reach and engagement?

- Email – How are they marketing to their customers through different stages of the sales cycle?

- Search – How do they rank for keywords? Where are they driving traffic to: blogs, web, or landing pages?

- Campaigns – Who are they targeting, what are their key messages and calls to action?

- Events – What events are they hosting, sponsoring, or exhibiting at? Events and conferences? Online or in-person events, or both?

Marketing competitive analysis		
Communication	**Branding**	**Proposition**
How are they engaging their audiences and getting interactivity? Are they using groups, pages, forums?	What is their tag line, brand look and feel, messaging, tone?	What are they offering to solve their customers' pain or problem?
Strategy	**Content**	**Channels**
What is their strategy/business model? What is their key objective? What tactics are they using?	How are they using content to attract, nurture, convert, and get repeat customers? Video, blogs, whitepapers, case studies, posts, articles, etc.	Where are they promoting their business? Where are they generating leads from?
USP	**Advertising**	**Social**
What is their 'unique selling point'?	Where are they advertising and what is their traffic and spend for this channel?	What networks are they using and how big is their reach and engagement?
Email	**Search**	**Campaigns**
How are they marketing to their customers through different stages of the sales-cycle?	How do they rank for keywords? Where are they driving traffic to... blogs, web or landing pages?	Who are they targeting, what is their key message and call to action?
Events		
What events are they hosting, sponsoring, or exhibiting at? Events or conferences – online or in-person events or both?		

FIGURE 3.1 Competitor analysis template.

Chapter 4

Developing your proposition

'The way to get started is to quit talking and begin doing.'
Walt Disney, entrepreneur

There are three goals that every business, regardless of industry or niche, wants to achieve (Figure 4.1). And digital marketing can help achieve all of them:

1. increase customer base

2. increase order value

3. increase purchase frequency.

So how does a business achieve these goals?

I meet businesses day in and day out that have amazing products and services on offer, but they quite simply don't have enough customers to make the business profitable.

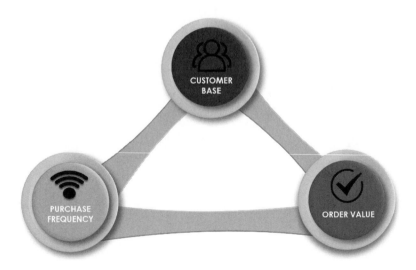

FIGURE 4.1   The three goals for business.

How can this be when we know there is demand and that the product or service solves a problem?

The two main reasons that a business fails are insufficient and ineffective marketing (Figure 4.2).

So how do we fix this? We need to nail down the 3Ps (Figure 4.3):

1. **proposition**

2. **presence**

3. **process.**

I always refer to this stage as the most important aspect of digital marketing.

INSUFFICIENT & INEFFECTIVE MARKETING

FIGURE 4.2   The two reasons businesses fail.

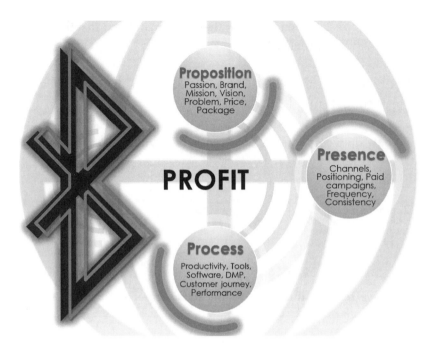

FIGURE 4.3   The 3Ps: Proposition, presence, and process.

Proposition

This is based around your **passion, brand, mission, vision, problem, price, and package.**

A **value proposition** shows how products and services create value for a specific customer segment.

So, from the **customer's perspective,** look at their **needs and insights:**

- What problems do they need to solve?

- How can they increase sales?

- How can they reduce costs?

- What's in it for them?

- What benefits would add value to your customer?

- Why should they care about your solution?

- Competitive differentiation – what are your points of difference?

- Why should they trust you?

The proposition needs to be clear and compelling. Quite often, when browsing the web yourselves, you type in a search question, choose a website from the list ... and when you land on the page its confusing or you aren't quite sure it is what you are looking for.

We see this a lot in service-orientated businesses, when there is perhaps no pricing, no clear package or options detailing what you'll get, and instead you are faced with an endless list of features – when really we need to know more about the benefits. And once we start getting confused, our automatic default is to retreat.

Consider instead our response when we are presented with a page showing Bronze, Silver, and Gold Packages and all they contain – with helpful green ticks and red crosses. Generally, then, our consumer behaviour is to go to the middle package.

And the reason this sort of proposition works – regardless of whether the business actually sells the package – is that they've succeeded in getting the web visitor to take action and contact them for more details.

This approach has just done a lot of the hard work for us – the basic fact-finding from your potential customer – because now you know how much they are willing to pay and roughly what level of service they require and you can create a bespoke, fully tailored proposal for them.

If a visitor is **presented with two or three options, they generally will choose one of them.** And this means your enquiry levels rise, because it takes away the customer's fears that perhaps this service is too costly for their budget or is not what they're looking for.

YOUR TURN – TAKE ACTION NOW

Try and map out your proposition looking at the 12 points in Figure 4.4 as a guide. I've given you an example below of how I would do it for my business.

EXAMPLE of Business Consort Digital Academy

- **Passion** – Making money from marketing.

- **Brand** – Real-world business marketing – it's digital marketing made easy.

- **Mission** – Bridge the huge digital skills gap – worldwide!

PROPOSITION　　　　　　　　　　　　　WHO * WHAT * WHY * WHEN

- Passion
- Brand
- Mission
- Vision
- Problem
- Price
- Package
- USP
- Benefits
- Tag line
- Why Now?
- Trust/proof

Maximise digital marketing profits to scale and grow your business

FIGURE 4.4 Developing your proposition template.

- **Vision** – Upskill 1 million youth of today – tomorrow's digital marketers.

- **Problem** – Not generating the profits you deserve.

- **Price** – Guaranteed at least 20% cheaper than any like-for-like CIM accredited course.

- **Package** – Fast-track digital marketing courses, plus gain a professional qualification with unlimited after-course support.

- **USP** – We practise what we preach – we are all CIM tutors and digital practitioners.

- **Benefits** – Guaranteed results in 30 days – Learn how to reach, attract, and convert profitable customers and turn your customers into your biggest advocates who don't just keep coming back but are actively referring new customers while you sleep.

- **Tag Line** – Maximise digital marketing profits to scale and grow your business.

- **Why Now?** If you don't act now, be fully prepared to see your competitors shine online.

- **Trust/Proof – CIM Study Centre of Excellence** – Learn from multi-award-winning digital author, speaker, and trainer – Ranked #1 on LinkedIn. Trained and certified over 25 000 professionals to date, Awarded Solution Framework of the Year for The Dynamic Digital Marketing Model taught at our Academy.

Presence

This section is all about channels, positioning, paid campaigns, frequency, and consistency.

To gain the ultimate presence, the ideal is to have positioning as an expert in your field – but how do you go from having a basic online presence to having people proactively promote you? How do you gain the positioning that will sell your products, services, and business for you? And, finally, how do you get people trusting you and choosing you over your competitors?

Well it's all about digital influence – online marketing has made achieving influencer status possible for anyone and in some markets this can be achieved fairly quickly … even overnight for so-called Instagram celebrities.

Look at Figure 4.5 regarding the stages of digital influence – and then let's examine what these terms mean for your business in more detail.

- **Presence** – Awareness of your business, products and service online.

STAGES OF DIGITAL INFLUENCE

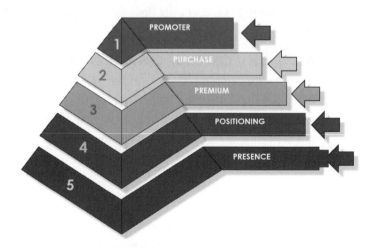

FIGURE 4.5 The five stages of digital influence.

- **Positioning** – Trust and credentials around you and your business/ adding value as an expert in your field.

- **Premium** – Never having to sell, as your presence and positioning are placing you as the premium product and service versus your competitors.

- **Purchase** – You have a steady sales funnel converting into profitable customers.

- **Promotor** – Your customers sell for you and are your biggest advocates.

You need to begin your journey through the stages of digital influence – or build on your existing influencer status – to gain all the benefits digital marketing can offer.

Once you have presence on all the channels your audience are using it's then all about positioning. Many see positioning as a tricky area, when they are perhaps new to a market or don't have a huge online presence – but actually it's about making yourself the expert in your own field and the credibility that then comes from trust; and trust itself comes from feeling understood.

That's why the actual content you use to market is critical in achieving influence. People buy people, and if we feel that someone is genuinely helping us and not selling to us, this again deepens the relationship.

In an era when there is masses of content to consume online, you need to stand out from the crowd and reach and attract new audiences every day. You can do this by creating marketing content that is:

- **Proactive** – For instance, if someone types in a search term or query into Google Search.

Two types of online engagement

FIGURE 4.6 The two types of online engagement states.

- **Reactive** – For instance, if someone was scrolling through their social media feed and saw an advert or post that caught their attention and triggered them to react or take action.

Marketing is only marketing when a customer can see it.

In an increasingly competitive arena a great option to gain vast presence, exposure, and positioning is using paid advertising – which is by far the best option as you can create uber-targeted campaigns where you only pay for results and the **returns are fast and vast!**

The key to a successful advertising campaign is to remember that it's not just a one-step process, but actually a series of ads that guides the customer seamlessly through their journey and shortens the sales-cycle.

FIGURE 4.7 Marketing quote by Dawn McGruer.

And last but not least, **frequency and consistency are critical** to achieving the presence and positioning to become a successful online marketer and profitable business.

In the world of digital marketing you need to keep momentum and must remember that you need to be in front of your audience each and every day in some capacity – think of it like keeping on their radar. This greatly helps with not only presence, but also positioning, as the **when a customer sees a business a lot, they automatically position them as scaling, growing, and successful.**

Nowadays, you wouldn't ever choose a business on page 2 on Google. Consider what would happen if someone asked you to recommend a restaurant, and you'd just driven past a brand new restaurant with huge 'launched today!' sign outside – you wouldn't be able to help yourself, you'd want to suggest they try it. You haven't been, you've no idea if it's any good, but perhaps it looked nice. **That is the power of presence and positioning.**

Process

Process encompasses productivity, tools, software, decision making process, customer journey, and performance.

How many businesses focus on the entire end-to-end funnel from lead to conversion? I see many businesses focused on generating leads and the moment is lost and money is left on the table because they haven't seized the **opportunity of shortening the sales-cycle and actually closing at the point of lead generation.**

This process looks at taking them through the entire **customer journey,** guided step-by-step based on using your **customer avatar,** which means you are able to target your audience using focused **advertising channels,** and finally enables you to capture the lead through using **premium content** that is entirely focused around their specific problem that your solution solves.

Most businesses stop there; and that's the biggest faux pas made in marketing every day.

It is really important when you have your ideal **customer's attention** to take this opportunity to sell. I don't mean hard sell, but offer them a one-time-only offer or opportunity that is too good to refuse or a natural step to enhance the premium content you have already given.

The key here is that you are trying to liquidate your advertising cost at the point of lead generation by guiding them through to a seamless opportunity that will solve their problem and provide a huge benefit that they wouldn't ever want to refuse.

An example of this from my business is where is we offer instant access to our online 'digital strategy session' as our premium content; but as soon as they sign-up, on the 'Thank You' page where you have 100% of their attention and provide the link to access their strategy session, we offer a '1:1 strategy call' with me to discuss achieving their business goals – which a large percentage take up. (I'd like to point out that unless it is a customer there is no other way of talking to me by phone or email so exclusivity helps with this process.)

We then ask them to complete a detailed online survey to ensure we have a very well-qualified lead and we have a good view of their business and whether they indeed fit our ideal customer profile.

They use an online calendar to book the call and we email confirmations and reminders as well as texts. And many who complete the call will then convert to customers on our coaching and mentoring programmes too.

So, when thinking about the process for attracting, nurturing, and converting customers, Figure 4.8 shows the most successful route to market.

- **Avatar** – Create your ideal customer profile/avatar.

- **Advert/channels** – Choose your channels and create advertising campaigns.

- **Premium content** – Create content that matches demand; could be a free guide, event, webinar or workshop, or even a strategy call.

- **Interaction** – That's when you can focus on conversion and not before.

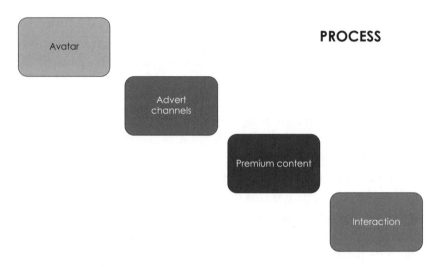

FIGURE 4.8   The process of reaching, attracting and converting customers.

So, the 3Ps are a way of getting your business fit to achieve your goals and ultimately = Profit.

YOUR TURN – TAKE ACTION NOW

Answer these five questions to evaluate demand and viability for your product or service or how to improve your proposition.

1. Does my product or service solve a specific problem for a specific set of people?

2. How competitive is the market and is there room for more businesses?

3. What are the costs associated with this business?

4. How long after starting will I become profitable?

5. How can I be innovative in this pre-existing market?

YOUR TURN – TAKE ACTION NOW

- Look at the main lead-generation sources for you and your competitors (this will be where you see the main concentration of their marketing efforts).

- Think about the acquisition, nurture to conversion strategies, and the tasks that need to happen in that sequence.

Uniting the three elements of proposition, presence, and process effectively, to promote your brand's unique value, will help your business stand out from the competition.

Chapter 5

Decide on key digital channels

'It is better to be a master of one channel than dilute your efforts across multiple channels.'
Dawn McGruer, founder of Business Consort

There are several areas of digital that will pave the way for marketing in the future and you need to consider carefully not just what will work now – but what will work in the future and what will give you the cutting-edge over your competitors. We will be covering all your potential channels in detail in the Part II of the book. These are just a couple of areas to consider.

Artificial intelligence

This is where machines think and work like humans – and it has been revolutionary in automating repetitive tasks such as auto-responding to social media comments, automating site chat using FAQs, appointment setting, tagging people and segmenting them into demographic and interest-based audiences, and creating automated conversion funnels (Figure 5.1).

Examples include **Facebook Messenger tools like 'Mobile Monkey'** where you can drive digital engagement through leveraging AI for user intent as you can match content to keywords and interactions; this embraces – and leads us onto – one of the most successful types of marketing: 'behavioural marketing'.

Behavioural marketing

This is when you market to potential prospects or customers based on their **actions.** Rather than trying to pre-judge their interests, you are aligning your content with **what you know they have previously interacted with.**

FIGURE 5.1   Chatbots and artificial intelligence tools are the future.

You can use behavioural marketing to run contests, promotions, and quizzes, customer surveys, webinar registration, nurture leads with drip campaigns, capture advert leads, and send notifications, updates, and promotions through tools such as Facebook Messenger.

Messenger marketing

MailChimp conducted research spanning millions and millions of emails, and they announced that the average open rate for an email is 20%. That means for every five emails you send, one will be opened by the recipient. Messenger, on the other hand, has open rates that are regularly in the 70–90% range. Almost everyone opens their messages on Messenger. **Messenger has a four times higher open rate than email.**

As part of that same research, MailChimp tells us that the average click-through rate for email marketing is 2.4%. That means you have to send over 41 emails just to get 1 single person to click through. But not on Messenger. We're seeing click through rates of 20–30%. And that's a strong signal that people don't just open these messages – they read and interact with them. **Messenger has an 8 to 12.5 times higher click-through rate than email.**

Email campaigns

None of this means that email campaigns are pointless – far from it. But it does mean that they have to be exceptionally well thought out to deliver the results you want. And, crucially, an email campaign needs to be a strategised series of communications to engage the customer.

Look at what needs to happen to educate, entice, and convert a customer and think about plotting out strategies – such as how you could use frequently asked questions in a series of emails when someone enquires to address sales objections head on.

Questions to consider when developing an email series:

1. Are there FAQs you know people always ask that you could front load in emails to overcome objections?

2. What information does someone need when they first become aware of you?

3. What free resources would assist them through the decision-making process?

4. Is there a way you can interact with them – can they respond to the email via email? Can they schedule a call?

5. If you are not already using **'marketing automation tools'** start researching options such as **MailChimp** which are free to use and are very user-friendly even for complete novices. MailChimp allows you to create a landing page and automated email sequences.

Customer experience marketing

This focuses on the customer journey and engagement strategy for your audience.

Marketers are always looking for ways to enhance how customers interact with their products and services, so time-saving tools like voice-enabled search, story-telling through video, augmented reality – where you can superimpose computer generated imagery into real-word scenarios (such as furniture retailer, Wayfair, who launched an augmented reality feature to allow customers to visualise furniture in their own home ahead of purchase) – social proof to aid conversion and shorten the sales-cycle.

The 3Ts

A modern-day marketer should be focused on optimisation strategy to constantly fine-tune campaigns to improve lead quality and conversion.

There are lots of reasons a business fails or marketing fails to achieve results, but the main things that prevent a business being successful in their digital efforts can be broken down into three categories (Figure 5.2):

1. time

2. training

3. tactics.

FIGURE 5.2   The three things that contribute to business success or failure.

Time

In your working day, it is very difficult to take large chunks of time out to strategise and plan and it is very easy to move tasks and projects to the side if there is no consequence. We see people getting caught up in fire-fighting in their role – and then all their best intentions of taking an hour out to work on digital marketing go out the window.

This isn't down to the person – but is more to do with psychology. And that's because psychologically it's much easier to think about taking 10 minutes out of a day than a whole hour.

So, allocating bite size chunks of time is a commitment that is easy to stick to and in turn becomes a habit. Magically, it is now part of your day.

Training

Since the arrival of social media, there has been a stigma around allocating a budget for training; because social networks have always been free to use and therefore there was less financial risk involved as there was no up-front investment. However, we've noticed that if software is purchased, there tends to be more of a structured implementation, upskilling, and strategy around getting a return on that investment.

Tactics

Next comes actually knowing what the tasks or tactics are that you need to complete in order to carry out the project.

We found that sitting down to 'do your social media' caused people huge issues because – when we delved deeper into what that involved for them – many had no idea which direction to take. There were two main reasons for this: one was that they had no documented social media strategy so had no idea what the objective they were trying to achieve was and what success could possibly look like. And second, they had no idea of the action steps and tasks required to carry out successful social media campaigns and what order and with what frequency they should be carried out.

YOUR TURN – TAKE ACTION NOW

It is estimated that we spend about 15% of our time in meetings, so try some time-saving tools to reduce time wasting and increase your time focused on actions that have impact.

Instead of listing out line-by-line items on never-ending 'to do' lists, try managing projects with timeline actions. I find this is the easiest way to manage multiple activities simultaneously without getting overwhelmed and I feel it helps keep to deadlines as well as flag potential pitfalls.

Time – tactics – training activity
There are lots of tools on the market, but **Basecamp and Trello** are my favourites.

(continued)

Basecamp and Trello: Project collaboration and management tools. Instead of sending emails with my ideas, I pin them to my trello board or post in basecamp for team discussions.

- On a piece of paper, draw out a grid and write down each project you are working on. Then set-up projects and list out all the steps of the project (but remember, these will be ever evolving).

- Then, on a daily basis, review the projects. You will find this brings structure to meetings and calls as you can visually see progress. Each day you will add to the flow of actions and delegate these to the relevant team member with a deadline.

- As you go through the actions and specific tactics for your project, you will be able to identify any skills or training gaps by reviewing the steps. Look at whether you will allocate elements of the project internally or externally.

- Project management tools will enable you to set up reminders for ongoing tasks, plus these tools also have notifications to alert you when projects have updates or completed actions, allowing better time management and huge time savings.

These sorts of tools bring other benefits – such as the ability to collaborate – and also act as a great place to braindump any project ideas for team discussion. This is far better than sending emails and saves so much time as everything is in one portal and you don't have to trawl email threads to find responses.

This approach will help you think more strategically, as opposed to getting bogged down in the minutiae – as that's all under control. We are so busy in our daily work lives that it is sometimes easy to forget what you have achieved and who in your team has excelled and these tools will help you see the bigger picture. It is important to step back and have the ability to recognise when a project or a campaign may need a tweak; re-focusing your efforts can often make big differences.

'Life is like riding a bicycle. To keep your balance you must keep moving.'
Albert Einstein

A project can lose momentum easily when not managed effectively and efficiently; and using tools to aid your journey will keep you moving.

Chapter 6

Review internal processes

'Innovation distinguishes between a leader and a follower.'
Steve Jobs, Apple co-founder

Marketing doesn't stand still, and nor should your business processes. If you look at online marketing and how it has changed since the evolution of the web back in the late 1990s, you can see the vast opportunities that the internet has presented (Figure 6.1).

Many businesses are still not harnessing the true power of digital marketing because they are held back by limitations or technology. **Growth in 91% of companies is being held back by technology concerns, according to the latest Dell Technologies research.**

The ability to be dynamic in your approach to digital marketing is vital to adapt and take advantage of market opportunities, trends, techniques, and tools.

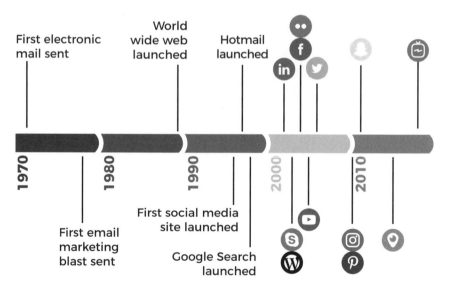

FIGURE 6.1 The evolution of digital timeline.

If you find your business is being held back by internal processes, such as outdated systems that are not fit for purpose, then you need to address this as a priority.

The reason businesses are held back digitally centre around budget restrictions, data security, lack of resources, and insufficient tech skills in the workplace.

An internal process needs to satisfy both your customers as well as those working in the business.

YOUR TURN – TAKE ACTION NOW

A good exercise to carry out is mapping out the tools and processes in your business that are aligned to your customer journey, while considering the experience from the consumer's viewpoint as well as that of the business.

Look at the complete end-to-end process: from how you are reaching, attracting, nurturing, and converting your ideal customer; through to after-sale, support, satisfaction, and repeat and referral.

It should be easy to identify any obstacles or time-sapping, repetitive activities where you can look at automating tasks.

A useful tool that can be used to help connect software and tools across the business is **Zapier:** this integrates software and automates repetitive tasks. A bit like a bridge to pass on information or trigger activities without the need for humans!

Look at interim and ideal options to bridge any gaps. If you can see areas that will instantly save you time or money, then that's a good case for immediate change. Likewise, if you spot a change that will generate more leads and help convert more profitable customers, as well as improving overall customer experience, then making these changes will be worth the effort and investment.

A customer-centric approach to the acquisition process will reap the best results.

Here are some suggested questions to focus on when reviewing your processes:

1. How does your company attract, engage, and convert customers?

2. How do customers experience a product or service?

3. What are the internal processes to move prospects through your sales funnel?

4. What are the departments involved in the entire acquisition process: from marketing to sales teams to customer support?

5. What tools and software are integrated and how do these align and support the customer journey?

'If you do build a great experience, customers tell each other about that. Word of mouth is very powerful.'
Jeff Bezos, Amazon founder

Chapter 7

Calculate your ideal sales revenue

*'Business must be run at a profit, else it will die. But
when anyone tries to run a business solely for profit, then
also the business must die, for it no longer has a reason
for existence.'*

Henry Ford, Ford Motor company founder

What's a good profit margin for a business?

Many new business owners believe you should expect to have a lower profit margin in the beginning. Of course, it depends on your field – but, in most cases, that's surprisingly not true. In the service and manufacturing industries, profit margins decrease as sales increase. The reason for that is simple. Businesses in these sectors may see a 40% margin until they hit around £250 000 in annual sales. That's about the time when the business has to start hiring more people.

According to an article by Investopedia, each employee in a small business drives the margins lower. One study found that 90% of all service and manufacturing businesses with more than £500 000 in gross sales are operating at under 10% margins, when 15% to 20% are likely ideal.

Marketing as a revenue generator – the maths of selling

A common misperception is that marketing is a cost to a business, when in fact your marketing should be a revenue generator.

It is a difficult shift to get your mind round – switching marketing as a cost centre to marketing as a revenue generator – as its normally associated with the sale of products and services, not the vehicle used to achieve the sale.

Most businesses will budget about 5–10% of their revenue as their marketing spend. But what if for every £1 you made a return on that investment of £10 or £100 or more?

It's about thinking around the **'maths of selling'**. It's about seeing sales and marketing under one roof and not as separate entities. For many years they have been seen as distinct departments within a business, but this is where the mind shift needs to start.

Revenue is vanity and profit is sanity.

Every business will have a target profit that they need to achieve in order to be successful; but all too often daily tasks get in the way of being laser focused on actually achieving this. There needs to be a very strong correlation between the activities you do each day and the money you earn each day, otherwise your business is out of sync.

I always encourage marketers to think about 'profit' at the beginning of each day and to break down achieving that magic number into specific tasks that will be part of a marketing campaign.

For instance, if a business needs to generate £1.2m a year, then we break it down to £100 000 each month and then again to £5000 a day (assuming average 20 working days a month).

It is much easier to focus on generating £5000 a day. And its then simple to take it to the next level and figure out how many products or services are required to achieve that goal each day.

So, an easy example to work to would be, for instance, that our daily rate is **£4999 + VAT** for an in-house strategy session (excluding travel and expenses so 100% profit – business costs = **87% profit** margin **£4349.13 profit**). So, if we use our business as the example, we need to generate enough leads to convert 20 in-house strategy sessions a month.

Let's assume that out of every **10 leads we take each day, 5 (50% of leads) go to proposal stage each and out of those 5 we convert 2 (20% of leads).**

Using the 'maths of selling' we'd be converting 10 profitable customers taking up strategy sessions **per week.** Which means we'd be doubling our target figure.

Return on investment (ROI)

So if you know how many leads you need a day, how many of those need to convert, and how much revenue and profit that earns you, then you need to work out what is the most efficient and effective way of achieving that goal.

At the Business Consort Academy, we generate a **lead approximately every 8 minutes** using a proven advertising method that we can turn on or off or increase or reduce in a matter of seconds.

So, using the example we gave you earlier, if we generate a lead every **8 minutes, that translates into about 7 an hour. Based on a 6-hour day, that means 42 leads a day. If 50% go to proposal and 20% of those leads convert into in-house strategy sessions, that equals 8 sales per day.**

We know we only need to achieve one sale a day, but this takes us eight times over our target – assuming we can cope with that level of customers. And this now takes you to the possibility that goals are meant to be exceeded and many businesses could indeed be hitting target but still not reaching their full potential.

So, what was our marketing return on investment (Figure 7.1)?

Simple MROI

Gross Profit - Marketing Investment

Marketing Investment

FIGURE 7.1   Marketing ROI calculation.

Advertising/marketing ROI calculation:

Let's look at return on investment

If a lead cost us £1.50, that's £63 invested in advertising (notice the terminology is invested not spent).

So, what was the return on that investment?

8 sales = £4999 Sales Price × 8 = £39 992 Gross Revenue

Deduct our normal business costs of 13% (£4349.13 Profit per sale) = Gross Profit £34 793.04

Gross Profit £34 793.04 − Marketing Investment £63 = **£34 730.04 Net Profit**
Marketing Investment £63 = **MROI 551%**

So that's a pretty good ROI! And if you consider that more of those leads may convert further down the line, then even if we added in

FIGURE 7.2 Digital marketing is a revenue generator.

additional costs to nurture and convert those leads – such as inviting them to a free event, webinar/workshop or strategy call – we have quite a bit of room for manoeuvre and we still get an amazing ROI.

Later in the book **I will teach you that exact formula and template** so you can start generating leads to maximise your ROI. The great news about this method of advertising is that it works whether you are brand new or an established business (Figure 7.2).

If you are generating leads that convert each day then you'll always be generating revenue from your marketing investment.

YOUR TURN – TAKE ACTION NOW

You must now do your own figures! If you haven't sold anything yet, use estimates. Then, as you create campaigns and test them, you will develop your figures and cost per lead to calculate your MROI.

Calculate your maths of selling figure

- Revenue per £_____ a year

- Revenue per £_____ a month

- Revenue per £_____ a day (based on 20 working days per month)

- Product or service price to customer £ _____

- Product or service profit to YOU £ _____

- Number of leads required a day _____

- Number of sales required each day _____

Chapter 8

Review your skills bridge

'Tell me and I forget, teach me and I may remember,
involve me and I learn.'

Benjamin Franklin

Back in January 2018, Damien Hinds – the Education Secretary at the time – spoke about the digital skills gap we are facing and the need to upskill in schools and businesses (Figure 8.1).

Digital skills are becoming increasingly essential for getting access to a range of products and services.

- However, there is a digital divide where up to 12.6 million of the adult UK population lack basic digital skills.

FIGURE 8.1 Cartoon highlighting the importance and need for digital marketing.

- An estimated 5.8 million people have never used the internet at all.

- This digital skills gap is costing the UK economy an estimated £63 billion a year in lost additional GDP.

- A recent study by O2 suggests that the UK will need to fill more than 750 000 new digital jobs by 2020 and train almost 2.3 million people to meet the demand for digital skills.[1]

So why invest in digital?

- 82% of prospects can be reached via social media (InsideView).

- Over 70% of B2B decision makers use social media to help them decide (Dell).

- Digital marketing spend is forecast to reach £240 billion pounds worldwide by 2020 (Forrester).

And why invest in digital training?

Professionally trained marketers can achieve:

- 44% increase in web traffic through effective blogging and content marketing;

- 60% increase in web sales conversion with a responsive and high converting website;

- 40% increase in sales leads, through improved management and digital lead funnels.

- Assuming a clear strategy is in place!

These statistics are based on results our clients have achieved at our academy.

[1]*Source:* https://www.ageing-better.org.uk/news/digital-skills-life.

Train or recruit in new skilled staff?

Consider that the average salary of a Digital Marketer is £38K. Then review the facts about recruiting a new team member and look at that against the cost of training someone in your organisation.

- New hire productivity is less than 100% for the first five or six months.

- The first three months' productivity is less than 50%. This can be a significant drain on your financial resources.

- Eric Koester of MyHighTechStart-Up estimated the cost of a new employee is approximately one and half to three times the cost of their annual wage.

So, the cost of hiring a new digital marketing specialist could be as high as £112 500.

Compare that to training a member of your current workforce: professional qualifications in digital marketing cost a little over £1500.

A recent survey by Hays Recruitment revealed that only **15% rate their digital skills as very good** and **34% reported skills gaps as being the biggest challenge** for marketing leaders.

It also cited that **42% of marketers are looking to develop their IT and systems understanding,** reflecting the greater role technology plays within marketing. There is definitely an awareness of the importance of digital across a multitude of job roles not just specific to marketing but across the business.

So, if you are looking to upskill your workforce, this is an investment that should pay dividends if done correctly. The big mistake in business is not getting team buy-in for training programmes at inception and not adequately auditing skills gaps – because often those procuring training are in need of upskilling too.

Whether to upskill your workforce

There are four key factors that influence a person's decision when choosing an employer or role

1. pay

2. culture and reputation

3. career progression

4. benefits.

It's perhaps surprising that **59% of a professional's decision to accept a job or stay in their current role is based on factors other than pay.** Their top considerations are around flexible working, health and wellbeing, training, and professional development.

If you have a team already established in the business, then upskilling is the obvious answer. A common route to upskilling a team is through interim team members gaining more on-the-job learning as well as coaching and mentoring across a few months.

I have used this option successfully over the past 20 years for my clients, because if you consider the stages of learning then just attending a course over a few days will have impact if digital skills already exist in the business.

If, however, there is more a need for digital transformation – in a situation where team members are experts in their own field but possess less digital experience – then more assistance on implementation and management may be required.

Utilising internal resources coupled with external expertise can be a good balance for the budget and the business, as training, preparation, and guidance is coming from outside the current resource thus saving time and money. This way often provides an accelerated route, as strategy is being driven and adapted from a specialist who has honed their expertise and has a series of case studies to draw knowledge from.

Many businesses now operate across virtual environments and the need for teams to be based in one office is no longer there, so building a team of freelancers who are experts in their fields and who work together can be a very cost-effective option – especially if you don't have a team or don't want to employ and manage your own staff.

If you are looking to recruit external resource, then make sure your proposition is appealing for your ideal employee. This is not dissimilar to attracting your ideal customer. Ensure you showcase the perks across the four factors: pay, culture and reputation, career progression opportunities and benefits such as health and wellbeing, as well as training and professional development programmes. Businesses often wait until the interview or even the offer letter to showcase these perks, but to ensure you attract the very best talent they need to be in the job advert.

Employee performance is critical to the overall success of the company, so it is important to empower the team you have to be self-motivated and successful in their role within the business. Recognising the motivation of your employees for their own professional development and wellbeing will be a critical success factor too.

YOUR TURN – TAKE ACTION NOW

Upskilling your workforce through training and professional development

To ensure you adopt the right programme for your business, budget, and team, here are a few tips you can follow:

- **Is the course accredited by an industry body?**

    Learning best practice with a clear understanding of the implications of regulations and legislation and how these impact on your business is crucial. A syllabus developed around industry with key leaders' input and the investment of accrediting bodies is paramount. A non-regulated training provider may not have the infrastructure to advise competently across these matters.

- **Is there certification provided or a qualification?**

    Giving employees the ability to gain a worldwide recognised professional qualification is an amazing incentive. A key human need is to develop and to continuously progress, so instead of ad-hoc training courses think about continuous professional development for you and your team. Especially in the digital marketing arena, this is not a one-off learning experience but ongoing, so CPD (continuous professional development) programmes provide benefits for both business and employee. Having a team that is not only current in their knowledge but who feels invested in is a huge asset to the business.

- **Is the course leader a practitioner or lecturer?**

    In the world of digital marketing, those with real-world business experience are key to success simply because of the sheer pace

    (continued)

of change. It would be impossible for those not involved in marketing from a practitioner level to keep abreast of the latest tips, trends, tools, and technologies – never mind the ever-evolving tweaks in strategy to align to market and industry changes.

- **Have the courses been designed by professionals for professionals?**

Experience and expertise are key factors when selecting a training provider, but are they testimony to their own training? Check them out online and see what their own marketing looks like. Are they a digital influencer or thought leader? The proof is in the pudding – because you wouldn't hire someone with no social media following to advise on your strategy, nor would you work with a training provider who hadn't got a proven track record with customer success stories. If you feel inspired by the trainer and you can see their success, then you will have trust in their guidance.

Chapter 9

Implement
time-management strategies

'You may delay, but time will not.'
Benjamin Franklin

Right, now I really want you to focus on getting a handle on your TIME.

Look into time-management techniques – these are techniques I use to save time in my working day and to work efficiently and effectively. As an entrepreneur you must **make time for 'mindset'** because it is as important as any strategy you will learn in this book. It took me a while to realise I was on the edge of burn-out, but I can honestly say it was life changing when I made these changes.

1. Making time

Know when to say 'no'

It is easy to get swept along in someone else's priorities, but remember these aren't necessarily yours.

Go through your diary and make sure you have daily slots for you and your priorities.

Use a weekly planner to mark out:

- breaks;
- lunch hour;
- exercise;
- personal appointments;
- calls;
- emails;

- small to-do items that are quick and easy to do;

- larger project time to focus on a bigger goal;

- don't forget to box off ad-hoc time for those unexpected joys that enter your day;

- write in any known meetings or appointments and see where you are at.

	Monday	Tuesday	Wednesday	Thursday	Friday	Saturday	Sunday
9.00am							
10.00am							
11.00am							
12.00pm							
1.00–2.00pm	LUNCH	LUNCH	LUNCH	LUNCH	LUNCH		
2pm							
3pm							
4pm							
5pm							

If you don't have any ad-hoc time, then you are doing too much and something will have to give.

If someone asks for something, never give precious time away – but look at your ad-hoc time. If it's a priority, put it in this week; but if it is not, move it to later in your schedule. Always ask for deadlines to see if the person just wants it or actually needs it.

Start thinking about what you want to spend time doing and what you don't. **And take time out.** I used to plot my day in hours and work out what I would do per hour, but never thought about actual breaks and time to rest and rejuvenate.

Delegate and exchange

I love my job, but as a business owner I design my role so it would be my fault if I didn't! It is easy to get caught up in being too busy, so I write a list every week with anything I didn't enjoy and delegate that – and then take on something new in exchange.

Create headspace – the art of being bored will make you more productive

I block out time in my diary every week because often my best work ideas come to me when I have this headspace. I used to spend time in bed running through what was on my mind, but this didn't help my sleep much.

I literally sit and do nothing and just run through all my thoughts and feelings. When you're bored, it sparks significant activity at the subconscious level. Those quiet, boring times allow your mind to wander, rewiring your brain in ways that help you achieve more.

This just creates space to think clearly and without emotion. I sometimes walk or do mindless tasks and let my mind drift. I run through conversations, visualise events or steps in a process.

I then just jot down all my ideas in bullets. Sometimes, if I get myself really in the zone, I allow myself to use that time to get creative and start working on what is motivating me at that second.

2. Time savvy NOT time waster

Emails

I never delete any emails. As I write I currently have a red notification on **my emails app = 29 887.**

I hear those of you who love a clean and clear inbox gasp; but imagine the hours of your life you are wasting reading and deleting pointless emails that you never wanted or have no positive impact on your life.

Just think: if you spent an hour a day clearing your inbox, in a year **you've wasted 260 hours – but worse, in the average lifetime over 22K hours –** when you could auto-archive them and spend 60 seconds doing it once and never lose an email again.

Don't let your working day be driven by emails, **simply set aside three times a day or even once a day** that you check and respond to emails.

Auto-filter incoming emails

I also filter all my emails on rules and contacts. Most people have about 10–20 contacts that are important clients, suppliers, etc. that they want to always see emails from.

I would say 80% of my incoming emails are simply trash and don't require any response, so for the 20% I set a rule for all my VIP contacts to go to one email inbox and then the rest are dealt with by my PA.

If you are managing your own email then a tip would be to set rules for subject lines, company, or contact names.

Another is to have a default auto-responder that states that if its important, contact you through your preferred method, or if it is about X,Y, or Z, perhaps contact the relevant team member; or include a specific subject so that you have a rule in place that again these go to your specified 'to reply' inbox.

The rest of my emails are then very quick to work through and don't hinder my working life; if I'm on the train, I'll perhaps have a quick scan and then set a rule to auto-archive to 'old messages' that if required can easily be searched and accessed.

Meetings and calls

I have to say that meetings and calls are my biggest bugbear in working life and even more so the request of meeting for a coffee.

I never ever answer my phone to incoming calls, but I set aside one hour a day to return any calls that require a verbal response. It's not that I have lost the art of communication and want to shun human contact, its more down to time being a precious commodity that I don't want to lose or waste on pointless tasks.

Efficient communication has many plusses, such as the fact that the conversation carries far more enthusiasm and energy when I am in a convenient time and space to talk and my mind is more engaged on the matter in hand. It is about getting the best out of yourself and other people, so quite often my calls are scheduled at mutually beneficial times by my PA.

I also don't ever listen or respond to voicemails. My emails and voice message both state this and request that if it is urgent, text or WhatsApp me if nobody else can assist, or email me if it is not urgent but you'd like me to respond.

You wouldn't believe how much this reduces unnecessary interruptions.

Set up a calendar/online diary system – calendly.com

I have been using Calendly for years now and every week I have three times I will accept calls where people can go online and book a call at convenient times for me. If someone wants to schedule a call, I send them my calendly link and it avoids the back and forth emails agreeing best times etc. too.

I also ask them to call me and provide the best number and this way all parties get reminders and it auto-adds the appointment to my outlook calendar too.

3. Focus and digital distraction

It is important to have laser focus on achieving just one goal rather than trying to do everything at once.

It's easy to get wrapped up and excited about lots of great ideas but it is always better to focus your efforts on one key goal.

If you wake up every day with just one key focus, it helps you to avoid overwhelm and it means you have better clarity around what you have to do – and it is also much easier to drill down specific daily actions relating to achieving just that one goal.

If you are a serial browser, then this is a great tool: **Google Keep** – capture what is on your mind. Available for desktop (as browser extension – just click the lightbulb to keep) or app for mobile. Add notes, lists, photos, and audio to Keep.

A Digital 2019 report by HootSuite and We Are Social revealed that the average internet user spends **more than a quarter of their life on the internet.** The same report further shows that consumers are **online an average of 6 hours and 42 minutes** each day.

The numbers above equate to more than **100 days a year of online time for an average internet user.** That is more than 27% of our lives each year.

What on earth did we do with ourselves before the internet began?

So, don't waste your life – if you have ever monitored your time spent online then you will be appalled at how much time you dedicate out of your incredibly valuable life to your wireless devices.

Turn on screen time:

1. On your iPhone, iPad, or iPod touch, go to Settings > Screen Time.

2. Tap Turn On Screen Time.

3. Tap Continue.

4. Select This is My [device].

You can now get a report about how you use your device, apps, and websites, any time you want.

Or use **recuetime.com** to get an accurate picture of what you spend your time doing online – the lite version is free to use.

Stay Focusd – App Block is a self-control, productivity, and app usage tracker app which helps you focus by restricting the usage of **blocked apps** or **overall phone time** based on daily usage limit/ hourly usage limit/limit on number of launches/in specified time intervals and a limit on the number of phone screen unlocks. It is available for desktop or an app for mobiles or a Chrome extension that restricts the amount of time you can spend on time-wasting websites, so you have to stay focused.

4. Organise your work environment

For me, I feel when my desk is tidy and organised, I am much more focused and feel calmer and less stressed even when I have 9 million things I need to do.

A third of your life will be spent at work. That's 90 000 hours over the course of an average lifetime.

My other cathartic ritual is **throwing something away each day** – it sounds strange, but I like to allocate one hour a day to clearing out something and getting it organised. I like everything in its place and less is more.

In terms of my working environment I **only ever have one to-do list which is my master** and has every idea on it that I use to write a daily list. I then throw away the daily list, score off the done items on the master, and start a new list every night before the next day. This helps me recognise my daily progress and a reducing list helps motivate me on to the next day.

I do use a digital calendar, but again for me I love visual maps and plans so I always have paper monthly planners and a daily planner/list. For some reason, I don't feel as connected to to-do lists online. There is something about the act of writing that makes me feel connected to the task at hand. Perhaps because cognitively the way our brains work is that to understand something, we deepen our connection through writing it and processing the emotions around that task.

I also feel that when I write my list I **visualise, brainstorm, and evaluate,** which triggers me to list bullets or ideas associated with it or key points and helps me remove any vagueness and become more specific around the actions required in achieving the goal, project, or task. This helps my mind associate the right level of time to the item and not over-stretch myself. This process helps me clear my mind and takes away the panic of forgetting my great ideas or important tasks that should have my attention.

5. Reduce your personal stress

Stress is a huge contributor to disease and illness and the less stress we have, the more productive we are.

Each person is different; but it is important to know what keeps you sane and what adds to your worry or stress.

Strangely, I feel most stressed on holiday when I am not checking in on work and emails. I have realised that for me, going from 100 miles an hour to nothing is my anxiety inducer. For me to feel in control, I cannot have any build up or pile of work to come home to. I like to put all the steps in place for annual leave and dip in to avoid any issues and manage items as they come in so I can return knowing its straight back to work with no back log.

The other aspect of holiday for me is I use it to step away from the day to day to look at the bigger picture, and I always come up with great plans and ideas. The important aspect of this for me is that it makes me feel uber-motivated and excited, so I like to record it – just jotting down my ideas and sometimes getting them actioned through the team while I am away.

6. Motivation

It can be easy to feel life is a bit monotonous – and believe me, I have been there.

I like to have two or three large projects on the go, not one, because when you split your focus across several then, even when one may not be going to plan, you can quickly get motivation from another and rotate them. Also, having one project is all encompassing, and you feel every-thing relies on it, so again any obstacles along the way feel less impactful when you have two or three other things to move to.

Set deadlines

It's always advantageous to set realistic deadlines. Regardless of the task or project at hand, setting clear deadlines will help you to better prioritise and dedicate your time. Furthermore, if you work and collaborate within a team environment, then, of course, this will also be a great signal to your colleagues, as they'll know the proposed task completion date.

7. Create goals for key areas in your life

It is easy to drift through life, but you only live once – so make it a life worth living.

If you really want to be the best version of you and find your own nirvana, whatever that may look like, you need to set yourself some goals.

It's about having compelling and exciting goals – but these will look different for everyone. It is NOT about being ostentatious and setting materialistic goals, but instead goals that really motivate you.

Every month I sit down and **using a grid with eight sections** I set a goal for each of the key areas of my life. Do this for yourself in the Take Action task at the end of this chapter. This type of approach really makes you look at what areas of your life need improvement and also focus on how you feel about each of these areas.

One goal I use every year at Christmas is for **Adventure:** I make a list of 12 things that I really want to do in the next year – I research fun activities, places to visit, and new things to try. My partner does the same and the only rule is the items on the list have to be really specific and aligned to the month we have to do them in. We now don't buy presents for each other at Christmas but exchange our lists, and I promise you it's so much more fun seeing what your loved one wants to do; it really makes you plan your year, giving you so many things to look forward to and create amazing memories.

Far more satisfying than a one-off gift, we get 12 months of action-packed fun!

8. Get creative and think BIG

We have looked at short-term goals, but now it's time to look at the bigger picture! I understand this may not a task that instantly appeals to everyone, but nevertheless I think it really will bring some real value to all aspects of your life and success!

So, my next suggestion is to **create a vision board:** this can be done for all eight areas of your life or for digital campaigns.

The psychological benefit of actually seeing your future is a great aid in gaining clarity to concentrate and maintain focus on a specific goal. It is as simple as using pictures to represent the results of realising your vision and can also be useful when getting team buy-in on projects.

I would then use a yearly planner to break down your vision into more manageable chunks, followed by monthly then weekly steps that you can then incorporate into your daily planner.

Other life resources you may find useful

- **Evernote:** when I am writing articles, I use evernote to capture sources for specific sources that I can always refer back to.

- **Drink more water:** get a daily health hydration tracker app on your phone!

- **Alexa** or Google Dot: My Alexa can perform tasks and remind me with alarms in the day – literally over 4000 tasks can be carried out through simple speech commands. Alexa calls people, adds items to my calendar, updates me on the latest news, finds facts for me, orders stationary, plays my favourite music, and even does a quick 7-minute workout for me at my desk! Oh, and brightens my day – don't forget to Google 'Alexa hacks'; she speaks like Yoda, sings to me, and makes me laugh with her responses! I take her everywhere. **My very own virtual friend when working away!**

Productivity is so important as it not only helps performance but ultimately impacts on your profit!

YOUR TURN – TAKE ACTION NOW

Go back to basics and make a list of what is important and not important to you.

This will help you get some clarity around your priorities so you can start setting some goals.

FOR EXAMPLE

Important to you

- Seeing friends and family
- Spending time with my partner
- Keeping healthy and cooking and exercising
- Improving myself and learning
- Freedom to live life the way I want

Not important to you

- Going to every social event
- Negative and draining people
- Letting others set expectations for me
- Conforming to the status quo of society
- Leading a routine lifestyle of endless tasks

(continued)

Create a grid with these eight topics

Each month, set a goal for each of these areas of your life.

FOR EXAMPLE

Wellbeing	Family
Work	Friends
Relationships	Adventure
Money	Home

Chapter 10

Safeguard against digital pitfalls

'To succeed in business you need to be original, but you also need to understand what customers want.'

Richard Branson, Virgin Group founder

A staggering 100 million businesses are launched annually, according to figures from GEM Global Report, which is about three start-ups per second, and SMEs account for at least 99.5% of the businesses in every main industry sector.[1]

Why does digital fail?

As a digital marketer, I not only train but also work with clients as a practitioner, and I see so many businesses failing in the world of digital marketing.

According to the Small Business Administration, close to **66% of small businesses will only survive their first two years and about 50% of businesses fail during the first year in business.**

One of the biggest reasons for business failure is **insufficient and ineffective marketing** (see Chapter 4): failing to attract paying customers in a cost-effective way. A business might have a product or service people are willing to pay for, but if they can't figure out a way to market it in a cost-effective way, the business will ultimately fail.

These days, your web and your social media presence can be just as important as your company's physical presence. People shop, search, and research online for everything these days. So, if the demand is already there, the virtual availability and visibility of your business is crucial.

[1]*Source:* https://www.fsb.org.uk/media-centre/small-business-statistics.

I pay little attention to revenue, but I always encourage my clients to look at their profit margins because sometimes it is better to scale to a certain size and retain profit margins than take that next step – because you can end up actually spending more money, more time, and more effort in managing teams to generate larger revenues and ultimately end up with the same or less profit.

So how can you succeed in digital marketing?

Well, there are seven easy-to-remember steps I want to take you through to give you the essentials you need to succeed (Figure 10.1).

These will help you understand the trends and opportunities available to you; from channels, investment, growing your audience and followers, testing campaign performance, to automating tasks and the best ways to quickly generate leads.

DIGITAL marketing

D Digital
I Invest
G Growth
I Innovate
T Test
A Automate
L Leads

FIGURE 10.1 The Seven Steps for Digital Success.

They have all been covered briefly in the previous chapters – and we will focus on them in more depth in Part II of the book. But this checklist should be at the forefront of your mind when you consider your digital strategy – and will help you avoid the mistakes made by companies that fail.

1. Digital – In Part II, I will be taking you through **eight powerful ways of marketing your business online** and the proven strategies for each of the key digital channels; as well as saving you time, effort, and money by showing you the exact tasks that need to be carried out daily to get the best results and profits.

2. Invest – You must **invest in training** for you and your team, focus on the **top ROI channels** such as search marketing, social media marketing, email marketing, and paid advertising. If you are not prepared to pay for social media advertising, then you won't gain the reach you need on social media such as Facebook and Instagram. (LinkedIn does tend to be much easier as there are fewer users and less content to reach your audience, but this won't always be the case as the network grows!)

3. Growth – It is fundamental to understand that – especially with social media – the power in building a network will only be recognised if you turn that audience into your tribe, your group of followers that you can ultimately generate leads from. This has a very different feel from a network, as your tribe has taken the step not just to connect or follow, but to join an interest group.

4. Innovate – Digital marketing is an ever-evolving arena and it is important to harness any opportunities ahead of your competition. Plus, there's the fact that such advanced technologies are available at entry-level pricing, where traditionally these were only available to enterprise-level businesses.

5. Test – The power of split and multi-variation testing in digital marketing is often over-looked, but this is an extremely important aspect of getting the best ROI and conversion.

6. Automate – Repetitive tasks such as emails, social media, and other website actions should be automated using software.

7. Leads – A business that is performing well will have a steady flow or funnel of leads coming into the business that are converting to customers. Acquisition of leads with poor conversion will not result in a profitable business, so attracting quality leads is just as important as nurturing leads.

TAKE ACTION NOW

Use the grid below to carry out a mini pitfall and opportunity audit.

Take a look at the digital channels you are currently using and any opportunities you feel you are missing out on. Look at current use and pitfalls, as well as future opportunities, for each element.

TIP:

Try and come up with immediate actions as well as a longer term wish list. So, if you can see any interim fixes or opportunities, as well as longer term ones, list them below.

	Now/Potential Pitfalls	Future Opportunities
Digital		
Invest		
Growth		

(continued)

	Now/Potential Pitfalls	Future Opportunities
Innovate		
Test		
Automate		
Leads		

Part II

The Dynamic Digital Marketing Model

The
Radical
Results
Reaper®

The
R.A.P.I.D.
Traffic
Generator®

The
D.I.R.E.C.T.
Digital
Marketing
Dynamo®

The
Proven
Positioning
Process®

The
Brilliant
Brand
Booster®

The
C.L.E.A.N.
Customer
Cultivator®

The
Ultimate
Reach & Retention®

The
C.R.E.A.T.I.V.E.
Content Communicator®

SCORE · SEARCH · SOCIAL · SEND · SUBSTANCE · SELL · SPONSOR · STRATEGY

DYNAMIC DIGITAL MARKETING MODEL®

FIGURE I The Dynamic Digital Marketing Model.

L et's now talk about **how YOU can reach digital marketing nirvana.**

I've discovered over the years that are are just eight key areas you need to master in order to become a fantastic digital marketer whose efforts **consistently generate an abundance of leads which convert into profitable customers.**

We call these strategies, which form our Award-Winning Solution Framework, **'The Dynamic Digital Marketing Model' (Figure 1).**

PROFESSIONAL SPEAKER AWARDS 2018

SOLUTION FRAMEWORK OF THE YEAR

We teach these strategies at our academy and they have been developed from addressing the common pitfalls we see in business.

As I discussed in Chapter 5, the **3Ts of Time, Tasks, and Training** are the key reasons that digital efforts don't generate the level of leads and customers required to provide a profitable ROI. So I developed this model to combat the common pitfalls that a business can fall into when marketing their business online.

What is the Dynamic Digital Marketing Model?

Each of the eight areas is a powerful way to market your business online and, in essence, each area is a digital marketing channel:

1. Search – search marketing and SEO (search engine optimisation).

2. Social – social media marketing.

3. Send – email marketing.

4. Substance – content marketing and creation.

5. Sell – social selling.

6. Sponsor – online advertising.

7. Strategy – digital marketing planning.

8. Score – digital metrics and analytics.

For each of these areas we have created an easy to follow, and remember, methodology for a business to follow. Each methodology is a proven strategy that we have devised based on our experience and is tried and tested and supported by case studies. These are the most efficient and effective routes to reach your digital marketing goals.

These strategies are broken down into steps that need to be carried out in order.

I will walk you through each area of marketing your business online, supported by practical exercises and planners, so you can start to implement each strategy as you read the book.

I will also provide a list of all the best digital marketing tools that you will need to manage and measure your success to ensure you are leveraging profitable returns on your investment.

In business, it is very important to have the right systems and processes in place to ensure you are maximising the resources, time, and money available.

Systems and processes play a significant role in building a company. They serve as the company's essential building blocks and support. Hence, it is necessary for entrepreneurs to incorporate them into their businesses. It is also important to consider the efficiency and accuracy of the business systems.

Some of the key reasons to have well-defined business processes in place are to:

- identify what tasks are important to your larger business goals;

- streamline them to improve efficiency;

- streamline communication between people/functions/departments to accomplish specific tasks.

I decided to create my unique branded solution for a number of reasons.

- Crucially, to empower people with my **knowledge in a consistent manner** that would be the same for each person I shared it with.

- **So others can also teach it** and not be reliant on me sharing my knowledge but on learning a system.

- So people could refer back to **a step-by-step process that is easy to follow and remember.**

- Each of the eight areas is built around **proven strategies** that I have tried and tested in my own businesses and in clients' too, so I can determine how successful the outcomes will be.

- Help others mitigate and **avoid the potential pitfalls** I faced.

- The model can be taught using all **four types of learning styles** – visual, auditory, reading/writing, and kinesthetic. This is extremely useful as each learning type responds best to a different method of teaching.

The Dynamic Digital Marketing Model is a system which encompasses the procedures, processes, methods, and actions designed to achieve a specific result. Creating effective marketing systems is the only way to attain results that are consistent, measurable, and, ultimately, generate profitable customers.

If you focus on the right processes, in the right way, you can design your way to success.

YOUR TURN – TAKE ACTION NOW

Take the eight areas from the model and place them in order based on your knowledge and expertise in that specific area.

As training is a critical success factor, as we discussed in Chapter 8, it is important to carry out a digital skills audit that you can refer back to after completing the training in the subsequent chapters.

1. Search – search marketing and SEO (search engine optimisation)

2. Social – social media marketing

3. Send – email marketing

4. Substance – content marketing and creation

5. Sell – social selling

6. Sponsor – online advertising

7. Strategy – digital marketing planning

8. Score – digital metrics and analytics

Take our quick digital quiz to see how you score.

1. What is an *algorithm*?

A. Section of a computer program

B. Set of steps or instructions to solve a specific problem or achieve a specific goal

C. Rule that is used in computer science

(continued)

2. How do you describe the position of a website in search engine results?

A. Prominence

B. Placement

C. Position

D. Ranking

3. What is used to make *webpages*?

A. HTML

B. JQuery

C. Python

4. You want to increase sales, what has an instant ROI?

A. Search engine marketing

B. Google Ads (PPC)

C. Email marketing

D. Mobile marketing

5. When running Google Ads (PPC), when are you charged?

A. When someone searches for the keyword and the ad is displayed

B. Upon impression of the ad when someone reads it

C. When someone clicks the hyperlink for the ad

6. **What tool would you use to make bulk edits to Facebook Adverts?**

   A. Facebook Ads Manager

   B. Facebook Insights

   C. Facebook Platform

   D. Facebook Power Editor

7. **Which social media platforms have the ability for LIVE video streaming?**

   A. Facebook and Instagram

   B. Instagram, Twitter, and YouTube

   C. Facebook, LinkedIn, YouTube, Twitter, and Instagram

8. **What types of content will get the most engagement in social media?**

   A. Photos and video

   B. Graphics

   C. Quotes

   D. Blog articles

   E. Text

9. **What is the process called when someone subscribes to your email marketing communications?**

   A. GDPR

(continued)

B. Opt-in

C. Sign-up

10. **You want to get a steady flow of new leads coming into the business – what is the quickest and most effective option?**

A. Write a blog

B. Create a social media advert

C. Send an email campaign

How many did you get right? If you didn't score 100% don't worry, because we promise you will learn everything you need to know to become a digital champion in the coming chapters.

Answers: 1.) B, 2.) D, 3.) A, 4.) B, 5.) C, 6.) A, 7.) C 8.) A 9.) B, 10.) B

Chapter 11

Search – The R.A.P.I.D Traffic Generator

Introduction

If your business can't be found on Google, then you are missing out on one of the biggest opportunities of free website traffic.

The words **'search engine optimisation' or 'SEO'** often create a confusion. For many years this process of optimising blogs and webpages has been sold as a dark art, but this chapter aims to demystify and simplify the whole process.

Google Search

Consider the journey for potential customers of either business or consumer products or services. Many will not even know what the solution is for the problem that they are trying to solve; so, they won't initially be searching for a product, service, or a brand.

The customer is potentially unaware of what is on offer – or that a solution even exists.

The R.A.P.I.D. Traffic Generator®

> **Reach**
> **Audit**
> **Paid**
> **Invite**
> **Dominate**

FIGURE 11.1   The R.A.P.I.D Traffic Generator.

For instance, if I asked you to go and find me a projector, it would be unlikely – unless you are so some sort of projector enthusiast – that you would type in a specific make or model; but you might opt to search a term like 'best projector' because you are trying to evaluate what is the best solution.

So how does a consumer ever find a solution to their problem? Generally, they search for advice, ask a question, or try and weigh up the options through searching for the best or event reviews etc.

And so your business needs to be able to be found online – and the most obvious search engine is **Google, which reaches about 90% of the internet's audience (Figure 11.2)**.[1]

FIGURE 11.2 Google reaches approximately 90% of the internet's audience.

[1]*Source:* http://gs.statcounter.com/search-engine-market-share.

How does Google Search work?

Google gets information from various different sources, including:

- webpages and blog posts;
- Google My Business and Maps;
- books and academic resources;
- public databases on the internet.

A common misconception is that every website will appear in Google Search results. However, a business won't necessarily appear in Google because, if you are searching Google, you aren't actually searching the web...

When you search Google, you are actually searching and seeing results that Google has **indexed** on the Google **search engine results page** (SERP).

First, Google crawls the web using software programs called **'spiders'** to review pages, and follow the links on those pages, and so on, until it has managed to **index** a fairly large section of the web. It then analyses the content it has found to try to understand the pages. This information is then stored in the **Google index,** a huge database, a bit like a vast online directory.

This process of discovery is called **'crawling'** and Google uses it to see what is new before adding to its list of known pages (its index). **Only now will a website appear in search results.** And even then, it's important to realise that this doesn't necessarily mean all the pages of your website will appear.

Google doesn't accept payment to crawl a site more frequently, or rank it higher, but it does allow you to submit a sitemap for your site and you can ask Google to crawl a single page or your entire site by submitting your homepage URL. This is useful if you discover that your site or some of its content are not appearing in Google searches.

Submitting to Google to appear in Search

The great news is that you can check your site and what pages of your site are indexed in Google, and then submit any missing pages for Google to crawl and index.

This can be done through **Google Search Console** which does all of the hard work for you, such as monitoring and troubleshooting errors on your site's presence in Google Search results.

It's free to use and easy to register and it will help you understand and improve how Google sees your site. It will, however, require you to include a snippet of code on your website for it to track and report on your website. If you are not technical, it would be wise to ask your IT team or website developer.

Search Console offers tools and reports for the following actions:

- Confirms that Google can find and crawl your site.
- Fixes indexing problems and requests re-indexing of new or updated content.
- Views Google Search traffic data for your site: how often your site appears in Google Search, which search queries show your site, how often searchers click through for those queries, and more.
- Receives alerts when Google encounters indexing, spam, or other issues on your site.
- Shows you which sites link to your website.

- Troubleshoots issues for Accelerated Mobile Pages (AMP), which are basically pages specially created to load superfast and enhance usability, mobile, and other search features.

YOUR TURN – TAKE ACTION NOW

Check for errors and troubleshoot any issues that are impacting on your presence in Google's search results – it is crucial to understand how Google sees your site: https://search.google.com/search-console/about.

What actually happens when you search on Google?

Well the answer, quite simply, is a lot!

The actual process between you submitting your search to seeing results is about half a second, but Google is working hard behind the scenes. When you type your search term or query into Google, you will be searching Google's index, so Google's software will find every page in its index that contains your search term or query and then decide which options to present in search results.

How does Google decide which results to show in search results? It uses questions, and there are about 200 of these which we refer to as **ranking factors.** It also uses an **algorithm,** which is a process or set of rules to be followed in calculations or other problem-solving operations, especially by a computer.

So how does Google's algorithm work?

Search algorithms look at many factors, including the words of your query, freshness of content, relevance and usability of pages, expertise of sources, and your location and settings to present the best-matched options for your search.

They will be looking at the pages that include the terms and assessing which are the most relevant by reviewing how many times your term or query appears on those pages, if synonyms of those terms appear, and the quality of that page using that page's current rank – which will tell Google how many websites link into those pages.

Then, just half a second later, you are presented with a list of results.

SEARCH or search marketing

This basically refers to appearing in search engines like Google. This could be via two routes:

- The process of gaining traffic and visibility by appearing when people search for your business, service, or product – which accounts for 25% of searches.

- But also appearing for people who are searching for a solution, or to solve a problem, to get advice, or to ask a question – which actually accounts for 75% of our searches.

Search engine optimisation (SEO) and pay-per-click (PPC) advertising

There are two different types of search marketing (Figure 11.3):

- **Search engine optimisation (SEO)**

  It doesn't cost anything to appear in Google, but you can opt to have a page 1 appearance through paid advertising, whereupon your advert will appear at the top of the page when someone enters a search term you have selected to appear for.

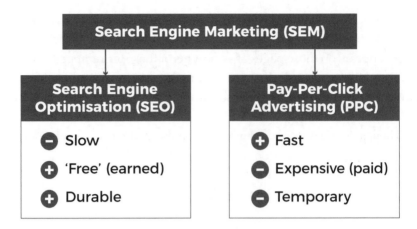

FIGURE 11.3 Search engine optimisation versus pay-per-click advertising.

- **Pay-per-click advertising (PPC)**

You will only pay when someone clicks the link for that specific advert – hence the term **'pay-per-click'** – while your **'impression'**, which is the amount of times your advert appears in searches, is free. As soon as you turn the advert off, your visibility disappears; so, it's often the best strategy to try and rank in searches organically; not paying for your position but achieving it naturally by optimising your content. This is generally possible if you don't operate in a competitive niche.

What does 'optimising content' mean?

Optimising your content involves **researching, analysing, and selecting the best keywords or search terms** for your audience to drive traffic to your website or blog posts.

If you are not ranking on page 1 then it's a real issue – as your competitors are getting those prospects. But how do people choose which listing to visit from the results? The way most people choose is by scanning for the most relevant words. Some will not only read the headline, but also pay close attention to the description that appears under the headline. This is where a business can really stand out from the crowd: by using this description to sell themselves by customising descriptions for each and every page.

If you include the **specific answer to a search query/question in the page description,** such as the example below, you can increase your chances of ranking and gaining enhanced visibility in search results (Figure 11.4).

There are around 200 factors that affect your ranking on Google. But we have broken down the exact steps into an easy to follow **five-step plan – The R.A.P.I.D. Traffic Generator** – that will help you to:

• optimise every webpage and/or blog post for Google;

• increase your online visibility and traffic in just a matter of weeks.

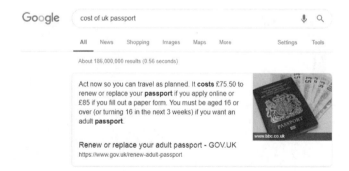

FIGURE 11.4   Screenshot of 'cost of UK passport' Google Search.

SEARCH Step 1: The R.A.P.I.D. Traffic Generator – Reach

Search remains one of the most popular methods of research and plays a crucial part of the customer journey for many businesses. There are a few priorities you need to consider if you want to rank on page 1 and reach your customer.

HTTPS and SSL certificates

HTTPS has been a confirmed Google ranking factor since 2014; but, in 2016, Google Chrome began marking non-secure pages containing password and credit card input fields as Not Secure in the URL bar.

If your website doesn't collect sensitive data, like credit cards, you may not have needed an SSL certificate in the past. However, with the new browser notices, it's now important to ensure every website has an SSL certificate and is loaded via HTTPS (Figure 11.5).

http   https

FIGURE 11.5   Http versus https.

- **HTTPS websites:** Hyper Text Transfer Protocol Secure (HTTPS) means all communications between your browser and the website are encrypted. All secure websites are denoted by a green padlock in your browser. If a site is not secure, a warning is given to the website visitor before landing on the website that it may be harmful – which will obviously greatly reduce traffic and ranking.

- **SSL certificates:** Secure Sockets Layer. Every website owner must have an SSL certificate to encrypt users' information and keep them safe and secure on the internet. Generally, your web host will offer SSL certification and automatically configure all website links to HTTPS, but you may need to seek help from IT professionals depending on your website provider.

- Any business that stores, processes, or transmits cardholder data is required to be **PCI compliant.** Trust Wave offers Trust Keeper to ensure you are PCI complaint. The software will regularly scan your site to ensure there are no vulnerabilities.

Google My Business

Google Search offers local search visibility too, so when you search on your phone, tablet, or computer you see a listing for your business with your address, contact details, photos, reviews, and map/directions, etc.

This will really help you stand out from search results in your region or area, and it is important to control what information is displayed here.

This information comes from **Google My Business** and you can create a free business profile here which helps you reach and engage with local customers across Google Search and Maps. This means you can fully control what people see when they do a local search for your business. You can include business information, photographs, or products inside and outside of your business, manage and respond to reviews, publish posts, as well as access insights to track interaction with your profile, like calls, direction requests, enquiries, etc.

YOUR TURN – TAKE ACTION NOW

- Check your site is secure and has an **SSL certificate:** https://www.sslchecker.com/.

- Check out Trust Wave who offer a free trial for cyber security software as well as **PCI compliance certification and vulnerability scanning:** https://www.trustwave.com.

- Check your **Google My Business** profile is created or updated: https://www.google.com/business/.

SEARCH Step 2: The R.A.P.I.D. Traffic Generator – Audit

As with most aspects of strategy, the audit plays a big part in success.

This can take some upfront investment in time and should be repeated around every three to six months to adapt to changes and keep up with trends (Figure 11.6).

SEO: 'the process'

Research and analysis

Search has always offered a window into what people **need, want,** and **intend to do,** so it is really important to consider consumer search trends when researching keywords and phrases. You will also need to benchmark how you compare to competitors in terms of site traffic, keywords, and ranking.

FIGURE 11.6 The SEO process.

Identifying keyword opportunities

There are on average 3.5 billion searches per day and 1.2 trillion searches per year worldwide.[2] In terms of the average search, **over a third of Google search queries are 4+ words long.**

Long-tail keywords or phrases are longer and more specific keyword phrases that consumers are more likely to use when they're closer to a point-of-purchase or when they're using voice search. These are things

[2]*Source:* http://www.internetlivestats.com/google-search-statistics/.

that people in your industry may be searching for on Google and you can drive valuable, qualified traffic using a long-tail keyword strategy, as these tend to be lower competition and therefore – if you are using these for adverts – they'll be at a lower cost-per-click.

Consumer behaviour and trends

Let's take a look at consumer behaviour trends for Google Search. There are three main types of search queries:

1. **Navigational search queries** – a search query for a particular website or webpage.

2. **Informational search queries** – a search for research related content, such as a **blog post full of tips,** a **how-to video, a step-by-step guide,** or **an infographic** that illustrates a concept like how something works.

3. **Transactional search queries** – searching for the exact brand or product name, which indicates they are ready to make a purchase.

The three most searched trends are queries that start with:

1. How to …?

2. Where is …?

3. What is …?

Question-based searches play a key part in search behaviour, as we use search engines for resources like an online library or knowledge centre to find the answer or to learn more.

There is an ever-increasing rise in personal searches that fall into three main categories:

1. solving a problem

2. getting things done

3. exploring around me.

When trying to source a solution, many searches are still around finding the **'best'** option or **'brands like'**, as well as the use **of 'I', 'me', 'to avoid', 'worth it'**, or **'should I'** and **'can I'**.

As Search is a normal part of most people's daily life, we put a lot of trust in Google and the content it shows us. We are always looking for the most relevant solutions, and by using these more specific and personal search terms we are constantly looking to drive our digital experience. People are a strong force behind the constant evolution of technology, not just as pertains to Search, but also the future development of our online experience.

So, how do these trends help with developing your online research for your search marketing strategy?

For your industry, you will need to research:

- What people are searching for.

- How many people are searching for it.

- In what format do they want that information?

YOUR TURN – TAKE ACTION NOW

Keyword research plan

1. Start by making a list of broad topics for your industry – such as 'social media'.

2. Then, around those topics, **extend the list into search queries** like 'How do I get more social media followers?'

3. Research these terms using Keyword Tools (see below for helpful tools) and check what people are searching for using Google Trends – for instance, a hot trend in digital might be 'influencer marketing'.

4. Look at how your competitors rank for these terms and benchmark them against how you rank.

5. This plan will form the basis of your content marketing strategy.

6. Now, create content based on successful content for your industry and get others to link to it by identifying influencers.

Useful SEO tools for research

- Just start typing your primary keyword into the Google search box and see what variations Google suggests and also check out Related Searches at the bottom of the page.

- Find out about website traffic, statistics, and analytics: https://www.alexa.com/siteinfo.

- Check out Google Trends: https://trends.google.com.

- Analyse what content performs best for any topic or competitor and find the key influencers to promote your content: https://buzzsumo.com/.

- Check out Internet Live Stats: http://www.internetlivestats.com/.

Free keyword tools

Use the volume of searches to identify demand for content.

- Moz Keyword Explorer: https://moz.com/explorer.

- Google Keyword Planner which is part of the Google Ads platform: https://ads.google.com/home/tools/keyword-planner/.

- Keyword Explorer: https://www.wordstream.com/keywords.

- Keyword Niche Finder: https://www.wordstream.com/keyword-niche-finder.

- Keyword Grouper: https://www.wordstream.com/keyword-grouper.

- Free Negative Keyword Tool: https://www.wordstream.com/negative-keywords.

- Popular Keywords: https://www.wordstream.com/popular-keywords.

Onsite coding and implementation

Once you have developed your keyword strategy through your research, it is time to look at the actual 'technical' implementation of how will you use those words and terms to enhance your online visibility in Search and where you should place them for Google to understand and optimise your webpages.

The technical aspect of SEO has been sold as the most complicated digital marketing art, that only those with 'technical expertise' should embark on. The irony is that when looking at how to technically optimise a page or post to appear in Google Search, this process actually takes about 60 seconds and is one of the easiest aspects of digital marketing.

Optimising your page

To 'optimise' your page you will need an 'SEO tool' installed on your website to guide you. The most well-known tool is 'Yoast' which is free and works on most websites such as WordPress as a plugin and Drupal – but if your site isn't one of these and Yoast isn't compatible, simply choose a 'Yoast Alternative' from page 1 on Google. Your site may already have one built in, or speak to your web team or developer for support on installation.

What does an SEO tool give you once installed? It will add an extra layer of admin onto your page editor (Figure 11.7). This will enable you to add a keyword or search term you want that page to rank for, and it will guide you through optimising your content for Google to index and rank your page.

The traffic light system in Yoast means that as you are going through and writing your content, Yoast will intuitively change the SEO score of your page showing red, moving to orange and green when good to publish or update.

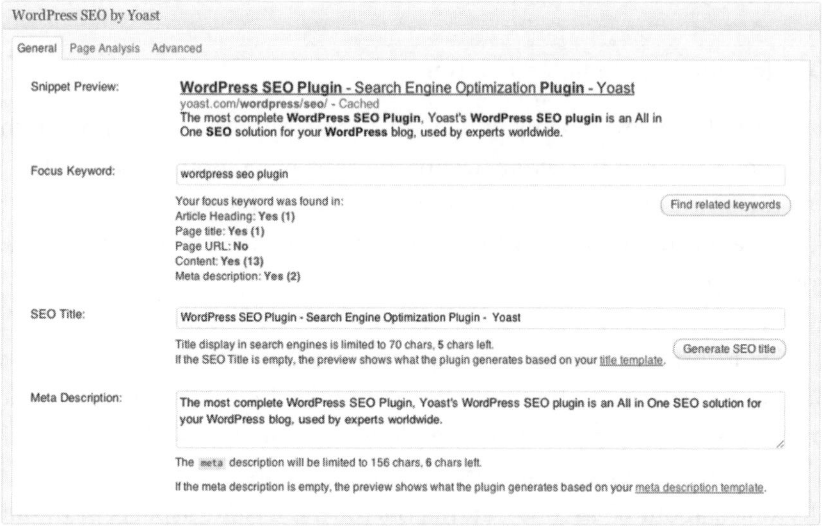

FIGURE 11.7   WordPress admin panel for Yoast SEO tool.

It will take you through steps to optimise structure, such as:

- title tag

- meta tag

- content of page

- URL

- image alt text.

How do you make sure you are 100% appearing in Google Search results?

TIP:

– For every new piece of content you create, make it a habit to create a **'Google Alert'**. This is a free tool where you enter the keyword you used to optimise the page for and as soon as Google has indexed your page and its ready to view in Search, you will receive an email alert.

There are two types of SEO:

- **On-page SEO** (also called **onsite SEO**) refers to the actual build of your site to make it search engine friendly. It involves optimising your webpage titles, description, image, tags, content and keyword use, internal linking, etc.

- **Off-page SEO** (also called **offsite SEO**) refers to actions taken outside of your own website to impact your rankings within search engine results pages (SERPs). This includes marketing and link building activities, which we will cover within the section below on Marketing and Link Building.

Copywriting and implementation

We've covered the technical aspects and how to use SEO tools to optimise the content, but here are a few tips to remember when actually writing your copy because it is important that content is created for the consumer and not just the search engines.

SEO is when you research keywords, select a particular keyword/s, and then use that keyword to write content; but writing for the web is slightly different to writing for offline consumption for many reasons.

The keyword will be the initial focus, but you must consider what the purpose of the blog is or piece of content you are writing. Then write an overview of the piece that really tells the reader what they are getting. Think of this like standing at the front of a room and presenting your work and selling it to your audience.

Questions to consider when planning your content for you and your audience

- Who is this for?

- What is the purpose of your article? Why are you writing the article?

- What is this about? What will be the main message of your post? What is the key question you want to answer?

- Why should they read it?

- How will it help them?

- When should they take action?

- What do you want to achieve?

Once you've considered these questions, plot out a **basic structure, research quality references and sources,** and just start writing as you would speak.

Tips when writing online content

- There is a temptation to use words that we wouldn't normally use to almost formalise the article, but do write in plain English. We generally scan through an article, and when you use uncommon words you are slowing the pace and making it more difficult to read and comprehend.

- Also consider accessibility to the reader and, if there is no need for complicated terminology or acronyms, try and avoid these.

- Take any quotes or key points and turn these into images and graphics that stand out from the text. These are any key takeaways you want the reader to remember.

- You must make it easy to read, so styling is important too.

- Keep sentences and paragraphs short and use subheadings every 100 words.

- I would also encourage the **'wiggly left margin rule'** which basically means use indents and bullets to keep intrigue and break large amounts of text into readable chunks and create white space around your article.

- If you are using sources and references to substantiate and support your article, then link to the external sites – but ensure these are from trusted and quality websites. This is also useful when there is a newer version of your article; don't ever un-publish content to replace with new, as you will lose your ranking for that content in search engines. Instead, utilise the ranking of the older content and include a revised link at the top of the old article linking to the new or related content.

EXAMPLE

Check out this post _I wrote on how to_ **write actionable content for your blog**_, it's packed with amazing tips._

TIP:

Read your post aloud, because your brain will be working quicker than you type. This may stop you missing words and encourage you to look at your writing style and grammar, as well as highlighting key points you want to emphasise. This method also means that you need to breath and this is helpful when ensuring you have adequate punctuation.

Inverted pyramid

I would recommend using this popular writing style guide – the **'inverted pyramid'** – which many historians say was invented by nineteenth-century wartime reporters, who sent their stories by telegraph, to get the most important facts across before transmission was interrupted (Figure 11.8).

It will help you to get your message across faster. Put your most important point at the top, followed by your next most important point, and so on, in diminishing order of importance.

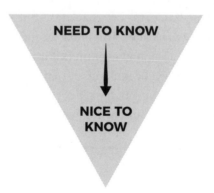

FIGURE 11.8 The inverted pyramid writing guide.

Calls to action

Every article or blog has a purpose and if you have captured the interest of the reader now is the time to get them to take action. But don't leave it to the end of the article, because remember approximately **80% of people will read the headline and only 20% will actually read the article.**

If a reader has been captivated by a specific point then it would be wise to put a 'call to action' (CTA) near the top, middle, and bottom, and perhaps use a combination of links and buttons.

Common calls to action would be:

- Facilitate comments or discussion, spark a debate.

- Share or connect on social media.

- Subscribe to the blog/join a mailing list (think about what the audience may want to subscriber for as a newsletter is not that enticing but free resources like – *sign up to receive our video series on seven steps to social media success*).

- Offer a free trial, demo, or product tour.

- Download free content or register for free resources like webinars, events etc.

- Interactive content, like completing a quiz or a poll are great for engagement too.

- Inclusion of offers: enquire now or buy now are also popular CTAs depending on the purpose of the blog/article.

Remember: calls to action should be prominent, valuable, and needs-focused to really get good results and get people taking action.

Summary

Once you have written the article, go back to the top and write a summary of all the key information and key points you absolutely need the reader to know.

Use the summary to really sell the article with juicy statistics and facts that will entice your audience to keep reading.

Over the years there have been numerous studies and speculation around the ideal number of words that Google's algorithm prefers; but generally, longer content, when going head to head with shorter posts, will perform better in ranking.

Blog posts with over 1000 words generally do better on average than shorter posts; but a minimum of about 500 words would be a good benchmark.

YOUR TURN – TAKE ACTION NOW

Now it's your turn to create an article or blog for your website. Here are a few pointers to help you structure your content and get the layout in place.

Structure of a blog/article:

- headline;

- attention-grabbing video or picture;

- subhead – introduction/summary;

- lead in – after the introduction, segue into your main points and actually frontload a bullet point list;

- subheads – main content (main points);

- subhead – conclusion.

Use the 5Ws and How to structure your article:

(The 5Ws and How were long attributed to Hermagoras of Temnos.[3])

1. Who?

2. What?

3. Where?

4. When?

5. Why?

6. How?

Headline creation

Your headline will be the first element of your article a reader will see, so it is important to make it really attention grabbing as well as SEO-friendly.

Think about the way people search as your headline will be what people would type into a search engine to find your content.

Headline/blog title examples:

1. **List:** ? Ways To {Do Something} That Will {Produce Desirable Effect}.

2. **How to:** How To Make A {Thing} To {Produce Desirable Effect}.

3. **Question:** What Can {Thing} Teach You About {Unrelated Thing}?

4. **Controversy:** Would You Do {Unimaginable Thing}? {XYZ} Did.

5. **Numbers:** ? Easy Ways To {Do Something} That Will Skyrocket By ?% In {timeline}.

[3]*Source:* https://en.wikipedia.org/wiki/Hermagoras_of_Temnos.

Once you have your blog constructed and you've finished with a strong conclusion you will have hopefully compelled your reader to take action.

The next step will be to actually drive readers to the blog – so when writing your article, think about where people will come from to land on the article and what information would entice them to click a link to visit and read your blog too.

TIP:

Don't name your article after an event or something specific to your business, but flip it so you think about not what your article is about but what it does for the reader – the outcome or solution.

Speed and site performance

The next factor that will impact on ranking and needs to be considered in your search strategy is speed – your website ranking will be affected by how quickly your website loads: 15.3 seconds is the average load time for a mobile page (Figure 11.9).[4]

- **A 1-second delay in mobile load times can impact mobile conversions by up to 20%.**[5]

- **More than half of visits are abandoned if a mobile page takes over 3 seconds to load.**[6]

[4]*Source:* Google Research, Webpagetest.org, sampled 11M global mWeb domains loaded using a globally representative 4G connection, Jan. 2018.
[5]*Source:* Google/SOASTA, 'The State of Online Retail Performance', April 2017.
[6]*Source:* https://www.thinkwithgoogle.com/data-gallery/detail/mobile-site-abandonment-three-second-load/).

FIGURE 11.9   Average speed index.[7]

It's not just conversion that you need to worry about, as page load speed can dramatically increase bounce rates too.

In particular, images can slow a page load speed down considerably; but there are a few checks your web developer or IT team can make to ensure faster loading times:

- Avoid landing page redirects.

- Enable compression.

- Improve server response time.

- Leverage browser caching.

[7]*Source:* Think Google https://www.thinkwithgoogle.com/marketing-resources/data-measurement/mobile-page-speed-new-industry-benchmarks.

- Minify resources (**minification** is the process of removing all unnecessary characters from source codes of a page without changing their functionality).

- Optimise images.

- Optimise CSS delivery (**CSS** stands for Cascading Style Sheets and it describes how HTML elements are to be displayed on screen).

- Prioritise visible content.

- Remove render-blocking JavaScript.

These items may require some more technical expertise to ensure your website's settings are maximising load speed opportunities, so your web developers and designers should be reviewing and monitoring them when maintaining your website.

The best option for reviewing your websites overall performance is **Google Search Console** which also has modern web technologies like **Accelerated Mobile Pages (AMP)** and **Progressive Web Apps (PWA)** which allow you to create engaging websites that load quickly for an enhanced user experience and are easy to implement.

Mobile responsive

Mobile responsive means your website can be easily accessed and viewed on any mobile device from smartphones to tablets etc. and means it will also rank much higher (Figures 11.10 and 11.11).

Remember that Google has customers, just as a conventional business does; it's easy to understand that the better the user experience, the happier the customer, and so Google will always aim to serve the most immersive and accessible websites at the top of the list.

FIGURE 11.10   Mobile friendly versus mobile responsive.

People who have a negative experience on a mobile website are 62% less likely to purchase from that brand in the future than if they have a positive experience.[8]

Here are the six most common issues that prevent a site being mobile-friendly:

1. It uses incompatible plugins.

2. The viewport not set – which tells browsers how to adjust the page's dimension and scaling to suit the screen size.

3. The content is wider than the screen.

4. The text is too small to read.

5. The clickable elements are too close together.

---

[8]*Source:* Google/Purchased, U.S., 'How Brand Experiences Inspire Consumer Action,' April 2017.

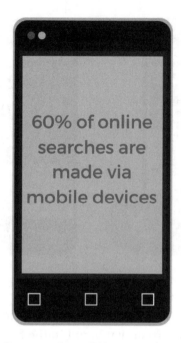

FIGURE 11.11   Of online searches, 60% are made via mobile devices.[9]

YOUR TURN – TAKE ACTION NOW

• Test your website speed: https://developers.google.com/speed/ pagespeed/insights/. A score of 90 or above is considered fast, and 50 to 90 is considered average. Below 50 is considered to be slow.

• Use the Think Google Tool to provide insights into the impact of your site loading speed on users: https://www.thinkwithgoogle .com/feature/testmysite.

[9]Source: https://www.statista.com/statistics/284202/mobile-phone-internet-user-penetration-worldwide/.

- The Google Test My Site tool also offers a recommendation report and the ability to benchmark the site speeds of industry leaders and competitors, as well as evaluating the impact a faster site can have on your business.

- Think Google also brings together Consumer Insights and Trends using Google Analytics date and research: https://www.thinkwithgoogle.com.

- Check your website is mobile responsive: https://search.google.com/test/mobile-friendly.

- Monitor mobile traffic and conversions as a KPI (key performance indicator) on a weekly basis to see if it is improving. And as part of your optimisation strategy, don't forget to test the customers' experience yourself by browsing on your mobile and timing how long it takes to complete typical customer tasks.

- Continuous A/B testing will be important in finding out what your customers really want, and by giving them multiple options you will be able to see what performs better over time (see below).

Continuous A/B testing

A/B testing is a method of comparing two versions of a webpage or app against each other to determine which one performs better.

First you will need to pick a variable to test. Here are seven items you could test on your website:

1. headings and subheadings (length, content, location);

2. calls to action (length, content, location);

3. buttons (colour, size, location, text);

4. images (size, content, location);

5. text on page (length, content);

6. forms (location, size, number of fields);

7. pricing.

> **TIP:**
>
> Identify your goal for testing and create a 'control' and a 'challenger' – such as the unaltered webpage as it exists and a new version.

Then split your sample groups equally and randomly and determine your sample size and how long to run the test campaign. Also don't forget to decide on what would be a significant result that identifies the winning version.

Tools like Optimizely (https://www.optimizely.com) are useful and many software applications such as MailChimp have these testing features built-in.

Marketing and link building

The term **back link** or **link building** refers to websites that have a link back to your website. Google uses back links as a ranking signal, so quality back links will definitely improve the prominence of your website in search results (Figure 11.12). Think of back linking as anywhere your content exists outside your website that links back to it.

Search success

FIGURE 11.12 The three main factors that will help search visibility.

Typical back link examples are:

- **Local listings and directories** – easy to rank for your region.

- **Industry-specific directories** – such as associations, accrediting or governing bodies.

- **Existing relationships** – any suppliers, customers, or partners.

- **Guest posting** – for magazines and popular blogs.

- **News and press releases** – in local, national, or international publications.

- **Donations** or **sponsorship** – prizes or events.

- **Networking/building new relationships** – social profiles such as LinkedIn and Twitter etc.

- **Rich content** – any long form or reports/white paper studies or infographics that others may reference on their blogs and websites.

YOUR TURN – TAKE ACTION NOW

Example links that I have in place can easily be seen in Google search. Just type my name into Google search – 'Dawn McGruer' or my business name 'Business Consort'. You'll see back links from:

- Judging for Digital Experience Awards;

- RSA – Royal Society of Arts Fellows Directory;

- CIM – Chartered Institute of Marketing Accredited Study Centre Listing;

- Digital Marketing Institute – Global Partner;

- Manchester Evening News and other press like Business Cloud, Chamber of Commerce;

- guest articles on Brand Quarterly, Training Journal and Customer Experience Magazine;

- Reed, Independent, Find Courses, Eventbrite;

- YouTube and Social Profiles;

- Apple iTunes podcasts.

Now type in your name/business name and see what back links exist for your business.

Ranking report and tracking

The last part of your audit will be actually tracking and reporting on your **rank, traffic, and sources**.

A well-known and commonly used tool for monitoring websites is **Google Analytics,** mostly because it is free to use; but there are a few quick tips I want to share in terms of actually ensuring you have it set up correctly so it collates and displays the data you actually need and want.

Google Analytics will display a vast amount of data. When visiting the software dashboard, don't be worried if you feel slightly overwhelmed as we can filter out some of the 'white noise' so you can see a more concise analysis of how your website is performing.

You will be able to measure and monitor all aspects covered in this chapter:

- performance on mobile sites;
- site speed;
- site search;
- search terms/top organic keywords;
- traffic and traffic from organic search;
- bounce rate.

If Google Analytics is new to you, don't worry as we cover it later in the book in Chapter 15.

YOUR TURN – TAKE ACTION NOW

You will need SEO monitoring tools to assist with tracking and reporting as SEO is not a one-off task but very much an ongoing process.

- Use **SEO monitoring tools** to evaluate your search engine visibility, competitor research and analysis. Two great analysis tools for ongoing SEO are www.semrush.com and www.moz.com.

- See where you **rank versus your competitors** for all of your keywords (weekly email alert showing ranking changes) – www. woorank.com – and what needs fixing on your site and each page of your site. Woorank provides an overall score out of 100 to aim for and step-by-step checklist of what to do, why, and what level of difficulty versus what impact it will have on your website's presence when fixed.

SEARCH Step 3: The R.A.P.I.D. Traffic Generator – Paid

Pay-per-click Google Ads are very quick to set up and can often drive instant results.

The main aim of advertising is to get the top placement and high visibility on **Google Search results pages** to increase traffic to your chosen landing pages for the keywords and phrases you want your audience to find you under.

Google also offers **Search Ads** which appear in search results, **Video Ads** which appear in You Tube, **and Display Ads,** which appear on the **Google Display Network** – which are third-party websites that have partnered with Google and agreed to have Google ads appear on their websites.

If you are selling online, then you can also choose **Shopping Ads,** which appear in across Google's Search and Shopping results.

Once you create an advert, you will then pay every time a Google user clicks on it, which is where **PPC** originates and you are charged a **cost-per-click (CPC).**

Your competitors will also be bidding to appear in these results if they are using Google Ads, so it is a bit like an auction to appear in the top spot as there are normally up to four adverts (depending on the competition and popularity of the keywords you have chosen) that display at the top of the SERPs (search engine result pages).

How is PPC worked out?

When you create an ad, you will **bid** on keywords, basing each bid on how much you are willing to pay for a Google user to click on your ad. This combined with a **quality score** of your proposed ad then determines which Google ads appear in results.

The **quality score** is Google's rating of the quality and relevance of both your keywords and ad. It is used to determine your CPC and multiplied by your maximum bid to determine your ad rank in the ad auction process.

You can use Google Ads to:

- get more calls to your business;
- increase visits to your store;
- drive people to your website.

Creating a Google Ad

The actual process of setting an advert up is relatively simple.

1. **Set up** your Google Ad campaign – Select 'Campaigns' from the navigation and press the '+' – select 'new campaign' and select a goal for your advert (sales, leads, traffic, product and brand consideration, brand awareness, app promotion).

2. Select the **type of advert – Search, Display, Shopping, or Video.**

3. Select the **ways you'd like to reach your goal** – web traffic, shop visits, calls, app downloads.

4. Choose **where ads appear.**

5. Choose your **targeting locations, languages, and audience.**

6. Set a **daily budget** + **bidding** which is what you are prepared to **pay-per-click.**

7. **Highlight key info** about your business – use **ad extensions** to include additional information, like business location, links to specific pages on your website, product reviews, etc.

8. **Create your Google Ad.** You can set up versions to test against each other which is always a good idea. You can set up **Ad Groups** which contains one or more ads which target a shared set of keywords for testing.

9. Set up **keywords** and phrases. You can get help here by entering keywords or your website URL and Google will provide suggestions.

10. **Track within Google AdWords and adjust** to optimise for better results.

The advert set-up process will also allow you to select **'negative keywords'**, which will restrict the appearance of your advert so you are only reaching the specific target audience relevant to your business and advert, which will avoid wasted ad spend. You can also set the **match type** of each negative keyword as part of the ad process.

For example, if the keyword is 'social media':

- **Broad match** means that any search queries containing the words 'social' and 'media' will not show your ad.

- **Phrase match** means that any queries containing the phrase 'social media' (in that order) will not show your ad.

- **Exact match** means that only the exact query 'social media' will not show your ad.

YOUR TURN – TAKE ACTION NOW

Set up a Google Ad account and start researching using the free tools – you don't have to actually set up an advert, but you will have used Google Ad words when performing keyword research using the Google keyword planner tool https://ads.google.com.

Return on investment (ROI)

In order to set up an advert, you need to work out what you are prepared to pay per click based on the return on investment.

Calculation to work out your max CPC:

(profit per customer) × (1 – profit margin) × (website conversion rate)

- average profit per customer is £500
- out of 1000 website visitors, you convert 10 into customers
- 1% website conversion rate
- 30% profit margin

$$\mathbf{Max\,CPC} = £500 \times (1 - 0.30) \times 1\% = £3.50$$

SEARCH Step 4: The R.A.P.I.D. Traffic Generator – Invite

Your business may be appearing on page 1 of Google Search, but are there any other ways of getting visitors to your website?

One option is your **Google My Business** profile, which gives you much more than visibility in local searches, but you can also **publish posts and updates for offers, events, news, etc.** directly to your Business Profile on Google to entice visitors to visit your website or physical location.

This turns Google into a social network of sorts with posts appearing in Google Search results attracting visitors to the post link or destination.

Alternatively, you could look to use **web push and notifications** to re-engage with users. These are similar to app notifications. When new content is published, it proactively reminds the user to return to your site.

Web push notifications can be set up by your developers or there are an array of web push notification tools available online that require little technical knowledge and are easy to set up.

If you consider that 60% of internet use is through mobile channels, app notifications could be used here; and then for the 40% of internet usage through a desktop, you could use a web push notification.

Web visitors must opt-in when they see an opt-in box which is triggered on their arrival. If the visitor clicks on 'Allow', he/she is added to your subscriber list.

Search for your brand and business on Google

As you must see your customer journey from your customers' perspective, it's your turn to go and see how your business appears in Google. Go and search for your own business name, you will see your website appear in the searches and often underneath your main website you will see indented links below referred to as **'site links'**.

These are where Google uses your sitemap to display quick links to information they think will be useful to the user. These tend to be the most visited pages, so Google is frontloading them to make your site more accessible and navigable without needing to actually visit the homepage first (Figure 11.13).

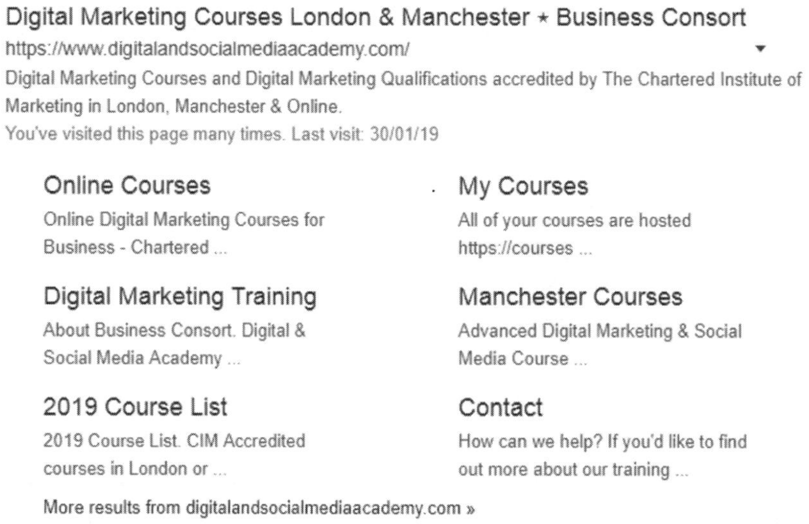

Digital Marketing Courses London & Manchester ★ Business Consort
https://www.digitalandsocialmediaacademy.com/   ▼
Digital Marketing Courses and Digital Marketing Qualifications accredited by The Chartered Institute of
Marketing in London, Manchester & Online.
You've visited this page many times. Last visit: 30/01/19

> **Online Courses**   **My Courses**
>
> Online Digital Marketing Courses for   All of your courses are hosted
> Business - Chartered ...   https://courses ...
>
> **Digital Marketing Training**   **Manchester Courses**
>
> About Business Consort. Digital &   Advanced Digital Marketing & Social
> Social Media Academy ...   Media Course ...
>
> **2019 Course List**   **Contact**
>
> 2019 Course List. CIM Accredited   How can we help? If you'd like to find
> courses in London or ...   out more about our training ...

More results from digitalandsocialmediaacademy.com »

FIGURE 11.13 Google Search for 'Business Consort' showing quick links below main listing.

> ## TIP:
>
> If you are researching how your business appears in Google for key-
> words, phrases, or even the company name, it is important to use an
> **'incognito window'** on your browser because Google Search is intui-
> tive and it will try and present the best results for you based on your
> past and recent search behaviour as well as your current location.
> So, to see an accurate view, it is important to remove your search
> history so you can see how your business presents as a brand new
> visitor would. If you use your own browser, you will get a distorted
> view of your ranking which could perhaps lead you to believe you are
> positioned far more prominently than you actually are.

Continue Google searching to see opportunities to attract your audience

After you have searched for your business and brand, you need to really
start delving deeper into other keywords relevant for your business and
evaluating how you perform for the products and services you offer.

Then move onto typing in searches for frequently asked questions
again that relate to your business, products, or services and compare
against your competitors.

Remember: searches for your brand, product, and services only relate
to around 25% of global searches and the content the consumer would
visit would be your web pages. These are specific searches when the consumer is aware of your existence and what they are looking for and are
further down the decision-making process. The other 75% of consumer
searches are when they are looking for answers, solutions, advice, etc. and
they may not even be aware of your business – never mind the product or
service you offer – so their state is different in terms of their motivation
and goal. Generally, the types of content they will be visiting will be helpful articles usually hosted on a blog page within the website.

YOUR TURN – TAKE ACTION NOW

Check out the Google My Business 'publish a post' feature by ensuring you are logged into your Google My Business account – then on the Google search homepage you'll see the feature.

Look at ways of **attracting visitors through notifications** by creating an app or mobile push notification.

SEARCH Step 5: The R.A.P.I.D. Traffic Generator – Dominate

The question that I get asked most is: How can I dominate Google and knock my competitors off the top spot and push them to page 2?

The answer is 'hard work'; but there is a system that has been proven to help you dominate the search engines using the key principles of SEO that you have learned so far – you know that linking plays a part as a ranking factor.

Stacking and linking

The process often used to dominate search engines is through stacking search results through linking related articles.

If you think about your **main keyword categories or topics** – for instance, for our business: social media, digital marketing, internet marketing, etc. – there will be key phrases within these that we would want to rank for.

The key is to create a series of related articles based on the most popular keyword phrase for your business. So, an example for our business would be using 'digital marketing' from our categories above and extending it into a more specific search such as 'digital marketing diplomas'.

We would then use a keyword tool to establish the volume of searches and related keywords for this phrase, and create an article using the initial phrase and then using the related keywords in order of popularity based on search volume then a second article, third, fourth, and so on; and then link each article to the next to form the process of stacking in search results.

YOUR TURN – TAKE ACTION NOW

Create a strategy to dominate search engines

Step 1 – use a keyword tool to research the category and then come up with a phrase.

Step 2 – list the popularity of the related phrases in order or search volumes.

Step 3 – create blog/article headlines for each of these related phrases.

Step 4 – write articles and link these together using hyperlinks so a reader can click to the next relevant article on a related topic and so on.

Not only are you writing for demand, using SEO-friendly headlines, but Google Search will have related articles show in search results, meaning you could end up having multiple listings and more opportunity for driving traffic. This strengthens brand awareness, which we know is a persuasive factor when choosing results in search. A user will almost certainly have a stronger alliance to a brand they have seen or heard of before.

You don't want to be on page 2: 75% never scroll past page 1.

'Being second is to be the first of the ones who lose.'
Ayrton Senna, racing driver

SEARCH: CHECKLIST

Google Search Console – no errors/all pages indexed.	
Website fully secure – SSL certificate/ security software.	
PCI compliance certification and vulnerability scanning.	
Google My Business profile created or updated.	
Keyword research plan and SEO tools for research.	
SEO tools for onsite coding and implementation installed (Yoast).	
Insights and trends researched for consumer trends.	
Content marketing strategy and plan content for articles/blogs.	

(Continued)

Website speed good and fast loading and performing well on mobile.	
SEO monitoring tools to evaluate your search engine visibility, competitor research, and analysis.	
Website tracking in place using Google Analytics or other analytics tool of choice.	
Google Ad strategy and set up (if using paid advertising).	
Google Search domination strategy for keywords you are not appearing in search results for.	

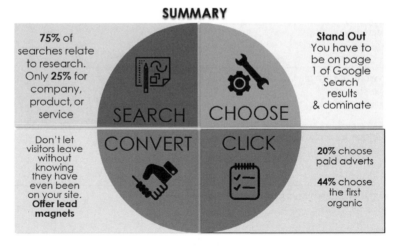

FIGURE 11.14   Summary for The R.A.P.I.D. Traffic Generator.

R.A.P.I.D Traffic Generator

FIGURE 11.15 The R.A.P.I.D. Traffic Generator Process.

Chapter 12

Social – The Proven Positioning Process

The Proven Positioning Process®

> **Increase**
> **Interact**
> **Influence**

FIGURE 12.1   The Proven Positioning Process.

Introduction

Social media is often referred to as a 'free' media marketing tool, which has resulted in lots of people trying to set up channels with no clear direction or focus.

We still see a number of self-taught social media marketers – and some succeed – but most will benefit from formal training because the reasons social media normally fails is due to a lack of the following:

- strategy

- knowing what daily social activities are

- time

- resource

- content

- frequency.

This is a marketing channel where consumers spend on average **two hours of their life a day,** so it's a huge opportunity for businesses to benefit in terms of visibility to their target audience.[1] Nowadays, it would be a rarity to find anyone without access to a smartphone and social media, so everyone has the opportunity to establish themselves as a key influencer in their sector and share content wide and far whilst building their brand and a loyal audience.

If you are not already using this channel, then your business is seriously missing out on growing relationships with your prospects and customers.

Social media strategy

There has recently been a definite shift in the importance of social media within marketing and overall business strategy. This is largely down to the fact that substantial budgets are now being allocated to social media advertising campaigns, which means that there is accountability around ROI (Figure 12.2). And this has resulted in an increased focus around creating a social media strategy.

Some businesses still think they're not suited to this market. I would, however, beg to differ and my business case for using these networks is extremely simple. I have a quick test that will allow a B2B who is considering the network to see if their audience is indeed reachable through either of these mediums.

YOUR TURN – TAKE ACTION NOW

Use any Facebook account to do a quick search for your ideal customer's interests. Interest Groups can be a good indicator; check out your competitors and search for your current customers and any influencers or partners: https://www.facebook.com/search/groups. Groups are ideal to gain more reach for your posts because by posting in groups you will constantly be reaching new audiences – and if these audiences

[1] *Source:* https://blog.globalwebindex.com/chart-of-the-day/daily-time-spent-on-social-networks/.

are part of an interest group, then they should have a higher natural engagement with your content as it should be more relevant.

You can do this activity across all of your social platforms, using 'keywords' and researching interest-based topics to see their audiences, content, companies, competitors, etc.

If people in your industry are there, then this suggests the network works for them. We will discuss another way of seeing if your markets are on Facebook when we look at targeting.

FIGURE 12.2   Research suggests 44% of businesses can't measure social media ROI (return on investment).[2]

[2] *Source:* Forbes https://www.forbes.com/sites/andrewarnold/2018/06/25/44-of-businesses-cant-measure-social-media-roi-heres-how-to-quantify-your-impact/.

'We don't have a choice on whether we do social media,
the question is how well we do it.'
Erik Qualman, author

So why invest in SOCIAL?

In brief, here are the main social media benefits (Figure 12.3):

1. Builds brand awareness.

2. Increases your customer base.

3. Connects and engages with current customers.

4. Offers a fast and cost-effective means of communication.

5. Reaches your target audience.

6. Enhances brand loyalty.

7. Promotes networking and development of partnerships.

8. Establishes you as a thought leader and identifies and connects with influencers.

FIGURE 12.3   Reach your audience through social media marketing channels.

9. Helps stay on top of industry news and competition.

10. Aids targeted advertising and retargeting.

11. Facilitates getting and giving product and service referrals and reviews.

According to Nielson, 39% of heavy social media users believe that finding out about products and services is an important reason for using a social network.[3]

Social media influence is all about positioning and being recognised as a leading expert in your own field. This channel has changed the way we communicate and taken one-way, static communication and turned it into an interactive, immersive, conversational experience where brands and social media users can really build meaningful relationships.

We turn to our peers for recommendations, help, advice, and support, especially in our consumer purchasing journey. We rely on reviews and testimonials from our trusted network to evaluate and ultimately assist in ensuring we are buying from the best provider.

Social media has opened up a non-intrusive way of keeping you and your business in front of your audience without the need for constant marketing emails. The level of interactivity on social channels can vastly speed up the sales cycle and also give users the true feeling of 'knowing' a brand or person.

---

[3] *Source:* Nielson https://www.nielsen.com/us/en/insights/reports/2017/2016-nielsen-social-media-report.html.

YOUR TURN – TAKE ACTION NOW

Success in social media marketing requires all of points below, so it will be a good idea to look at how you are doing in these areas and identify which you could improve on.

- **Reach:** Refers to the number of users who have come across a particular item of content on a social platform. Measure the reach of any given post, then divide the reach by your total number of followers and multiply by 100 to get your post reach percentage. A good tactic to aid reach is posting in Groups – but also leverage your employees to spread your message and brand.

- **Authority:** In order to gain authority on social media, you will need to increase your visibility and keep growing your network, so remember to include social media links in email campaigns, signatures, and on your website and proactively encourage connection through all online and offline channels (business cards and printed materials). Adding comment, like, and share buttons and making your blog articles portable will help too. A large proportion of content that you see in social media doesn't originate from the author but is seen on a website or blog and 'shared back in' to their audience, giving that brand or business added reach and authority outside their own network. It will be important to focus on your niche and establish yourself as an expert in your field by providing real value, consistently posting and engaging your community, as well as building relationships with influencers (your customers can be your influencers, as can your employees and other contacts in your network).

(continued)

- **Credibility:** Build trust around the brand through your social content and ensure you are presenting a strong but transparent and approachable image. Gaining credibility will include being an active networker and showing you are competent and knowledgeable about your industry by writing opinion and thought-leadership articles. Don't just focus on the news: tell people what the news actually means to them. Showcase yourself as a leader!

- **Influence:** A very controversial metric as a whole. A brand or business could have a large audience, but are they actually taking any action that impacts on the organisation? Engagement, however, is a good metric to measure to understand if the content you are sharing is resonating with your audience. Just remember to think about whether you focused more on generating interaction (replies, comments) or on spreading a message (shares, retweets, and posts).

TIP:

If you are looking to measure reach for social posts, these are all provided in the social media platforms analytics or you can use social media monitoring tools.

What not to do on social media

Do not fall into the posting for the sake of posting trap.

I cannot stress enough that having an actual purpose and objective for your social media is vital. It is not enough jump on the social media bandwagon just because others are. Social media content needs to exist for a reason; otherwise you will end up posting pointless, unengaging content that doesn't match your audience's needs.

The key to success lies in human interaction and connection, not promotion of business and brands – which is just a by-product that comes from social networking.

Think outside the box and really try and view your social media like a documentary, a window into your life, a brand or business.

A great approach to adding value and become a key part of your networks' content consumption and engagement is through thinking: **'Have I done any good in the world today?'** This will help you focus on the reason you are on social media and what your network stands for. Providing help and support will not only strengthen your brand awareness, but also form bonds and confidence within your network.

Think demand and your customer needs and problems and how your social network can serve your audience.

YOUR TURN – TAKE ACTION NOW

Social media audit

Use the 5Ws for your social media audit.

Create a simple table with these as your five headings. Record your findings under each heading in the column.

- **Who** – You/your business (brand), customer, influencer, competition.

- **Where** – List all of your social media channels.

(continued)

- **What** – Record what they are posting.

- **When** – Review when they post: frequency and times and days of week.

- **Why** – Look at calls to action and the purpose of the posts plus engagement.

You can add a notes section to record any observations and ideas.

EXAMPLE

I have included a sample audit below. You will need to fully complete yours. If you don't already have a social media presence, then just leave 'You' out of the audit.

WHO	WHERE	WHAT	WHEN	WHY	Notes
You	**All Channels** LinkedIn Facebook Twitter	Video	Daily	Event Sign-Up	Currently getting 300 landing page visits and 60 sign-ups. Review landing page to optimise and increase conversions
Customer	**All Channels** LinkedIn Facebook Twitter				

WHO	WHERE	WHAT	WHEN	WHY	Notes
Influencer	All Channels LinkedIn Facebook Twitter				
Competi- tion	All Channels LinkedIn Facebook Twitter				

YOUR TURN – TAKE ACTION NOW

Once you have completed your audit, it is time to establish what the goal for your network existence is.

Creating a **social media marketing mission statement** is a fantastic starting point.

When writing your mission statement think about the following:

1. Why does your social media profile/page exist?

2. Who is your content for and what does it help them achieve (specific benefits)?

Be specific; but aim to inspire. And keep it short and simple. Plus, it should always be closely aligned to your business mission and vision.

EXAMPLE

Here is an example mission statement:
Connect with us on social media where we share tips, trends, tools, and techniques to help entrepreneurs and businesses to maximise their online presence to accelerate their success in order to profitably scale and grow.

Social communities

There are lots of different types of **social communities,** but they can be broken down into six main categories:

- **Pleasure:** These are just for fun communities.

- **Problem:** Most customer service communities are based around solving a problem. The majority of business communities are trying to solve a problem or pain. These tend to be built around a common interest or topic.

- **Hope:** Health, fitness, and personal improvement communities are a good example for hope. These are action-based communities of people trying to bring about change.

- **Pain:** Support group style communities supporting people in a time of need; brought together through external events or situations, or perhaps around new technology or regulations, these communities help people in a time of fear or worry.

- **Social acceptance – peer groups:** These are exclusive communities made up of people in the same profession or undertaking the same activities.

- **Exclusive:** An alumni group is an example of this type of community – as you couldn't join an alumni community or group unless you actually went to the academic institution.

Now, answer these questions to establish the 'purpose' and type of community your business will be:

- How will social media align with helping you achieve your business goals?

- Who are your competitors and what are they doing on social media?

- If you are using social media currently, what's working and what's not?

- Who is connecting with you on social media?

- Which networks does your target audience use?

- How does your social media presence compare to that of your competitors?

- Who is your social community for?

- Why will your community be unique?

- Does your social network or community serve a higher cause? Are you on a mission? What is your vision?

- What will you help them with?

- Who will be the content creators?

- What are the key benefits to joining your network or community?

This isn't just about creating content, as you need a clear idea about what your outcome is to develop your approach. This could be one or a combination or all of the below:

- brand maintenance;

- community building;

- influencer outreach;

- reputation management and development;

- big-splash creative campaign that generates a lot of short-term attention.

Posting strategy

Now you have a clear idea about the goal of your social network or community, it is time to think about the content you will post and the strategy behind it. This stops you posting on the fly and reminds you and your community what you will post, when, and why (Figure 12.4).

Timing is everything - when are
your customers reading and
engaging with your content?

FIGURE 12.4 Do you know when your customers are engaging in your content?

TIP:

On Facebook, the 'When Your Fans Are Online' feature will tell you the optimal time to post. Use this data to increase your **reach.** On your Facebook page, click on 'insights' in the top navigation, then 'posts' in the left navigation on desktop, and then you will see at the top 'When Your Fans Are Online' tab.

A simple strategy that lays out markers for content is **'theming your days'** so you have specific content on each day of the week.

Example of 'themed days':

- **Motivation Monday** – Simply try to make people smile on a Monday: aim to inspire and motivate after the weekend.

- **Tips Tuesday** – People want to make their lives more efficient and effective and anything around saving time, money, or effort works well on Tuesdays – once they have cleared the backlog from the weekend on Monday.

- **Wisdom Wednesday** – This is a great day for sharing your own wisdom and we find webinars and lives tend to be well received midweek. We all love learning!

- **Throwback Thursday** – People love to see 'olden days' imagery versus today. Amazing statistics and facts about how the world has evolved always inspire intrigue.

- **Freebie Friday** – Strangely enough, Facebook has found that through extensive research we hit a so called **'happiness index'** on Thursdays – whereas people tend to check their emails a lot after 2 p.m. on a Friday – so this is a great time for email digests, and we've also found that free resources on a Friday afternoon or interactive polls or quizzes are also popular.

Posting on weekends?

There is no hard and fast rule about posting on weekends; just consider who your audience are and what they will be doing. For instance, sport is one of the highest engaged topics on a Saturday for obvious reasons, as many games and matches are happening.

Posting about activities or days out can work well, but more corporate-focused posts may not be so well received because people's minds are on leisure pursuits and activities rather than their working day. It is about testing and seeing what will work for your audience and gaining insight to perfect your posting cycle.

Why post?

So: what do you want from your social media posts?

A common response I hear a lot is: 'get more website traffic'.

And this is where social media fails a business – when the goal is to drive traffic from the social network outside to websites.

Consider the **actual** behaviour of ourselves and our customers within a social media network: most of the time we stay in our social media feed. **We don't leave and visit external websites unless there is a very good reason.**

Which posts will make us leave the social network?

1. **Breaking news** – If perhaps you caught sight of a post about an earthquake in your hometown, then I'd bet you would more

than likely chance a look at the full article. We see social media users visit articles that are relevant to them and their current circumstances.

2. **Tips and articles** – A common reason to visit external content is seeing blogs or articles that are helpful to us. We love tips and quick learning. Or headlines focused around what we should never do – we can't resist a sneaky peek just to check we aren't doing anything wrong.

3. **Buy products or services** – Impulse buys or consumer-focused products tend to be the most popular type of purchases. Basically, if we see something that appeals, we may check it out or leave to buy it.

4. **Sign-up for FREE resources** – Social media posts offering free events, webinars, or any added-value resources are a great pull and users will definitely click and visit external landing pages to sign-up for something they deem useful or relevant.

5. **Adverts** – Facebook has made it harder for brands and businesses to get reach for their content. This isn't for any other reason than the fact that Facebook doesn't want to saturate their users with content that isn't relevant. This could be seen as a disadvantage; but, to be honest, it's probably a good thing, because it will make businesses and brands target their content rather than posting to the masses. This in turn should reap better results. Advertising is also a very cost-effective means of reaching a highly targeted audience across social platforms.

Targeting your audience for free using social media

Let's cover the ways you can reach a larger and more targeted audience without paying for the privilege. A common misconception is that you can only reach or target your audience by paying, but that isn't strictly

Facebook tracks your audience's online behaviour, allowing you
to target your ads more specifically.

FIGURE 12.5   Target accurately through tracking.

true. Some of the most under-utilised tools in the world of social media
are 'targeting' in LinkedIn and Facebook, as well as Twitter and Instagram
(Figure 12.5).

The majority of social media posts are not targeted, perhaps because
people believe that in that way they will reach the masses; but actually
the opposite will happen. A post with no targeting will reach the fewest
possible people on that network or even in that brand or business network. Why? Because when you post, the social network needs to know
who that post is relevant for and who should see it. And you have to tell
them exactly this information.

How do you target social media posts for free? The simple answer is through using one or many of the options below:

- **Hashtags** – Used to identify messages on a specific topic (great for targeting).

- **Mentions** – Used to refer or reference something or someone (a shameless way of getting in front of other audiences too).

- **Including and excluding** – Limiting your audience through organic social media posting will actually increase your reach. Strange but true; because you are eliminating anyone it isn't relevant to by excluding them. Again, including the specific audiences you wish to target will have a positive impact on reach.

- **Targeting through behaviour and interest** – On Facebook and LinkedIn, you can target specific audiences based on their social media behaviour and interests. If you aren't already using these features, then they should be a priority to familiarise yourself with. Let's look at how you can do this.

1. **On your Facebook page**

   Where you 'Write a Post', you will see three dots to the bottom left of where you type your post – once you click on that, scroll down to news feed and click on 'Public'.

   This is where you can choose to restrict by age or location or target by interests (*Facebook can help you to reach specific audiences by looking at their interests, activities, the pages they have liked and closely related topics. You can choose up to 16 interests*):

   - **Restricted audience:** Only certain people on Facebook.

   - **News feed targeting:** People in your news feed with specific interests and their friends.

2. **On LinkedIn**

You can do exactly the same thing from your company page. Where you would 'Start a Post', above it is set to default to 'anyone'. When you click on this you will see the option for 'targeted audience'. Target options include:

- language

- location

- job function

- company size

- university

- industry

- seniority.

Basic posting strategies

A good rule of thumb is to break your content into categories, such as key topics for your industry, and do the following:

- Drive traffic to your blog articles about half the time.

- Then, split the rest of your time between sharing other people's content on your feed – remembering to comment – and posting promotional and lead generation posts. A small proportion of this should also be about your company culture, such as 'what is it like to work at XYZ'.

Another popular strategy is the 80:20 rule:

- 80% of your posts should add value for your audience;

- 20% can be promotional.

I use this rule to aim for **80% planned content** and 20% **live real-time content** to keep it dynamic.

Or you could use the rule of thirds strategy:

1. one-third promotional;

2. one-third shared content;

3. one-third geared to interact with your audience.

SOCIAL Step 1: The Proven Positioning Process – Increase

Using our simple three-step 'Social Media Strategy – The Proven Positioning Process' you'll be able to reap the rewards that this powerful medium has to offer.

We have calculated the perfect posting strategy, and we'll cover:

- Best posting times and frequency.

- The perfect media mix to ensure maximum audience reach and growth.

- How to engage with other people's content for your own benefit.

- The daily tasks behind this proven social strategy (and the best bit is this only takes 10 minutes a day!)

- How to double your engagement but also double your network.

- Why 'scheduling' could be destroying your reach by as much as 70%.

Optimise your profile and grow your network

Once you've decided which networks to focus on, it's time to create your profiles or improve existing profiles to reflect your **content marketing mission statement.**

Set up (and optimise) your accounts: first steps

- Make sure you complete all sections.

- Use keywords your audience would use to find your business.

- Make sure images render properly on each network.

Growing your network

The organic way to grow your social media networks and audience is through connecting or following. To continually grow your network, there are a few important steps you need to incorporate into your strategy and daily actions.

First, to build a quality and targeted audience made up of people who you feel are relevant, you need to make a concerted effort to seek and find new people to add to your network (Figure 12.6). This can easily be done by searching keywords and finding like-minded people, organisations, and brands in your industry or target markets.

Social listening allows you to track, analyse, and respond to conversations about your brand and industry online and will be extremely helpful in this process to identify suggested connections.

There are an array of **social listening tools** on the market that will help you easily see what people are talking about or interested in and will also help you keep an eye on your competition, such as **Hootsuite, Buffer,** and **Sprout Social.**

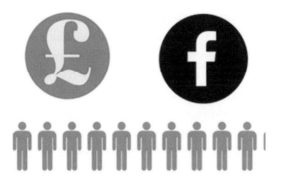

Consider your budget,
preferred channel, and
target audience

FIGURE 12.6 Choose your channel based on your audience.

These tools can be used to monitor:

1. customer feedback;

2. direct mentions;

3. discussions regarding specific keywords, topics, competitors, or industries;

4. analysis to gain insights that in turn create social media opportunities.

TIP:

Connect with or follow anyone who has interacted with you or your brand; proactively find new connections using keywords (I follow all my competitors).

Quite often, I am asked about who to accept connections from, especially on networks like LinkedIn. Social networking is about extending your existing contacts and reaching those you don't yet know. I would always recommend that when you receive a connection request, view their profile; and if they have completed it and have a picture – and they look legitimate – then why wouldn't you connect?

If you only want to connect with people you know you have a mobile phone for that.

Some people think they don't want to connect with others because they aren't their target market or preferred audience, but that is not what social networking is about. If you are looking to build a strong network who could introduce or recommend you to others, then you shouldn't be approaching connection requests thinking 'will this person buy from me' but 'is this person a good addition to my network because they are a keen networker, have an audience or influence in their sector etc.'?

Online networking is no different to offline networking: it is about getting awareness and positioning in your sector as the go-to person for 'xyz', so people who haven't even necessarily done business with you would recommend you as your positioning is so strong that they already perceive and consider you as trusted, worthy, and good at what you do.

YOUR TURN – TAKE ACTION NOW

Have a look at and explore these social listening and monitoring tools:

- **Native Analytics Tools** within the Social Media Platforms.

- **Tweet Deck:** https://tweetdeck.twitter.com (free).

- **Buffer:** https://buffer.com/business (free trial available).

- **Sprout Social:** https://sproutsocial.com/ (free trial available).

- **Hootsuite:** https://hootsuite.com/ (free trial available).

- **Tweet Reach:** https://tweetreach.com/ (free).

- **Followerwonk:** https://followerwonk.com (free).

- **SumAll:** https://sumall.com/ (free).

- **MentionMapp:** https://mentionmapp.com (free).

- **Boardreader:** http://boardreader.com (free).

- **Buzzsumo:** https://buzzsumo.com/ (free trial available).

- **Socialbakers:** https://www.socialbakers.com/free-social-tools (free tools).

Social media platforms

Facebook

Here are all of the Facebook page components and what they do.

- **Create additional company pages:** You can create multiple brand/ business pages (or a 'public figure'). You can collect Facebook 'Likes' for your page – this is different to a Facebook Profile which is always a person and requires you to accept 'friends': a Page allows anyone to 'Like' the page without the need to accept or moderate.

    As a Facebook Page, you can interact as the page; or if you also have a Profile, you can interact as a person. A Group must be managed by a person – and this is an advantage of using a separate work-related Profile: you can also connect with your work network and like pages (which you can't do as a Page).

- **Call to action button:** The button at the top of your Page helps people take an action. Choose from:

  1. make a booking with you

  2. contact you

  3. learn more about your business

  4. shop with you

  5. download your app or play your game

  6. join your community.

- **Recommendations and reviews:** Get feedback about your business with reviews.

- **Shop:** You can choose to promote and sell your products through Facebook.

- **Services:** If your business doesn't sell products, then set up your services. Now you can promote your shop, products, and services across your page without visitors needing to leave to find out more.

- **Inbox:** Send and receive private messages not visible to anyone apart from the sender and recipient.

- **Notifications:** Alerts to any activity on your page, such as interactions to posts, etc.

- **Insights:** Analysis of your page activity, such as followers, engagement, etc.

- **Publishing tools:** This feature allows you to create and schedule posts within Facebook itself, as opposed to using third-party tools which can reduce reach.

- **Creator studio:** Allows you to publish and manage posts, insights, and messages from all of your Facebook Pages in one place. Perfect if you manage multiple pages.

- **Settings:** Each business will have their own specific preferences for settings; so it is always best practice when setting up or managing a Page to review its settings.

TIP:

There are two settings I'd suggest reviewing.

Page Moderation: This allows you to prevent any posts containing certain words to be held in moderation for your review before making public. For instance, you could choose to block competitor brand names etc.

Profanity Filter: Set as 'strong' to avoid social media users using bad language on your page. Any posts will be blocked.

- **Group:** A Facebook Group will bring people who share common interests together as they discuss or interact with posts. Groups tend to get far more engagement because people have joined them because of a specific interest. For instance, someone joining our Business Consort 'Digital Marketing Made Easy' Group wants to be part of a community on that subject.

- **Live:** Facebook Live reach tends to be more engaged than uploaded video; perhaps because you can pre-announce that you're live, and your network gets a notification. It could just be the fact it is live and interactive, which is added-value content.

- **Event:** Create online or offline events. A bonus of creating an event is that it allows you to manage attendees in two categories (interested or going). Due to the fact that other people may be able to see who is interested or going to events in a news feed story, notifications, on the event itself, or in the Events section of a profile – depending on the event's privacy setting – this may alert their peers to an event of interest. If it's a public event, anyone on or off Facebook can see if you're interested or going.

- **Offer:** Create an offer, discount, or deal that you can fully customise with a link to redeem the offer.

- **Job:** Receive and manage job applications through Facebook.

- **'Write a Post':**

    1. **Post a photo/video:** individual photo, album, slideshow, or instant experience, which allows images and photos to be combined to create an immersive storytelling experience.

    2. **Stories** with **Facebook Stories:** you'll be able to see both how many people have viewed your Stories and the names of individual viewers. Like Instagram, Facebook will allow people to view Stories for 24 hours. These are displayed in a row at the top of your news feed.

    3. **Get messages** via messenger in your inbox.

    4. **Feeling/activity** which means you can explain what you are doing and how you are feeling.

    5. **Check in** (to a location) to show people where you are.

    6. **Get calls** on your business number.

    7. **Add directions** to your business location.

    8. **Tag a product** from your shop.

    9. **Get shop visits,** which encourages offline, physical location visits.

    10. **Event tickets** for promoting events either online or face to face.

    11. **Write a note:** this is like a blog article that social media users can view in their feed without leaving Facebook. If they click on the post the whole article appears in a drop down.

12. **Polls** to research and interact with your audience.

13. **Add a milestone:** an important achievement or accolade to record as your page history.

14. **Support non-profit** – great for charities.

15. **Start a Q&A:** use this tool to research your audience and find out what they want.

16. **List:** Choose from a list or make a custom list, i.e. this year's highlights.

17. **Watch party:** a feature that lets people in Groups watch live or pre-recorded videos together (and chat) in real time.

18. **Share the post to Instagram** too – which is owned by Facebook.

- **Advertise your business:** There is the option of boosting posts; but you are limited very much in terms of your campaign goals as this only gives the option of paying for impressions on others' news feeds. Take a look at Facebooks Advertising Page – https://www.facebook.com/business/ads – which is a useful resource to look at advertising options and success stories. Then, for greater control and objective options, 'create an ad' using the Ad Manager within 'Business Manager', which allows you to manage ad accounts and your page or multiple pages all in one place:

  1. Go to business.facebook.com.

  2. Click 'Create Account'.

  3. Enter a name for your business; select the primary Page and enter your name and work email. Note: If you don't yet have a Page for your business, create one.

  4. Enter your information in the rest of the required fields.

Twitter

Twitter Profiles can be for people, brands, or businesses. To subscribe to see **'Tweets'** from other users (Tweets are social media posts) you would **'Follow'** them and the aim would be to grow your **'Followers'** in turn. Either way, you can interact with others both from a point of view of following and interacting with tweets.

The easiest way to find people you may wish to follow is through the **search field,** or Twitter suggest **'Who to follow'** based on your network.

Twitter will also suggest **'Trends for you'** – again, based on your activity, which you can change to suit your own preferences.

Here are the most useful features on Twitter and what they do.

- **Twitter handle:** For instance, mine are **@businessconsort** or **@dawnmcgruer** which is my username.

- **Compose a 'tweet':** with a photo, video, gif, poll, or location. You can use hashtags too for targeting and categorising your post for a specific topic. On the Mobile App you can go live and in your settings you can choose to notify your followers when you do so.

- **Profile:** In here you can control and edit your header image, profile picture, your description or bio, and general details such as website etc.

TIP:

Complete all sections to improve your profile strength which increases as you add more relevant content. On your dashboard you will then see you have reach **'All Star'** status which will help with visibility on the platform.

- **Lists:** You can collate Twitter users into 'Lists' which can be private or public. For instance, I have lists of clients, influencers, journalists, etc. – it's a great way of just seeing a segment of your network for a specific topic. We also have a list called 'Retweet Relationships' where we collate all of our partners that we proactively **'retweet'** (which means to share) and interact with. These are alliances or partners that have audiences we would like to target and vice versa. We only link with non-competitive partners who we feel create quality content that adds value to our audience and that we think they will find useful. Lists are perfect for engaging with specific users' content and cancelling out the white noise.

- **Moments:** Allows you to collate multiple tweets into stories. Moments showcases what is happening around the world. You can create 'moments' and add a title, description, and cover image, a bit like a mini blog post, then select the tweets you want to attach. You can choose from tweets you've liked, from specific accounts, find via a Twitter search or by using the tweet's link. Then press publish!

- **Notifications:** Alerts you to any activity, such as interactions with your profile or tweets.

- **Messages:** Send and receive private messages that are not visible to anyone apart from the sender and recipient.

- **Bookmarks:** Bookmarks are private, so no one can see which tweets have been bookmarked. It is like saving tweets so you can view them in your bookmarked tab.

- **Promote mode:** For a flat monthly fee of £79, Twitter will automatically promote your tweets according to your preferred targeting (interests or locations).

- **Twitter ads:** Twitter advertising allows you to reach a larger audience and set up ad campaigns for different objectives. You can promote Tweets, Accounts, and Trends.

- **Analytics:** Analysis of your page activity such as followers, engagement, etc.

- **Media studio:** Allows you to publish, schedule, and manage tweets, insights, and content from your Twitter profile in one place.

- **Settings and privacy:** This is very much down to user preference but worth checking if setting up or managing a Twitter profile.

LinkedIn

This platform is very much more business focused and tends to be the one that users find most difficult to use.

On LinkedIn, like Facebook, you can have a profile and a company page.

- **Home:** General overview of your LinkedIn Profile and Page activity, hashtags, groups, trending news, and your news feed.

- **Search:** In the top navigation you can search LinkedIn for people, companies, schools, groups, jobs, and content.

- **Posting:** You can choose who sees the post by clicking on 'anyone'.

- **Start a post:** Choose to include a photo, upload a video, or go live using the mobile app. As with all social networks, you can write your post to include @mentions, #hashtags, and hyperlinks. There are also options to include documents, give kudos (to give recognition to a colleague), or share that you are hiring.

- **Write an article:** This allows you to create blog-style articles within LinkedIn which tend to get much more engagement as social users don't have to leave the platform. There is definitely more trust toward content housed within the platform.

- **My network:** Connections, groups, companies, hashtags that are currently in your network with LinkedIn's suggestion to grow your network using the 'More suggestions for you' and 'Alumni you may know'.

TIP:

On the desktop version of LinkedIn, you will see **'more options'** in the top left-hand corner of the screen. This is where you can upload or sync your contacts. This is a really fast way to grow your network and connect on LinkedIn with email contacts, prospects, customers, suppliers, partners, journalists, or anyone you have contact details for. If you are uploading using Excel, you must save the file as 'csv' otherwise you will encounter an upload error.

Use a business card scanner to quickly import details into an Excel spreadsheet and upload to connect with multiple people that you met at an exhibition or networking event. They receive a 'connection request' message through LinkedIn and you can add a custom note to make it more personal too.

- **Jobs:** Find or post a job and check out latest salary information.

- **Messaging:** Send and receive private messages not visible to anyone part from the sender and recipient.

- **Notifications:** Alerts to any activity on your page, such as interactions to posts, etc.

- **Me:** This is where you access your profile, membership subscription (if you have one), settings, manage posts and activity, job posts, and company page (if you have one set up) or sign out.

- **Groups:** Create a group or view groups you are a member of.

- **ProFinder:** Online directory to help you source freelance professionals for your business for specific projects.

- **Salary:** See a detailed breakdown of salaries by job title and location.

- **Slideshare:** https://www.slideshare.net/ was bought by LinkedIn and is packed full of presentations, infographics, and documents.

- **Create a company page:** Create your company or brand page.

- **Advertise:** https://business.linkedin.com/marketing-solutions/ads.

    1. **Sponsored content:** promoted content appears in news feeds and is very effective.

    2. **Video ads:** share videos adverts across LinkedIn.

    3. **Carousel ads:** swipe across a collection of images.

    4. **Text ads:** appear at the top of LinkedIn desktop and tend not be as well engaged with as sponsored content in news feeds.

    5. **Sponsored InMail:** send a private message to someone outside your network.

    6. **Display ads and dynamic ads:** appear on the desktop around main page content and sponsored content, and again tend to generate better results. Dynamic adverts can be personalised to contain LinkedIn user data to capture attention.

    7. **Advertising costs: sponsored content and text ads** – choose cost-per-click (CPC): you only pay when people click your ad; or cost-per-1000 impressions (CPM): you pay when people see your ad. **Sponsored InMail** – cost-per-send (CPS): you pay for each InMail message that is successfully delivered.

- **Elevate:** This feature allows you to involve employees so you can create content for your target audiences, employees will see content that is relevant to their interests and can easily share to Facebook, Twitter, and LinkedIn and it has built in tracking to view results.

In addition to these basic features, LinkedIn offers the following advertising features.

- **Conversion tracking:** View in your advert Campaign Manager.

- **Contact targeting:** You can upload up to 300000 email addresses. Once you're on the audience creation page in Campaign Manager, click on 'Create an Audience' and choose '**Match Based on a List of Email Contacts'.**

- **Lead generation and lead gen forms:** When LinkedIn members click on your ad, their profile data automatically populates a form they can submit with one click.

- **Website demographics and website retargeting:** In Campaign Manager, you can set up tracking for your website to get professional demographic data about your website visitors and which content they engage with the most. Create website visitors' audiences to re-engage.

- **Account-based marketing:** Reach decision makers at your target accounts by uploading your account list. You can upload up to 300 000 company names. Next, set up Account Targeting for your LinkedIn ads. Once you're on the audience creation page in Campaign Manager, click 'Create an Audience'. Choose '**Match Based on a List of Accounts'.** Your list may take up to 48 hours to match and become available for targeting.

- **Audience network:** Get your sponsored content in front of more people, on LinkedIn and across the web.

There are two basic membership options for LinkedIn: the **Basic (free)** account; or the **Premium Career** or **Business** Account. If you are an individual looking for a job, then Premium Career is good option.

Unless you have a sales team or are a recruiter, then the best paid solution is the entry level called 'Business Premium' which should be sufficient for the majority of businesses.

Business Premium features include:

- **Five InMails per month:** Send a private message to someone outside your network.

- **Who's viewed your profile:** Great to see who is checking you out.

- **Business insights:** Get exclusive insights into public and private companies on LinkedIn.

- **Job insights:** Compare your skills to the qualifications required for open jobs and see how you stack up against other applicants.

- **Unlimited people browsing:** With Premium, you can view any profile (up to third-degree connections) from search results or whilst browsing similar profiles.

- **LinkedIn learning:** Access LinkedIn online training courses.

- **Open profile:** Increases brand visibility as this feature allows any LinkedIn member to see your full profile and reach out to you, without InMail credits.

- **Resumé builder:** Turn your LinkedIn profile into an easily downloadable PDF.

- **Talent solutions:** Find, attract, and recruit talent with **LinkedIn recruiter.**

- **Sales solutions:** Unlock sales opportunities with **LinkedIn Sales navigator.**

- **Learning:** Develop skills for you or your team.

Instagram

Here's a list of the most useful features on Instagram.

- **Photo or video** (live or uploaded video): Videos in the main feed can run a little longer at 60 seconds. Followers can comment on or like your Live Video stream in real time, but the video is gone after you end it (it doesn't save to your account).

- **Instagram stories:** Video recordings are limited to a length of 15 seconds and stories allow people to view Stories for 24 hours. These are displayed in a row at the top of your news feed.

- **Push notifications:** Followers get a push notification telling them you're going live and you can get notifications from your favourite Instagram accounts you follow.

- **Geo-tagged content hashtags:** Help reach your target audience.

- **IGTV:** Instagram TV is an app within Instagram that gives users the ability to share videos that are up to an hour long – which is a bit like a TV programme.

- **Hyperlink username and hashtags in your bio:** When you type an @ or #, the username or hashtag that follows will automatically be hyperlinked. Link to recent premium content you are promoting too.

- **Switch to an Instagram business account:** Navigate to your profile in Instagram (for mobile), and under Account Settings you'll see an option called 'Switch to Business Profile'. You will then be asked to log into Facebook within the app. After that, you'll be asked to select which Facebook page you want to connect with. There are more features, plus anyone can follow your account – just like for Facebook pages – without the need to accept or moderate.

- **Shoppable tags in stories:** Shoppable tags allow businesses to tag their products in their photos.

- **Use @ mentions to tag other users in their stories:** These @ mentions can be typed on the image, or they can be added as Stickers.

- **Advertising:** You must have a Facebook Page and use Ad Manager to advertise on Instagram: https://business.instagram. com/advertising/. Check out the case studies and advertising options here too.

Interactive social media campaigns for network growth and engagement

Once you have connected with everyone you know, it can be hard to steadily grow your audience, so social media campaign tools can be a great addition to really drive interaction and reach.

There are two third-party tools that you can use to further enhance interactivity and take your social campaigns to the next level. I love them, because they make it so quick and simple to set up interactive social campaigns like contests, giveaways, coupons, polls, and quizzes.

Woobox

The easiest way to sign-up is using your Facebook account, which then will ask which pages you wish to connect to display the campaigns etc. you create using Woobox. Some tools are free; but this is a fairly inexpensive tool to access all features. Key features include:

- **Coupons, giveaways, contests, polls, quizzes.**

- **Facebook tabs** – Add further Pages to Facebook such as adding custom or campaigns as a tab or showcasing your YouTube, Twitter, Instagram, or Pinterest social media pages.

- **Forms** – Collect leads, sign-ups for free downloads, or anything you like!

- **Brackets** – A feature that you can use to create a vote of which results are displayed using leader boards.

- **Instant wins** give participants a chance to win a prize instantly **or Winner Picker** – randomly select winners from people who liked, commented, or both on one or more of your Facebook and Instagram posts.

ShortStack

Very similar to Woobox and again offers a free version as well as premium options to access the full suite. Use the templates to easily create contests, giveaways, landing pages, or quizzes.

TIP:

Creating content about you and your business will spark human interaction naturally. Accolade marketing is one of the best received types of post. Humans love to celebrate success of our friends, family and colleagues. So why would it be different online?

Put yourself out there. A photograph with people or a person in it has far more power to engage than a static image. Here is an example of a post I shared on LinkedIn about signing the publishing contract for this book with Wiley. At the time of sharing this with you, it was still getting visibility and interaction (Figure 12.7).

(Continued)

Dawn McGruer FCIM FRSA ...
Awarded Best Female Speaker - Digital Marketing Author & Trainer - Ranked #...
1w

Guess what I signed today! An amazing publishing contract with Wiley Publishers for my new 'Digital Marketing 'book! This really is a very proud moment in my career and I just couldn't wait to share it with you all! #publishedauthor #business #dynamicdigitalmarketing #marketing

with You

 66 · 14 Comments

Like   Comment   Share

2,689 views of your post in the feed

FIGURE 12.7   Example of a social media post celebrating success.

SOCIAL Step 2: The Proven Positioning Process – Interact

If you are a social voyeur, you will find that standing from afar and just watching what is happening is a slow journey through social networking.

The key is to be social. If you don't interact and actively join and participate in conversations, then this could be considered anti-social.

Every time you see a post in your social feed, imagine that the person is standing in front of you at a networking event and try and 'interact' with them in a human, positive, and engaging way to initiate two-way conversation or activity.

For example, if you see an amazing statistic or intriguing quote, try **'liking'** it to show that person you quite simply liked what they had to say; or **'share'** it to your network if you feel it would add value (but remember to always put your own slant on it by typing in a question like 'what do you think about this?' to try and initiate engagement from your audience, or a statement like 'I thought you may find this useful because I did').

Most people find it quite easy to like or share content, but when it comes to **'commenting'** then putting your name to a written statement scares people off. So, think about commenting as like having a conversation at a network event. If you see an article or infographic etc. then simply comment with 'great article' or 'really useful' – it doesn't have to be lengthy – but take normal offline interactions and use them online. If someone posts an amazing accolade or achievement, then celebrate their success and congratulate them.

Social networks use **notifications** about 'new job' or 'birthday' etc. to try and encourage social networking users to do this, so it is definitely an approach they're promoting. They also use it to entice us back into the social platform through App notifications.

If you are sharing information to your network, people won't mind that you are not the original author or post creator – but they will see you as a source of information that they either like or interact with. This means you don't always have to create original content – and you can see some of the most influential channels take this approach. It also brings a more interesting dynamic to your social media because it isn't 'all about you'. It is about being a one-stop-shop for your audience for a specific topic or interest.

If we look at how social networks perceive their users' influence, which in turn impacts on the visibility of what you post, remember that **the more active you are, the more social you are, the more you grow your network and the more people engage with you, then the better positioned you are in their eyes.**

Social networks reward users for using them as they were intended, so why not reap the benefits from doing what they want you to do and get a three-way win whereby your audience loves you, you and your business are benefitting through growing your network and building strong relationships, and the social network is also rewarding you with reach?

About 10 years ago, I developed a technique for my clients that had to be extremely easy to remember and use to ensure they incorporated the strategy into their day-to-day schedules and so that it didn't take up too much time or resource.

This unique and highly effective strategy is called **the 'MAGIC 10'**. It guarantees that if you do it every single day using the exact methodology I provide you with, you will absolutely 100% increase your network and audience engagement (Figure 12.8).

The 'MAGIC 10' strategy

I worked out the DAILY tasks behind a successful social strategy – AND the best bit is it only takes 10 minutes a day!

FIGURE 12.8   The MAGIC 10 social media strategy created by Dawn McGruer.

Every day you **MUST** interact across all of your chosen social media platforms.

- **ENGAGE** – Comment, like, and share 10 items in your news feed on each social network.

- **CONNECT** – Connect or follow 10 NEW people on a social media platform.

There are no best times to do this as such, but there are a few pointers you can follow. Insights in your social media platforms will build a picture of your most engaged content and you can see the peak times that received the most engagement.

The MAGIC 10 strategy means that instead of doing your social media in one hit at a certain specified time each day, you are mixing up your posting schedule. I want you to **engage and connect in the morning, noon, and at night.** This will also allow you to see the times that your own audience are most engaged, by analysing the times of your shared posts and the engagement you got.

Within a week you can see huge results: we have seen networks and engagement double in a month.

There are big advantages to using this process and it ticks many boxes from the social networking perspective.

- It ensures you have a really good and consistent posting frequency. This process doesn't even rely on you creating unique content, because you will be sharing content while putting your own slant on it in each post.

- It doesn't matter that it isn't your own content. It gives your feed up-to-date posts on a daily basis that your audience can interact with. Post nothing and you have a 100% chance of getting no engagement whatsoever.

- It automatically provides you with the perfect media mix to ensure maximum audience reach and growth. As you will be sharing content, this diversifies your feed so it isn't all about you but brings content relating to your industry from multiple sources to one place – making you a one-stop-shop for all their industry news.

So remember: engaging in others' content is for your own benefit to encourage interaction and therefore social networking.

YOUR TURN – TAKE ACTION NOW

Go and do 10 interactions using the **MAGIC 10 strategy** on your social media platform news feeds. Use mobile apps for speed and scroll through your feeds looking for content you can interact with. Then comment, like, or share (remember to post your own comment on the shared post). Every time you click like, or comment, or share, this counts as one of your 10 interactions for that network.

I'd suggest for any of those posts you interact with then you connect or follow them, as this is an indication that their content maybe useful or of interest in the future. Use search to find accounts to follow or connect with too. Connect or follow 10.

Repeat on your other networks.

SOCIAL Step 3: The Proven Positioning Process – Influence

So how do you become the most influential person in your network? Well, quite simply, if you are **increasing your audience and interacting with your audience** then you are halfway there. Once your audience interacts and engages with you, you have completed the circle and are influential in your network.

The next step is to gain influence in your sector and reach an ever-increasing audience through consistently and frequently creating added-value content that people actually want.

Every industry and topic have social media influencers, so you need to go and research and watch or listen to what they are doing and saying. If they are an influence, then the strategy they are using is working; so gain inspiration from their actions.

I always feel that to be a good social media networker and keep your posts fresh and innovative the more content you see, then the more dynamic you will be in your creation. Look at what content actually generates engagement from audiences. Remember that video will always reap the highest rewards – when you look at influencers like Gary Vaynerchuk, Tony Robbins, and Guy Kawasaki who are among the highest ranking in the world for their sectors, then you can see the majority of their content is video (or podcasts) followed by photos and articles. However, all of their content is added-value content and they are not selling anything.

Social media pitfalls

I want to share with you the most common pitfalls I see in social media so you can proactively avoid them. As long as you don't include any of these in your strategy, then you can be as creative as you like in your social networking, content, and posting.

- **Never plan your social media too far in advance** as you'll lose creativity and you won't be able to be dynamic and react to time specific and relevant topics or news – you'll end up with staid and boring and most likely promotional posts that nobody engages with.

- **Never opt to only post promotional posts:** try 20% – and then 80% should be added-value, as people don't want to be constantly sold to; you will sell your product or service more effectively through building a relationship and using content to educate them about the benefits you or your business can bring to their lives.

- **Never use third-party social media tools to automatically schedule your posts** because you'll miss out on great native social media tools and features that aid engagement. It is important to remember social networks want users to login to their platform, use their own tools, interact and socially network – and if you are using third-party tools then none of this happens – so they will reward your use of their platform for posting or scheduling with reach. Test your reach if you are using third-party tools and monitor the differences. We have seen 'scheduling' destroy reach by as much as 70%.

- **Never start political, religious, or inappropriate debates** (which is not be confused with being controversial, which can be a great engagement strategy when used to spark debate).

- **Never post without targeting your post,** otherwise it will just get lost and the social network won't know who it is for. Remember to use #hashtags, @mentions, and targeting and exclusion tools.

- **Never post just about you** without sharing content to your audience to keep content diverse and dynamic.

- **Never use social media without implementing a social media policy** and governance to protect your business, but also just as importantly to empower your team on how they can get involved through social media. Your employees or colleagues can be a key part of your successful social media strategy.

- **Never post without having a solid social media strategy** that has clear goals, target audience, tactics, and consideration to time, resources, and any training requirements.

- **Never stretch yourself too thin.** It is better to be a master of one social network with consistent presence than have ad-hoc low impact visibility on all.

- **Never post without measuring tracking using KPIs** (key performance indicators) that relate to your goals. We will cover this in more depth in Chapter 18.

- **Never create multiple social profiles on the same network** unless they are for separate businesses, as this just creates an often unmanageable amount of work. Have an umbrella brand and target posts to the correct audiences for each of the business categories or sectors so only the relevant parties are seeing the posts that are relevant to them. You can exclude segments of your network by age, gender, location, etc.

- **Never forget the power of customer reviews.** Every time you sell, seek feedback. Your customers can be your biggest advocates who proactively recommend or refer, so make it easy for them to do so, perhaps even incentivise them. Customer loyalty programmes are great to encourage repeat purchases too.

- **Never delete negative feedback;** always manage and respond. Even if the feedback is a personal attack and entirely unfounded, your response will only act to highlight the other person's backlash as spam.

- **Never try and argue a point in customer service issues.** Remember: the customer is always right. Perhaps it is something technical that they don't understand – never point this out publicly, always take the conversation to more personal interaction and just focus on solving the issue, even if you don't see it specifically as an issue caused by you. They'll love you for just helping them!

- **Never ever ignore comments or mentions** – these are great opportunities to interact and build those all-important relationships, research, and get your business in front of their network.

- **Never post just as a faceless corporation;** but bring a human touch to your social media. People buy people, we love to see who you are, what you and your team look like, what your office looks like, as well as what you do and how you do it. Visual storytelling is an amazing way of building brand awareness and recognition.

- **Never buy followers.** This is pointless as they aren't real so they can't interact or engage in your content and they are certainly never going to become customers. It may even negatively impact your social media visibility and reach because you will be seen to have a very unengaged audience who don't interact in any of your posts. Focus on quality not quantity!

- **Never forget to focus your content around current customers,** not just attracting or engaging prospects. Use your customers to help create content like case studies, reviews, interviews, etc.

- **Never post without asking for interaction.** If you want people to comment, like, and share, it's only fair to share and care yourself.

- **Never be negative or pick public fights with others;** it just doesn't look very inviting for new prospects.

- **Never have incomplete social media profiles.** Seeing a half-filled LinkedIn Profile with no photo is like viewing an empty page on a website – and people will judge you. Remember their first interaction with you or your brand could be through social media profiles. Do it properly or don't do it at all.

So now we have covered what never to do, it's time to give you my best social media tips which I call my '**Seven Steps to Social Media Success**'.

Seven Steps to Social Media Success

1. **Post once a day.** Consistency and frequency is important and the act of simply signing in each day will impact on what the network thinks about you. Take this opportunity to showcase your accolades and news. Show the world how you are scaling and growing your business.

2. **Frontload snippets from original content.** If you have taken the time and effort to write a great blog article, then make sure you get real value out of the content and make sure your network has multiple chances to see it. Take key points from your article and turn these into attention grabbing headlines to create social media posts across the period of a month to drive back to the article. Different messages will attract different audiences and you'll also benefit from consistent steady traffic back to your website which will help your search engine visibility in Google.

3. **Connect with partners and influencers.** Find, follow, and connect with all of your partners from suppliers, customers, associations, charities, accrediting bodies, print and online publishers, and journalists, to influencers in your industry. It isn't always easy find an influencer who will engage with you and your brand, but the initial steps would be to get on their radar by interacting with their

content. There is a far higher chance that they may ultimately work with you if they actually know who you are.

I would suggest **making at least 20 social media buddies** who can really help increase reach for your content. Try setting up informal relationships whereby you offer to interact and comment, like, and share content you deem useful for your network if they do the same. The only condition when finding potential buddies or influencers is that they have a network that aligns to your target market – and if your network isn't as large as theirs, it's probably a good idea to have another benefit to offer them to make it mutually beneficial for both parties.

4. **Generate leads through offering premium added-value content.** If you are offering content that you know matches your audiences needs and it is free then why would you not attract your network? Generally, the reason is a misalignment in content. The content needs to be premium that is highly beneficial for someone to take action. So ensure your offer is compelling and there is demand for it.

5. **Monthly campaigns: One theme – no selling – add value = big results!** Remember your **MAGIC 10 strategy** and think of this as the **maintenance** of your social media that builds the amazing foundations for growth and engagement without the need for content. This is the fundamental strategy that has to be done very day to empower you as a social networker who interacts and participates in a meaningful way.

6. **Growth and groups.** Once you have exhausted connecting with everyone you know, it is important to keep growing your network through reaching new audiences and attracting them to connect or follow you or your business.

Focus on growing your network daily and utilising interest groups to build a community around a common interest. It will be much easier to generate interest in your products and services when you have a ready-made and highly engaged audience that you know is interested in your subject matter.

7. **Monitor your social media.** Here are a few metrics to look at measuring and analysing as part of your social media monitoring (Figure 12.9).

- reach and growth of network;

- audience engagement (on and off network);

- media and post analysis;

- web or landing page visits;

- conversions – lead, prospect, or sale;

- campaign goals – reach, action, convert, engage, ROI (return on investment).

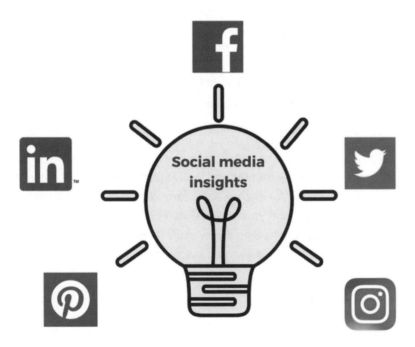

FIGURE 12.9   Social media insights across channels.

Calculate your social media ROI

Profit/total investment(people hours, ad budget, etc.)×100
= social media ROI (as a %)

YOUR TURN – TAKE ACTION NOW

The next level of the strategy incorporates each of these seven steps, but the key is to **break down your year into monthly campaigns.** So create **twelve themes, one for each month** so you have a focus for that entire month that runs alongside your maintenance strategy.

This step will be your **marketing strategy** where you choose a theme and create a whole month of added-value content which forms a campaign but doesn't focus on selling, and instead addresses a problem.

A campaign could encompass a challenge, taking a quiz, or learning from content you create.

The more your audience can get involved and participate the better; and ensure your campaign tag line is memorable and motivating.

- Look at social media campaign tools like Woobox or ShortStack for inspiration.

- **Map out twelve months and look at planning a content calendar** with a theme for each month; for instance, a high-level theme would be around your business goals and plans for that month. You will use this to align your specific theme nearer the time based on current trends, news, and events that you can hook onto.

- Now use **Google Alerts** and **Google Search** to research current trends, news, and events for your industry. You are looking for something relevant to your audience.

For us, if Facebook announced a new major platform change, we could theme a whole month around this and how our audiences could mitigate the change and prepare for the launch.

This would be very timely, specific to our audience, and uber-relevant. So, the chances of engagement are high. We would align this to our business goals and ultimately offer our audience this as an upsell option to the added-value content that they have been engaging with.

We would generate leads through data capture using free guides, webinars, or events etc. and then for our conversion strategy look to nurture them through with premium content and upsell opportunities.

This approach basically showcases our skills and expertise and builds trust and ultimately a relationship with our audience and this naturally impacts on conversion rates.

Remember, though, this is all about 'TELL' not 'SELL': No heavy promotion, just lead nurturing and relationship building.

Don't expect to post a piece of content and it to reach a huge audience on Facebook unless its boosted. Think about what the social networks want you to do – NOT LEAVE.

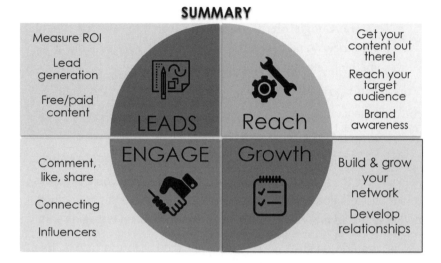

FIGURE 12.10 Summary of the Proven Positioning Process.

SOCIAL: CHECKLIST

Search for your ideal customer's interest groups on social platforms like LinkedIn and Facebook.	
Analyse your reach, authority, credibility, and influence on social platforms.	
Complete your social media audit.	

Create your social media marketing mission statement.	
Establish the 'purpose' and the type of community your business will be.	
Develop your social media content and posting strategy.	
Discover social listening and monitoring tools.	
Familiarise yourself with social media platform tools and features.	
Gain social media campaigns inspiration from examples on WooBox and ShortStack.	
MAGIC 10 strategy on each network.	
Create your content calendar.	

Research current trends, news for your industry to identify possible themes.	
Join interest groups for your industry to review ideas for your own business group.	
Calculate your social media ROI.	

Proven Positioning Process

FIGURE 12.11   The Proven Positioning Process.

Chapter 13

Send – The C.L.E.A.N. Customer Cultivator

It's hard to believe that email is nearly 50 years old and actually predates the internet!

The **C.L.E.A.N. Customer Cultivator is a simple five-step process** looking at the entire customer lifecycle and how to communicate your message throughout that person's specific interactions with your business or brand. The techniques we teach at the academy are centred around marketing based on your prospect's behaviour at a time when it's relevant and they are interested.

Marketo found that marketing automation emails had 59% better click-to-open rates, and a whopping 147% higher overall click rate, over bulk promotional emails.[1]

Benefits of email marketing

- It beats social by 40 times for customer acquisition according to **according to McKinsey.**[2]

- And for every £1, email marketing generates £25 in ROI **according to VentureBeat.**[3]

The main benefits are cost, speed, and almost instant returns on investment.

Every business will have a natural attrition of subscribers on their databases. To combat the loss of data, a steady flow of new prospects is important to maintain the levels of business required to be sustainable – and of course profitable.

[1]*Source:* Marketo https://blog.marketo.com/2013/09/get-more-email-opens-and-clicks-using-behavioral-targeting.html.

[2]*Source:* https://www.mckinsey.com/business-functions/marketing-and-sales/our-insights/why-marketers-should-keep-sending-you-emails.

[3]*Source:* https://www.campaignmonitor.com/resources/guides/email-marketing-new-rules/.

The C.L.E.A.N Customer Cultivator®

> **C**apture
> **L**eads
> **E**ntice
> **A**utomate
> **N**uture

FIGURE 13.1 The C.L.E.A.N. Customer Cultivator.

Also consider that not everyone who joins your email list will be ready to make a purchase or sign up for a service. Email gives you the opportunity to capture a new visitor's attention and nurture that relationship with helpful and informative content. This keeps you in front of prospects so that when they are ready to contact you, or make a purchase, the chance of them choosing your brand or business will be much higher (Figure 13.2).

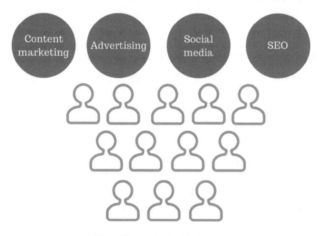

Use these platforms to
increase brand awareness
and build your database of
email addresses

FIGURE 13.2 Use digital marketing platforms to increase brand awareness.

201

Simplifying the law and best practice for data

GDPR (General Data Protection Regulation) is a legal framework that sets guidelines for the collection and processing of personal information of individuals within the European Union (EU). The principles are broadly similar to the principles in the Data Protection Act 1998 (the 1998 Act). So think of GDPR as an up-to-date approach to processing personal data. You can obtain a copy of the regulation here: https://eugdpr.org/.

The Information Commissioner (ICO) is the UK's independent body set up to uphold information rights. Every business needs to register with the ICO and pay the annual registration fee. The fee varies based on turnover but is on average £50 for most businesses.

'From 25 May 2018, the Data Protection (Charges and Information) Regulations 2018 requires every organisation or sole trader who processes personal information to pay a data protection fee to the ICO, unless they are exempt.'[4]

The GDPR sets out seven key principles: I will discuss each principle and what it means for your business.

1. **Lawfulness, fairness, and transparency:** collected for legitimate reasons.

2. **Purpose limitation:** collected for specified, explicit, and legitimate purposes.

3. **Data minimisation:** not used outside the purpose collected for.

4. **Accuracy:** personal data that is inaccurate are either erased or rectified without delay.

5. **Storage limitation:** keep data for no longer than is necessary.

[4]*Source:* https://ico.org.uk/for-organisations/data-protection-fee/.

6. **Integrity and confidentiality (security):** security of the personal data, including protection against unauthorised or unlawful processing and against accidental loss, destruction, or damage, using appropriate technical or organisational measures.

7. **Accountability:** the controller shall be responsible for, and be able to demonstrate, compliance.

Failure to comply

'Failure to comply with the principles may leave you open to substantial fines. Article 83(5)(a) states that infringements of the basic principles for processing personal data are subject to the highest tier of administrative fines.

This could mean a fine of up to €20 million, or 4% of your total worldwide annual turnover, whichever is higher.'[5]

YOUR TURN – TAKE ACTION NOW

1. It is crucial that you are aware of which legislation applies to your own country. If you are not exempt, check you are **registered with the ICO.** If you are not sure if you need to register, take a quick self-assessment to find out: https://ico.org.uk/for-organisations/data-protection-fee/self-assessment/

2. **Ensure you are GDPR compliant:** every business needs to demonstrate compliance and we use a tool called **'Trust Keeper'** which constantly scans our website and also ensures we review all measures regularly to keep compliant. I would suggest searching

(continued)

---

[5]*Source:* https://ico.org.uk/for-organisations/guide-to-data-protection/guide-to-the-general-data-protection-regulation-gdpr/principles/.

Google for 'GDPR compliance tools'. These tools will take you through the elements required to be compliant, addressing each of the seven principles as you work your way through.

SEND Step 1: The C.L.E.A.N. Customer Cultivator – Capture

Opting in

Once you are clear on how you collect and process personal data while complying with the relevant regulations for your business, how will you generate leads?

A business must get consent from a subscriber to send them commercial email marketing messages. Permission-based marketing or opt-in lists will definitely get much better response rates.

So, what does this mean for lead generation and data capture? Well, there are a few steps of best practice that need to be adhered to:

- Provide an **opt-in box** when subscribing to get consent to receiving future marketing communications. This is very important – especially around the actual language. Basically, any email containing a name is personal data, which means you must respect their privacy and ensure that they indeed wish to receive marketing emails. If they didn't opt-in and had, for instance, enquired about more details from your business, you are absolutely allowed to email them through a normal business one-to-one email **but never as a mass mailing.** A business can continue to follow-up person to person, but you can't add them to your newsletter list etc.

- You may have heard the term **double opt-in**. This refers to the process of the subscriber receiving an opt-in confirmation email where they must click a link to **confirm their opt-in**. This can be the best way to protect your business and guarantee you have user permission. Confusion occurs for some businesses when they assume a customer who has purchased from them has opted in. But if you have a database of customers who have not taken a deliberate action to opt in, you have not gained their permission.

- I recommend creative ways of getting permission and opt-in rather than sending an email asking for it. Try and add some value and an incentive, such as being part of an amazing giveaway, and then include an opt-in. Let's be honest, nobody lives to receive yet another newsletter, but we are quite happy to sign-up and give our data in exchange for something we deem to be of value.

Lead generation

The same goes for your lead generation strategy: it comes back to knowing your customer and their needs and problems. If you can create a proposition that is compelling, then why wouldn't people sign up (Figure 13.3)?

Around 97% of your visitors who visit your website are just browsing; therefore, most businesses are only recognising results from the 3% that are ready to buy or enquire. You could be letting some very valuable web visitors slip through the net by not offering content they want and are willing to sign-up for. Lead generation through your website is just as important as landing page lead generation from paid advertising. If you haven't got a good lead generation strategy, then the result will be that much of the traffic you have managed to attract will be lost forever and never be seen by you again.

Offer your subscribers useful content, such as cheat sheets, guides, or case studies in return for opting-in to your mailing list.

FIGURE 13.3 Offer useful content in exchange for subscribing.

It is crucially important to have mechanisms in place to enhance potential customers' website experience so those visitors don't just leave without you even knowing who they were and with no means of staying in touch. There should be a strong focus on every website towards how to actually **capture** their visit and the data needed to nurture the visitor through to the next stage of their journey.

There are plenty of opportunities that you can utilise to continue to communicate with visitors who are not ready to buy and enquire.

These are often referred to as **lead magnets,** such as:

- free content, such as downloads or resources;
- offers, coupons, or discounts;
- interactive quizzes or polls.

Don't forget other opportunities to connect, such as social media as well as commenting on or liking blog articles.

YOUR TURN – TAKE ACTION NOW

Take a look at your website and make a note of how many options you have for the 3% of your website visitors that are ready to buy and enquire – such as call, send an email, live chat, etc.

Then record all the items that relate to site visitors who are not ready to buy and enquire. Think about ways you could capture their visit so you can stay in touch and nurture them through to conversion.

Take a look at your where you are currently getting leads from, then review what are the sources you attract the most interest from and which has the best conversion to customer. The leads that come into your business feed into what is often referred to as a 'sales or lead funnel'.

This is just a way of expressing the volume of people at each stage of the sales-cycle.

Obviously, prospects go into the funnel and then reduce in numbers until ultimately filtering through to becoming a customer. The aim is to ensure you have enough volume of leads progressing through to each stage of the funnel to reach the level of customers required to sustain a profitable business.

I would also suggest aiming for six different engagement tools, such as lead magnets and ways of staying in touch, across a website.

For 3% of web visitors ready to buy or enquire	Stay in touch with the 97% of web visitors not ready to buy or enquire

SEND Step 2: The C.L.E.A.N. Customer Cultivator – Leads

Conversion rate

A common misconception is that a business will look at results based on those who have enquired or bought and then look to increase traffic to generate more leads and customers.

This would be completely the wrong approach as it's more cost-effective to look at implementing lead capture mechanisms and the overall conversion optimisation of the website.

Conversion rate optimisation (CRO) aims to increase the number of visitors who actually complete the desired goal or action you require for your marketing activity.

By optimising your conversion rate, you can:

• increase revenue per visitor

• acquire more customers

• grow and scale your business.

Calculating your conversion rate

It is pretty simple to calculate your conversion rate, because all you have to do is divide the number of conversions you get in a specific time frame, by the total number of people who visited your site or landing page, and multiply it by 100% (Figure 13.4).

$$\text{Conversion Rate} = \frac{\text{Number of Goal Achievements}}{\text{Visitors}}$$

FIGURE 13.4 Conversion rate calculation.

Ways of improving conversion rates on landing pages

- Include as few fields as possible and keep those other than name and email optional.

- Remove any elements that may distract from the key message, such as navigation.

- Have a main headline and a supporting headline.

- Create a unique selling or value proposition.

- Talk about the benefits of your offering as well as using emotionally charged language and storytelling to create excitement.

- Handle any objections or FAQs to overcome any conversion obstacles.

- Keep conversion elements above the fold (the part of the page visible without scrolling).

- Include happy and human images and video.

- Add a guarantee that their data (include a privacy policy and opt-in forms) is safe or a guarantee about your offering.

- Provide social proof, such as testimonials, ratings, awards, accreditations, and certifications.

- Create a sense of urgency or scarcity. Using motion countdowns is a great visual way of displaying offer deadlines.

- Have a reinforcement statement.

- Give a closing argument.

- Include a call to action using a button instead of links; and if it has a purchase option, include an option for data capture for those not ready to buy; or an option to register for more dates if you are promoting an event and the visitor isn't free.

- Include contact options to provide transparency and enhance trust.

- Test variations of the pages.

- Have live chat or interactive message tools.

YOUR TURN – TAKE ACTION NOW

Optimise your landing pages for high rates of conversion

Take a look at tools like **Instapage:** https://instapage.com/.

If you aren't using landing pages, tools like Instapage can help you create landing pages yourself. Instapage has a WordPress plugin so the landing page under your URL can be used with a custom domain name.

Even if you have in-house teams or designers that you use to create landing pages, you can use the Instapage selection of pre-tested high-converting templates for layout ideas.

Instapage also has built in analytics and landing page A/B testing tools that you can use to optimise performance.

SEND Step 3: The C.L.E.A.N. Customer Cultivator – Entice

Customer research

Enticing your subscribers to either become customers or to remain customers should be a priority in business.

How do you find out exactly what your customers want and what they think about you? The answer is simple: through prospect and customer research, which should be part of any marketing plan.

Using email will definitely be easier than telemarketing campaigns and is much more cost-effective as well as time saving. Use survey tools like **Survey Monkey:** https://www.surveymonkey.com/. Surveys tools have proved to be revolutionary in the way we measure satisfaction and perform market research.

Gone are the days of compiling huge amounts of data to produce meaningful customer insights.

Net Promotor Score

The Net Promoter Score® (NPS) is an index from –100 to 100 that is used to gauge the customer's overall satisfaction with a company's product or service and the customer's loyalty to the brand.

The positive and negative indicators of your overall customer experience will be reviewed and you'll receive a score. Based on global NPS standards, any score above 0 would be considered good, over 50 excellent, and over 70 world-class.

Your Net Promoter Score® can be obtained through customer survey using tools such as Survey Monkey, or any other customer feedback software which measures this score, and can then be displayed on websites and promotional materials to showcase your customers' feedback supported by reviews, testimonials, and case studies.

Behavioural marketing

The next stage of enticing your audience is to define what content you want to send to which people.

Traditional methods to do this would include segmentation and looking at key characteristics and trying to pre-judge what your customers will be interested in, but a more dynamic approach would be **behavioural marketing.**

Utilising what your consumers actually do can provide a far better indication of interests and a more time relevant option of marketing. Examples of behavioural marketing could include triggering an email when users not only visit content on your site but perhaps re-visit a specific page, product, or service numerous times. For instance, you could trigger an action using an email marketing tool like MailChimp.

Typical **triggers and actions** could be to send an email based on subscriber activity; for example, sending to subscribers who received, opened, didn't open, clicked, clicked a specific link, or didn't click for a specific campaign.

Triggers can also be set for moving subscribers to specific lists or groups for marketing based on recurring dates like birthdays, pre-purchase like abandoned cart reminders, or post-purchase follow-up to entice reviews, or for segments such as lapsed or VIP customers. You can also trigger to send the next email in an automation series. The list of options is literally endless and completely tailorable to your own business goals.

Personalisation marketing is around tailoring the customer journey to enhance the customer's experience and align content to their wants and needs. Suggested personalisation can be selected via algorithms and based on past consumer behaviour and activity. An example of this is when we see suggested content on social channels based on content we have interacted with; it could be digital TV suggesting options based on viewing behaviour, or suggested products on Amazon based on our web activity.

YOUR TURN – TAKE ACTION NOW

1. Create 10 questions that would help you assess your customer satisfaction and look at running a survey to identify your **Net Promoter Score® (NPS)** or to get overall customer feedback.

2. Make a list of triggers you could use for your business based on any repetitive tasks that you could automate. Also, look at how you could personalise the customer experience with your business or brand.

3. Look at each stage of the customer–buyer cycle and find these four main categories of subscribers. **For each of these categories of your audience, try and brainstorm ideas for automation and personalisation.**

   - **Suspect:** Could be part of your community, but hasn't proactively signed-up for anything; might be following your brand or business on social media. For instance, they might comment, like, and share your content.

   - **Prospect:** Matches your ideal customer profile, but hasn't yet expressed interest in your products or services.

   - **Lead:** Has proactively reached out and expressed an interest.

   - **Customer:** Has purchased or has met your ultimate conversion goal for your organisation.

	Automation	Personalisation
Suspect		
Prospect		
Lead		
Customer		

SEND Step 4: The C.L.E.A.N. Customer Cultivator – Automate

Automation opportunities

Every prospect and customer you have subscribed to your databases should have their own unique customer journey with your brand or business that aligns to their needs and goals at a time that is pertinent to them. Getting your business in front of a customer or prospect when they are ready to take action is obviously going to be far more effective than sending random communications with messages that just won't resonate.

It is quite remarkable just how many websites have the means to sign-up for newsletter or resources – and then don't actually send anything to the customer at the point of engagement. This is the moment they are in a heightened state of interest, and to leave contact for even a day is a huge opportunity lost that you have then handed on a plate to a competitor.

If you have mapped out your automation and personalisation opportunities, then the next step is to look at sales and marketing processes and how these can be incorporated.

Creating content on your website in the form of blogs or articles has search engine visibility and traffic benefits, but automating some of your methods of distribution can also be a huge time saver. If you have automatic publishing to social media through your blog, then remember to check how it renders on social media. I often see well-written headlines and articles that when they are shared into social platforms lose their impact, as the imagery is distorted or it isn't actually attention grabbing and gets lost in the news feed.

Another great automation is to set up an **RSS-to-email** from your blog (RSS is a standardised system for the distribution of content from an online publisher to internet users). So in this example you can simply add an **RSS feed** URL from any website or blog. All you need to do then is write your articles each week and they are pulled through from your blog and displayed in your email, which is emailed out to subscribers automatically.

All leading email marketing software options have this service, and this method means that your headline, featured image, and brief summary or description are pulled into a pre-designed email template with dynamic place holders for new weekly content. Assuming you have written the articles on your blog, then the software will send the email on a pre-defined date and time to everyone on your list. Depending on your blog set-up, it may require some technical tweaking to ensure the content pulls through correctly into your email template; but once set up, it will run forever until you stop creating content.

The internet has opened up such amazing ways of marketing and none more amazing than behavioural marketing. We can now time our marketing to perfection and target consumers based on their behaviour on websites, rather than purely by the content of pages they visit.

TIP:

If you send out client proposals as part of your sales process, then I suggest you look at using proposal software, which is not only great for pipeline analyses and follow-up, but plays an important part in timing that all important follow-up.

We use a tool called **Proposify** which means as soon as proposal is sent, we get notifications when they open it and read it. We can also see when and how many times they access it. This means you can rest assured that your prospective client has got your proposal, and you can interact with them when their mind is on it.

YOUR TURN – TAKE ACTION NOW

You are going to be your very own audience and consumer and go through the steps for sign-up for every channel.

- Check everything and make sure the responses to any leads or sign-ups are actually being satisfied.

- Ensure that where are people attached to these tasks, you automate them.

- Evaluate what is sent out and make sure there is no out-of-date content.

- Check there are clear response paths for consumers to have two-way conversations.

- Look at follow-up and any automation series that are in place.

- Is there an opportunity to automate your blog articles to send via email as weekly digest?

I have seen businesses who don't even know where their 'contact us' page enquiries land – make sure you do!

SEND Step 5: The C.L.E.A.N. Customer Cultivator – Nurture

The process of nurture can often be implemented in a way that actually has the opposite effect on subscribers. Email marketing in a manner that is not focused on the customers' needs at their own specific stage of their journey can result in unsubscribes.

Why do people unsubscribe?

The number one reason people unsubscribe from emails is that they simply get too many. But it may also be the case that the email is not relevant and in turn considered spam.

Every email marketing software will provide analytics for your campaigns. As best practice, always check whether you have a high unsubscribe rate/opt-outs or if you have received any complaints.

'Email is possibly the greatest owned media channel for brands.'

Joe Pulizzi, Content Marketing Institute (CMI) founder

Keeping data clean and safe is not only important but also the law, and I would always suggest integrating your **CRM (customer relationship management) with your email marketing software.**

This means that people can unsubscribe from your email marketing, but you can keep them on your CRM for one-to-one personal email communication. This gives you a more personal approach for follow-up; but automating this process can work equally as well as long as you are taking them on their very own customer journey.

My favoured approach is to create a series of emails for each customer segment. You will need to consider suspects, prospects, and customers and ways of maintaining communication for the entire customer lifecycle. This really doesn't have to be a difficult or time-consuming process, but there are a few key methods you can use to create effective emails that will stimulate engagement with little time and effort (Figure 13.5).

LEAD NURTURING

FIGURE 13.5 Lead nurturing for increased profit.

YOUR TURN – TAKE ACTION NOW

Check which **CRM** you are using and if it passes information across the software; or **identify a good CRM for your business.**

Nurturing your leads

Use your customer avatars or personas to establish your main audiences and messages. Using examples from our academy, we have:

- Tim the trainee

- Felicity the freelancer

- Tony the trainer

- Marie the marketing manager.

We have created detailed customer avatars/personas around each of them; from where they hang out online, to what resources they use, and what their goals, problems, and pain points are. This allows us to really drill down our key messages to each segment of our audience.

We can attract 'Tim the trainee' using a piece of content that is really relevant to him. This could be a 'free guide about getting into digital marketing', 'a day in the life of a digital marketer', or 'digital marketing salaries and career paths'. Once Tim signs up, we can send his free resource straight away by email. Then write a series of emails to follow-up and nurture Tim through to ultimately developing his digital skills with our academy.

The ideal is to create **conversational-style emails** that look very personal. They need to feel like one-to-one interaction and not like mass email communications. They don't even need imagery etc. They need to try and instigate an interaction from a two-way conversation to taking action and engaging with more content or ultimately buying or proactively enquiring.

The key is to fact-find and overcome obstacles of purchase by addressing any frequently asked questions as part of an email series that runs over a three-week period. We suggest around three weeks because after this point they aren't a hot prospect that is ready to convert. It doesn't mean they won't; just that it isn't the right time for them now. So you would still keep in touch but just not through such an intensive series. Ideally, move the non-converted subscribers to a nurture series – which could be a weekly digest email packed full of added-value content like tips, interviews, industry insights, trends, tools and techniques etc. which will keep your audience engaged and encourage web visits.

Over 21-day nurture, we would suggest sending emails:

- instantly
- 1 day later
- 7 days later
- 14 days later
- the final one on day 21.

If they get to the final email and haven't converted, then move them onto a digest series of added-value content. (A digest is the modern newsletter with lots of interesting articles to help them achieve their goals.)

YOUR TURN – TAKE ACTION NOW

Start to try and plot out an **email nurture series** for a specific audience segment and think about the content that would initially attract them too. This could be used in advertising campaigns as well as on your website as a lead magnet.

Consider drip campaigns

Instead of offering the generic boring newsletter, offer drip content through email. This could be a five-day challenge, a three-week course, or six steps to success; any form of content that helps showcase your brand as well as educate and entertain.

You could use pre-existing content and chunk it into steps, or utilise existing articles with several key points. These types of campaign, which someone has signed-up to receive, help you segment your audience and see what they are most interested in too. Self-segmenting always works better as they are proactively telling you what their pain or problem is; and you are positioning your solution accordingly at a time that is relevant.

Email ROI

You might be wondering if email is still a worthwhile marketing strategy.

In fact, according to a recent study by DMA (Data & Marketing Association) email **ROI has shot up from £32 to £42** – and marketers are measuring ROI more than ever – mainly because email marketing platforms have made it far easier to measure and therefore quantify the impact of email. In addition, marketers may have benefited from better quality email addresses as a result of GDPR.

Email marketing audit

If you have already been using email marketing within your marketing arsenal, then it would be useful to reflect on past campaign results. Most email marketing tools include heat mapping, which shows which links on the email template were clicked and also analytic reports within the platform.

- Compare your email campaigns against industry benchmarks and competitors.

- Identify problems with email creation and distribution.

- Improve key components of your emails to drive better response rates.

- Assess your current email marketing tool/email service provider.

- Create a plan for improvement within your email marketing strategy.

Compare your email campaigns against industry benchmarks

Understanding what the metrics in email marketing and what they represent is essential when evaluating their performance.

Here is a quick glossary of terms and metrics to evaluate in your audit:

- **Open rate:** opened email.

- **Click rate:** clicked on hyperlinks within the email.

- **Soft bounce:** temporary deliverability issue.

- **Hard bounce:** permanent delivery failure.

- **Abuse rate:** complaints.

- **Unsubscribe rate:** opt-outs from marketing communication.

In order to assess how well your email marketing is performing, it will be useful to get a handle on your industry benchmarks. These can be found within email marketing platforms such as MailChimp and Campaign Monitor.

According to Campaign Monitor's recent study, the average email benchmarks for all industries are:

- Average open rate: 17.92%.

- Average click-through rate: 2.69%.

- Average unsubscribe rate: 0.17%.

- Average click-to-open rate: 14.10%.

- Average bounce rate: 1.06%.

Further breakdowns across specific industry sectors are available, and to get an across the board view simply Google 'email industry benchmarks' – I would suggest searching across a specific year to ensure you are reviewing the most up-to-date statistics.

Once you have an idea of what results you should be aiming for – or if you are already running email marketing campaigns, then how you compare to the industry benchmarks relevant to you – then you need to develop an email marketing strategy utilising these benchmarks when considering your targets and goals.

In Chapter 3 we covered a tool to analyse your emails against competitors which it would be best practice to include in your email marketing audit: https://www.owletter.com/.

Take a look at successful email marketing campaigns for inspiration. Just search Google by entering 'best email marketing campaigns' and the year.

YOUR TURN – TAKE ACTION NOW

Identify problems with email creation and distribution

Look at the end-to-end email marketing process within your business, from how you build your list, through who is responsible for the creation and management of each element.

Email Marketing Process Steps	Questions: Who will do this? How is this decided? How will it happen and how much will it cost? What needs to be included and what is the goal or expected result or target? When will it happen? What will the follow-up be?
List building	
Target audience	
Design and build	
Call to action and landing pages	
Testing	
Sending	
Reporting	

YOUR TURN – TAKE ACTION NOW

Improve key components of your emails to drive better response rates

Look at your current email campaigns and compare how they perform against each other. Once you have a good cross-section for review, you can start to drill deeper into the campaign and look at each from name, subject line, and the actual email contents. Collating these results in this manner can be used as ongoing email campaign measurement tool, as well as identifying elements to test.

Cam-paign Name	Open Rate	Click Rate	Soft or Hard Bounces	Com-plaints	Unsub-scribe

Create a plan for improvement within your email marketing strategy

A basic strategy is summarised in Figure 13.6.

1. **Choose or upgrade your email marketing tool/email service provider**

   Procuring the right software is as important as the actual email campaign strategy, because if your email can't be delivered – never mind opened – then your campaign has failed before it even began.

   Investment in software over a given year is always a good indication of ongoing research and feature development, meaning your software is adapting and evolving to the market changes and trends.

FIGURE 13.6   Email marketing strategy.

Another good indication of whether a platform is performing is through feature analysis and testing them out via free trials.

The most common email marketing platforms are:

- Active Campaign

- MailChimp

- Constant Contact

- Campaign Monitor.

There are many more available and checking which has the best deliverability rate is a good way of shortlisting your options. Search Google for 'best email software for deliverability' and there are a variety of tools and reports that can provide up to date information across the platforms.

I am a firm believer in using a piece of software specifically built for the task rather than bolt-on email platforms that isn't their main service. The reason for this is functionality, user-experience, and features tend to be more developed within email marketing specific software.

2. Identify your target audience

Within your strategy, you will need to identify your target demographic for your email campaigns.

These are the six targeting options.

- **Customer demographics:** Socioeconomic characteristics of a population expressed statistically, such as age, gender, geographical location, education level, marital status, household income, occupation, and hobbies. If you were hosting an event in a specific location, you would segment your email list to target those with a specific location characteristic.

- **Customer lifetime value (CLV):** The worth of the present and future value of a customer considering current spend and potential future spend. You may choose to market an offer to your VIP customers who are your high-spend clients; or on the flip side you could have low-spend regular clients that form the lifeblood of your business through recurring revenues and you might wish to target this group with a specific campaign.

- **Customer lifecycle:** If you consider the three goals in business – to increase customer base, purchase frequency, and average order value – you will need to gear your marketing messages around the stage of the customer lifecycle. For instance, a person who may have signed up for a free guide has not yet expressed an interest in a specific product or service through an enquiry, so you would need to send email campaigns aligned to their journey and stage in the decision-making process. Again, sending a customer an offer to obtain repeat business would be very different to the email sent to a prospective customer.

- **Customer behaviour:** Marketing based on their activity and actions. These could be around frequency, monetary value, and category of products purchased. A campaign could be sent to those who opened recent emails, or visited your website or specific web pages etc.

- **Customer channel behaviour:** Look at your target audience and evaluate their channel preference from online to more traditional methods to social media usage and interaction. Some email marketing platforms allow you to create a social post to share your campaign through your social media channels so you can track interaction. Another option would be to look at social profiles for your email list. All the major social media platforms have an option to upload your list of contacts, which will allow you to deepen your relationship with them by connecting and engaging with them on social media. This takes the conversation across multiple channels and reduces the need to constantly bombard your list with emails.

- **Customer personas or avatar:** Develop a profile of your ideal customer using key traits of a large segment of your audience, based on the data you've collected from user research and web analytics. Creating email marketing campaigns with messages constructed around understanding your customer needs, goals, obstacles, and pain points will enhance the relevancy and engagement in your messages.

3. Choose list-building tactics

This is about looking at your current lead sources and getting creative about how you can use the less obvious methods such as web pop-ups, free content, etc. as well as adding more intuitive ways through analysing the interactions and touch-points of your customer journey at the different stages of the lifecycle. For instance, if someone joins a social media group, you could send them a welcome email through the platform to get them to sign-up for a free workshop or training series – and to sign-up they enter their email address. Ensure for every subscriber you obtain GDPR complaint permission to add them to your lists. They must always click a link or proactively tick a box to opt-in to further 'marketing communications'.

TIP:

Look at where you have communication or interaction with your audience but may not have their email address.

---

4. Create list segments

Using your target market criteria for specific email campaigns you can divide email subscribers into smaller segments. Typically, segmentation is used to personalise so you can deliver more relevant email marketing to your subscribers.

5. Create a send schedule

Email frequency depends on the type of email and what the subscriber has opted-in to receive – for instance a daily news digest, weekly or monthly newsletter – but added-value content is always going to be a more welcome email than a sales promotional campaign. It is about balance and adding value whilst promoting your products or services. Your **email marketing** frequency should be based on your typical customer's purchase cycle and profile.

6. **Define goals**

Think about why you are using email marketing and also your specific campaign goals. Generally speaking, your email list is one of your most valuable marketing resources along with consumer related goals. Include goals to optimise campaigns and focus on improving email open rates and email engagement as well as overall business results.

7. **Decide on the types of emails to send**

There are six types of emails that you can send and these vary on where your subscriber is in the customer journey and what the goal of your campaign is.

- Welcome series – as someone subscribes, send a series of emails.

- Promotional campaign – aimed at selling your products and services.

- Triggered – sending an email based on the subscriber behaviour.

- Post-purchase and surveys – customer emails to gain feedback or reviews.

- Newsletter or news digest – regular added-value articles or industry news.

- Pre-purchase/abandoned cart – capture lost sales to convert into customers.

8. **Design emails**

Email design isn't just about the look and feel of the email on your screen; it starts way before then from when a customer chooses to delete, open, or save for later. It is important to look at how the email presents in the inbox before it is even viewed as this will be the deciding factor for whether the person even reads it, never mind anything else.

Here are some tips for creating a winning email campaign:

- **Email width:** Use a width of 600 px (web images are measured in pixel dimensions – also referred to as PX – so 600px means 600 pixels wide), so your email will work with the majority of screen sizes and email platforms.

- **Preheader:** Add teaser text before your header, which will show up on the subject line in many email clients and give you another opportunity to influence opens.

- **Sender information:** Make it clear who is sending the email and make sure it is a person, not just a faceless brand, to increase the human feel. This increases the opportunity of interaction if you include a reply call to action, as your customer is more likely to do this for a person than a business. In addition, this reduces the automatic delete and lessens the feel of a marketing communication as it looks more personal and business as usual than promotional.

- **Subject line:** Best subject line length according to data from Marketo is 41 characters – or 7 words.[6]

- **Use Active Campaign's free Subject Line Generator Tool:** https://www.activecampaign.com/free-marketing-tools/subject-line-generator

- **Web-friendly fonts:** Use a standard font because there is a set of common fonts installed across all computers and operating systems (such as Arial).

- **Optimise for mobile devices:** Use responsive templates optimised for both desktop and mobile devices. Use your email marketing tool to test how your email appears on mobile.

According to a study by Adestra, poor formatting in mobile emails is the number one complaint. A poorly formatted email is likely to

---

[6]*Source:* https://www.campaignmonitor.com/blog/email-marketing/2019/02/best-email-subject-line-length/.

be deleted in under 3 seconds in over 70% of cases. As many as 15% of users will even unsubscribe, instead of delete. All in all, that's an 85% drop in potential customers on mobile.

- **Email layout:** An eye-tracking study by the Nielsen Norman Group found that people consume digital and web content in an F-shaped pattern after tracking 1.5 million eye movements of 300 web users. Use headings and subheads to maintain visual organisation. Make your content easy to scan, so recipients do not need to read every word to understand your email and click your CTA.

- **Text and format:** Keep blocks of text short and simple. The inverted pyramid writing style works extremely well. Use one column – single column emails work really well on both desktop and mobile as well as reducing overwhelm. Try adapting traditional horizontal styling and angle elements to add intrigue.

- **White space:** Adding white space around the elements in your email encourages click-through and helps focus the reader's attention on them at the right time. It can also increase the legibility of your email and improves the eyes' ability to follow the content.

- **Imagery:** Use JPG and PNG images in emails. Keep the image size small for fast download into the email. Have a balanced ratio for text to images – aim for at least 60% text to 40% images. Don't use images as your entire email, since they may not automatically display in many email clients. Make text descriptive enough to persuade recipients to allow images to be displayed. Use image alt text (written copy that appears in place of an image on the email if the image fails to load on a user's screen) so readers can read what your images are about if their email clients do not display them.

- **Video:** Use video in your emails using a clickable image linking to the video or animated GIFS. Animated GIFs are a great alternative to using video if you want to add moving content to your emails.

- **Calls to action:** Use hyperlinks within the email body as well as image calls to action to ensure they are displayed and clickable. Keep your CTAs high: place your first CTA above the fold.

- **Personalisation:** Use your subscriber's name in the subject line, when addressing them in the body of the email.

- **Dynamic content:** More advanced tactics of personalisation include changing the content of the email based on a subscriber's gender, location, or other things you know about them. Change entire sections of content within your email to make the entire campaign more relevant and more appealing to subscribers.

- **Utilise live content:** Tools such as motionmail allow you to quickly create countdown timers. https://motionmailapp.com.

- **Footer:** Include contact information, additional resources such as social media links and value-added links, unsubscribe links, and any legal fine print in the footer.

9. **Optimise email results through A/B testing**

A/B testing can be applied to many components of your email, but the subject line is one of the most popular, and easy, things to test.

Test your subject line and see which gets a better response:

- length

- topic

- promotion/offer

- personalisation – such as a first name greeting.

Then look at:

- from name

- email content

- calls to action.

Email marketing checklist

From Name
• Company domain included – authenticate your domain with your email marketing provider
• Personal, professional name
Subject Line
• No spam words
• Length
• Personalisation
Preheader
• Preheader to entice reader to open your email
Headline and Subheadings
• Increases readability when scanning online
Email Content and Layout
• Short paragraphs of text using bullet points
• Includes benefits to take action for the reader
Call to Action
• The call to action is a button as well as links within the body of the email
Images and Video
• Alt text included to encourage displaying images in email client
• Images are small in size and you are using jpeg or png (or if using animated GIF ensure it's small in size) for fast loading times
• Link clickable images in the email to video content on the web
Branding
• Your logo and company name that links to your home page
• Message and tone is consistent with brand, mission, vision, and values
Footer
• Unsubscribe button is obvious with contact information and clickable social icons to follow and share your email

10. Report and analyse

So what are the specific metrics or statistics you need to measure to see if your campaign was successful?

Here are the most popular email marketing metrics:

- **List growth:** Indicates how much your email list has grown over a given period.

- **Open rate:** These are slight vanity metrics as some email software has a viewing pane which means that when a consumer goes to delete your email it marks it open in your email marketing platform. But it can be used in conjunction with other metrics, such as click through rate, and will to a point show you how well you're engaging with your audience.

- **Click through rate:** This is an important metric only if you want your consumer to visit or click on a link to visit something online.

TIP:

One of the most popular consumer behaviours when viewing emails is to hit the reply button. This is just the same as having a 'contact us' page on your website, so don't worry, you won't be swamped with incoming enquiries, but it does open up conversation.

Email marketing tools like MailChimp have a 'manage conversations' option in the campaign set-up that allows you to remove all out of offices and just see 'real person' responses, so they don't get lost in someone's inbox but are available for all team members to view and manage.

- **Delivery and bounce rate:** This will give you a good view of list health and could indicate your email getting caught in spam filters (programs that are used to detect unsolicited and unwanted email and prevent those messages from getting to a user's inbox) or that your list has inactive email addresses.

- **Unsubscribe/abuse or complaint rate:** If all of your subscribers have proactively opted-in, then this should be extremely low.

- **Conversion rate:** To calculate the conversion rate, divide the number of recipients who took the action (this can be any goal you choose and does not have to be revenue based) you were looking for, by the number of emails delivered to recipients. Multiply the result by 100 to express the outcome as a percentage.

- **Forward/share rate:** How many people forwarded or shared the email is a good indicator of how your email was perceived as this indicates its contents were useful and deemed valuable to subscribers' colleagues or team members.

- **Social media interaction:** Email campaigns can be shared to your social channels as part of the campaign set-up within most platforms. This enables you to each audiences who you don't already have email opt-ins.

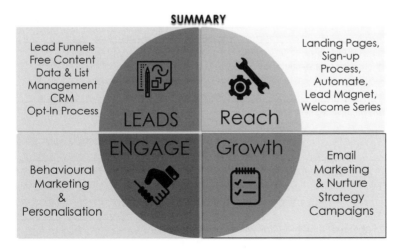

FIGURE 13.7 Summary for The C.L.E.A.N. Customer Cultivator.

- **ROI – return on investment:** Subtract your total investment from the amount of revenue generated, divide the number by your total investment, and multiply the result by 100.

SEND: CHECKLIST

Registered with the ICO or relevant equivalent for your business if required.	
Ensure GDPR compliant and have tools and processes in place for ongoing monitoring.	
Review the methods of interaction for your 3% of web visitors ready to buy or enquire.	
Review how you can stay in touch with the 97% of web visitors not ready to buy or enquire.	
Optimise landing pages for high rates of conversion.	
Collect your Net Promoter Score® (NPS)/ implement customer satisfaction surveys.	
Collect reviews, testimonials, and case studies.	
Brainstorm ideas for automation and personalisation.	
Go through the steps for sign-up for every channel as a consumer.	

Review unsubscribes or complaints for past campaigns.	
Check which CRM you are using and if it passes information across the software or identify a good CRM for your business.	
Consider drip campaigns and email nurture series to convert your leads.	
Find out your industry benchmark for open, click rate etc then carry out your email marketing audit.	
Email marketing audit and strategy creation.	

C.L.E.A.N Customer Cultivator

LEADS
Attract interest & build lead / sales funnel – Integrate on website - **Lead magnets (i.e. FREE content)**

AUTOMATE
Marketing Automation – Trigger email marketing based on behaviour or goal – Nurture with a welcome series

STRATEGY
Campaign objectives, KPIs, design, target - **Lead nurture strategy & campaigns**

ENGAGE
Keep in touch Using CRMS and behavioural marketing to send email marketing messages when it's relevant and personalise to increase engagement

SUCCESS

FIGURE 13.8   The C.L.E.A.N. Customer Cultivator Process.

Chapter 14

Substance – The C.R.E.A.T.I.V.E. Content Communicator

The C.R.E.A.T.I.V.E. Content Communicator®

> **C** onversation
> **R** eact
> **E** ducate
> **A** wareness
> **T** ips
> **I** nspire
> **V** isibility
> **E** ntertain

The C.R.E.A.T.I.V.E. Content Communicator®

FIGURE 14.1   The C.R.E.A.T.I.V.E. Content Communicator.

Marketing is impossible without great content!

Content marketing is an ongoing process integrated into marketing strategy, focusing on **owning media** through creating and distributing valuable, relevant, and consistent content to attract, educate, and engage your audience to ultimately generate profitable customer action and loyalty without selling.

Content marketing costs 62% less than traditional marketing yet generates three times the amount of leads.[1]

Benefits of content marketing include:

- media visibility

- competitive advantage

[1]*Source:* DemandMetric https://www.demandmetric.com/content/content-marketing-infographic.

- brand awareness

- website traffic

- client engagement

- leads and conversion.

Why invest in content marketing?

- It's got a far better ROI than search marketing, such as Google PPC.

- It gives a business the opportunity to appear in search for more terms.

- It drives traffic to the company website and blog articles.

- It not only attracts the target audience, but can also greatly assist in nurturing them through to conversion.

- It's a great way to get to re-engage with customers.

The content marketing process

An outline is given in Figure 14.2.

1. Create customer avatar; research and listening (see Chapters 1 and 3).

2. Decide on themes and topics.

3. Content creation.

4. Promote content.

5. Measure and evaluate.

6. Re-purpose content.

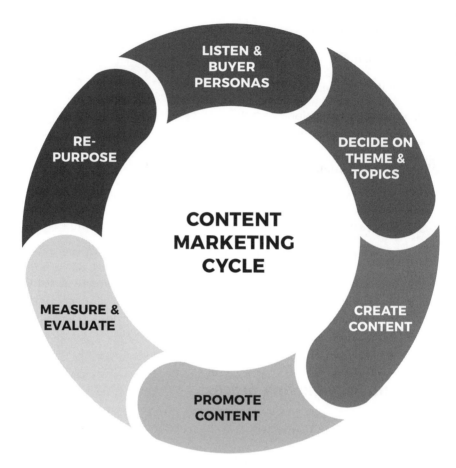

FIGURE 14.2 The content marketing cycle.

Content marketing techniques

Outbound marketing

Outbound marketing tends to be the most familiar type of marketing as it is the more traditional way of pushing your business or brand out in front of larger, less-targeted audiences who are not necessarily proactively seeking your particular product or service. It is often referred to as **push marketing** as you outwardly push your brand, products, or services to consumers through marketing in the hope of generating leads or customers. Basically, it is a style of interruption marketing whereby you disrupt someone with a marketing message to get their attention.

Outbound marketing tends to be more costly than inbound marketing and the ROI is much lower. Examples of outbound marketing include:

- email marketing

- online advertising

- outbound sales calls

- TV and radio adverts

- print adverts, flyers, and brochures

- tradeshows and exhibitions.

Inbound marketing

Inbound marketing is what every business strives for because it is one of the best and most cost-effective ways of attracting potential customers. It is about creating content that can be easily found by customers who know what they want and are actively searching. This is storytelling while they evaluate your brand versus your competition ultimately to enhance conversion (Figure 14.3).

An **inbound marketing campaign** is focused around a single message and goal whereby you promote something valuable and relevant for your audience through your marketing channels.

This method uses tools, technologies, and processes that work together to generate traffic to your website, nurtured into leads that you will ultimately convert into profitable customers. This tactic is often referred to as **pull marketing,** which is generally used when a customer knows what they are looking for; and its purpose is to draw the customer to your business over competitors.

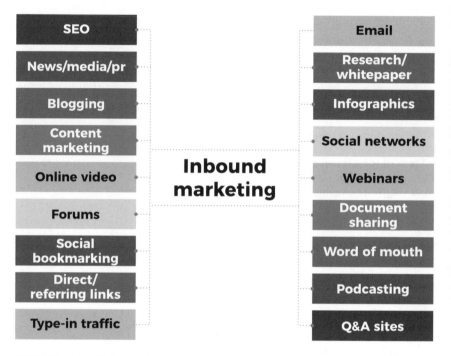

FIGURE 14.3   Inbound marketing channels.

Examples of inbound marketing tactics include: content marketing and social media marketing; and intent-based search engine optimisation, such as blogging, events, webinars, lead nurturing, and media coverage. In other words:

- **Brand storytelling:** telling your brand story to your prospective customers through marketing messages. Essential elements that you need to communicate through your brand story are telling your audience who you are, what you specifically do, how you solve problems, how you add value and care, how you engage and contribute.

- **Brand journalism:** showcase your success through case studies, white papers, social media, and websites. This is your accolade marketing, such as your news about what you have done and achieved and to constantly show the world you are scaling and growing through storytelling.

- **Branded content:** a form of entertaining storytelling that is relatable to the brand although not promotional, such as podcasts, YouTube shows, etc.

The customer's buying journey

We are very savvy online shoppers, whether for consumer or business-related products or services.

We use the internet throughout our decision-making process and often content that we are not proactively searching for that is presented in front of us will trigger us to move several stages further in our buyer journey (Figure 14.4).

Micro landing page

Mobile enabled

Contact details

Explanatory videos

Live chat

Testimonial imagery

FIGURE 14.4 Content marketing from your website.

Awareness **Consideration** **Purchase** **Retention** **Advocacy**

FIGURE 14.5 The five stages of the customers' buying journey.

There are five stages of the customer's buying journey (Figure 14.5):[2]

1. **Awareness:** the consumer becomes aware of the brand through channels, including advertising and word-of-mouth.

2. **Consideration:** realising that they have a need that must be met, the consumer actively considers whether or not to buy the product or service on offer.

3. **Purchase:** the consumer makes the purchase.

4. **Retention:** the customer uses the product, sometimes seeking guidance from provider or a user community, and perhaps being contacted by the provider to encourage brand loyalty.

5. **Advocacy:** the customer spreads the word about the product – whether their opinion is positive or negative.

Forrester Research says that 90% of the buyer's journey may be complete before a prospect reaches out to a salesperson.[3]

It is important that you have a clear customer avatar or customer persona in place so you can focus on building a solid **content marketing strategy** which aligns to your customer journey; and your focus should be to analyse and constantly evolve and improve to **maximise customer value** and continue to scale and grow.

[2]*Source:* CIM https://exchange.cim.co.uk/blog/five-stages-of-your-customers-buying-journey/.
[3]*Source:* Forrester https://go.forrester.com/blogs/15-05-25-myth_busting_101_insights_intothe_b2b_buyer_journey/.

Maximising customer value can be achieved through selling more to existing customers, retaining them for longer, and reducing the cost to serve – which with no acquisition cost should be relatively easy.

On average, roughly 20% of new sales come from repeat customers, plus it's less expensive to generate sales from an existing customer than to acquire a new one – so this is clearly a good strategy to focus on.

The Pareto Principle says, in general, 20% of your **customers** represent 80% of your sales, so if that is true for your business then looking after that 20% of customers will be a major focus to protect your business.

The **C.R.E.A.T.I.V.E. Content Communicator** is a system that ensures you are getting the most from your content.

Communication is the hub of digital marketing and it's the tool you will use across the entire **customer lifecycle** (Figure 14.6) to:

- attract interest

- capture leads

FIGURE 14.6 Seven stages of the customer lifecycle.

- nurture prospects

- convert sales

- deliver and satisfy

- upsell customers

- get referrals and repeat business.

Communication is the element that will get your audience's attention and help you attract and persuade your audience through engaging content.

YouTube

Why does content not get engagement?

Generally, because there is no demand or it is just plain boring and doesn't satisfy the customer need.

- **Over 80% of marketers use video marketing (Figure 14.7).**[4]

- The majority of video is watched on social media using mobile devices and **53% of consumers engage with a brand after viewing a video on social media.**[5]

- **Video gets around 87% more engagement than any other type of content.**[6]

Video has consistently proved itself as one of the best-performing forms of content in terms of engagement. **YouTube,** which is the second most visited site in the world, is probably the most well-known site for

[4]*Source:* Render Forest https://www.renderforest.com/blog/video-marketing-statistics.
[5]*Source:* https://www.brightcove.com/en/company/press/new-research-brightcove-finds-video-content-impacts-product-and-service-purchases-particularly-.
[6]*Source:* WordStream https://www.wordstream.com/blog/ws/2017/03/08/video-marketing-statistics.

80% of businesses currently use video as a marketing tool

FIGURE 14.7   Current business use of video for marketing.

Video Marketing.[7] It is owned by Google so is the only video visible in Google Search, so embedding You Tube video into your website has a huge impact on visibility.

However, uploading a video onto YouTube doesn't mean you will automatically get views – which is why you need a well thought out strategy.

Video marketing strategy

- **Who** is it for? Outline your target demographic.

- **What** is your video's aim?

- **Why** does it matter to your audience? What should your audience should take away from your videos? What's the value add of your content in particular? What does it help your audience do?

[7]*Source:* Alexa https://www.alexa.com/topsites.

- **When** will you create videos? As a weekly show? A how-to series?

- **Where** will you create video and distribute it? Live or pre-recorded? Uploaded or scheduled?

TIP:

The types of videos you should start posting on your channel should be around popular content like how-to, behind the scenes, experts and influencers from your industry. Don't just rely on YouTube traffic as much will come from search engines; and remember, in the first week you need to promote your video across every channel driving YouTube to get views and in turn higher ranking and visibility in YouTube.

YOUR TURN – TAKE ACTION NOW

Create a video marketing mission statement

A simple one-liner that sums up: what type of content you'll make. Educational videos? Entertaining? Practical? A mix? Your brand's tone and your audience's needs.

Write out your statement like this:

'At (Company name), we make (adjective) video content for (specify target audience), so that they (exactly what you want them to do).'

Your YouTube checklist for success

- Try SEO Tools like **TubeBuddy:** https://www.tubebuddy.com/.

- **Research channel and video keywords** and when you upload video add **video headlines** and **descriptions** and add **video tags** (these are simply more keywords that relate to your video).

- Include a **call to action** and encourage engagement, asking them to subscribe to your channel and comment, like, and share.

- Include your **social profiles and URL** etc. in the description.

- Make your video stand out from the crowd with an **attention-grabbing thumbnail** as this will be a key motivation to watching it or not.

- **Transcribe your video** as not everyone has the volume on!

- Use the **YouTube Editor** if you need to make any amends like adding music (but remember this must be copyright free).

- **Drive as much traffic** as you can for the first week (back to YouTube).

- Once you hit over 100 subscribers, you can **customise your YouTube channel URL.**

- Another great way of getting subscribers as opposed to just video views (this can be done through YouTube advertising) is to **add 'subscribe' buttons to video** using the Branding Watermark feature.

- Create a YouTube content marketing mission statement to **ensure your channel theme and subscriber benefit is clear** and add a **channel trailer.**

- Add **interactive calls to action (CTAs) to videos** using YouTube cards or annotations.

- Create consistent and frequent content and let people know when to expect it!

Video kit – what you will need

1. **Webcam:** Buy a webcam for laptops/computers for high-resolution images (search for HD webcam).

2. **Smartphone:** Most of the time you can just use your smartphone as they have amazing cameras.

3. **DSLR camera:** Can record videos as well as taking photos.

TIPS:

When selecting a camera make sure:

- **it has autofocus** so you don't have to worry about blurry images or video;

- **it has a flip out screen** so you can see yourself using the view finder without the need for a videographer;

- **it is Wifi enabled** for easy upload of imagery and video;

- **it has a lens** as part of the package, as these can be costly if bought separately;

- **it can produce GoPro** Slow Motion or Fast Motion (Time-Lapse) style videos.

---

4. **SD card:** It is important to have a memory card to save video and images on. Keep several on a shoot as you would not want to run out.

5. **Remote:** If taking photos or recording videos solo, then you need someone to press the 'record or take photo button', but an even better option would be to get a Bluetooth remote. You can pair this with your phone or camera and press the clicker to start and stop and even zoom in or out.

6. **Lighting:** The best light is outside or facing a window with no other light in the room. The easiest way to get good lighting is to block all light out and use ring lights with a phone or mount inside the ring. These are circular lights with a hole in the middle where you can mount your camera to obtain a source of uniform light that comes directly from the point of view of the camera. They are best used with collapsible tripods so you can vary height and they are portable. Selfie lights that clip on your phone are a must as you don't

have a flash when you take images and videos of yourself. They can be easily recharged with a USB connection.

7. **Back drop:** You can buy collapsible back drops online; but it's always best to use natural scenes as they look better and there is no need to edit.

8. **Microphones:** Portable **condenser microphone** that plugs into your phone, or computer. If you want a wireless microphone, then a **Lavalier microphone** would be the best option as it clips to your body and the cable runs into a small transmitter pack which you attach to your waistband or belt. The transmitter sends the audio to a small receiver that connects to your camera for crystal clear audio.

9. **Travel bag:** Ensure you have a travel bag that fits everything and is well-padded.

10. **Selfie/tripod:** A selfie stick with a remote and a multi-height portable tripod are essential kit.

Scene setting and stance tips

1. Always stand facing forward. That way, even when you turn to perhaps write on a flip chart you will return to face your audience.

2. Don't lean on one leg, otherwise you will look like you are on a slant on the video.

3. Stand slightly apart with your toes pointing out to stabilise yourself so you don't rock throughout your video.

Video editing desktop tools

The YouTube editor is still very popular, but here are some more options:

- Final Cut Pro X for Mac
- Adobe Premiere Pro CC for Windows
- Magisto Cloud-Based (and app).

Video editing apps

- Splice

- LumaFusion

- InShot

- Adobe Premiere Rush

- Videoshop

- Filmmaker Pro Video Editor

- VivaVideo – Best Video Editor.

Screen recording and editing tools

- **Camtasia** or **Movavi** for screen recording and screen capture.

YOUR TURN – TAKE ACTION NOW

Video planner activity

- What's the **goal** of this video?

- Who is the **audience** of this video?

- What's your video **topic**? Think about actual search terms. **EXAMPLE:** 'How to get more social media followers: Seven Steps to Social Media Success.'

- What are the **key takeaways** of the video? What should viewers learn from watching it?

- What's our **call to action**? What do we want viewers to do after they've finished watching the video?

Video Script Activity

- Set the scene: In this video . . . Make it the Best 10 Seconds Ever.

- 'Have you ever . . . ?' Relate to viewers.

- Introduce the AMAZING concept and validate it – why should they listen to you?

- ADD value: For example, three tips.

- Give a brief summary of your benefits.

- Handle objections.

- Sum up and give a strong call to action.

'Creativity is intelligence having fun.'

Albert Einstein, physicist

Substance Step 1: The C.R.E.A.T.I.V.E. Content Communicator – Conversation

It is important for a brand or business to build strong emotional connections with customers because this can lead to increased consumer loyalty and the ability to charge premium prices.

So how do you start the conversation and what will help build emotional connections?

It is just the same as in real life; so, when you are looking at doing this online, ideally you should be looking to inspire relevant and engaging conversations around your industry.

First you need to get to know your customers and fact-find to help you position your content to spark these conversations.

Here are a few pointers to help your customer get to know you and talk to you.

- Introduce yourself.

- Ask questions.

- Let them see what you and your team look like.

- Include bios on your blog.

- Make someone your figurehead or brand ambassador.

- Build a community, group, or forum.

- Include your customers in celebrations of success or anniversaries.

- Invite your customer to the conversation or spark a debate.

- Use Q&A websites and respond whilst checking out what questions people are asking.

- Look at the most searched keywords using Google Search and Keyword Tools.

- Customer polls, quizzes, and surveys are a great way of fact-finding and researching.

- Use listening tools like social listening to see what conversations are happening.

- Use live chat and messenger tools.

- Host live streams and ask viewers to post questions.

- Use social media @mentions to start a conversation.

- Comment on posts to get conversations going.

- Ask for feedback on content and ask about their thoughts on shared content by posting your comment when you share it to encourage responses from your network.

YOUR TURN – TAKE ACTION NOW

Use this template to do a content marketing audit and brainstorm some ideas.

WHO	WHERE	WHAT	WHEN	WHY	Notes
You	All Channels Blog Facebook Twitter LinkedIn Email	Bio with picture	Host a live video Q&A		CTA for article engagement. Use a poll for research and follow-up article content
Cus-tomer	All Channels				
Influ-encer	All Channels				
Com-petition	All Channels				

*'If you're not putting relevant content in relevant places –
you don't exist.'*

Gary Vaynerchuk, entrepreneur

Substance Step 2: The C.R.E.A.T.I.V.E. Content Communicator – React

It is important for your consumer to take action when consuming your content, but also for you to react to any interactions.

Notifications on social networks will keep you up to date with real-time interactions and social media tools can also be used to monitor conversations.

The level of reaction will help you quantify whether your content is having an impact on your business, and this is as important as any other tracking or reporting across channels. If your content is not getting engagement, then you know there is a problem.

One of the most highly engaged types of content is when a social media post is about a genuine success or achievement as people love to support and congratulate their peers. And if the reaction is a lead, then you need to have processes in place to instantly respond and nurture the lead through to a sale.

If you have good traction with a particular piece of content, then respond to that trend by re-focusing future content. Another great way of re-purposing content is to reply to any questions in an article.

Analytics is brilliant for tracking how many visitors land on your content – like webpages, landing pages, or blog articles – but you need to see exactly what they are doing when they get there. There are some very important questions that you need to answer before changing any design or content related element on your pages.

- Are they clicking the back button?
- What is the most persuasive area on that page?
- What calls to action are working?
- Is there any content they are scrolling past and ignoring?

- Is your content positioned in the order a customer wants to consume it?

- Is your website easy to navigate and can the visitor locate content they are looking for to create a positive customer experience?

- Where is my traffic coming from and what does that segment of my audience do on my site?

The answers to these questions will be invaluable in terms of actually enhancing conversion and creating the optimal customer experience.

Analyse what content appeals to your web visitors

Website conversion optimisation has never been easier. There is an amazing tool that you can use to help optimise your website. The tool is **Crazy Egg:** www.crazyegg.com.

Simply sign up for a free account (free for 30 days) then install the tracking code and for a period of about a month collect a snapshot of what your users are doing.

This tracking will form the basis of any changes you need to make to your site to improve conversion and test variations of the same page.

Crazy Egg gives you:

- **Heatmap report:** See the most and least clicked on elements of the page.

- **Scrollmap report:** See where interest is on the page to see where people stop scrolling to consume or scroll past and ignore.

- **Confetti click reports:** See each and every click on your page by traffic source.

- **Overlay report:** See the numeric quantity of clicks on a clickable element.

- **List report:** Basically, a list of all page elements with interactions and activity for each page.

- **User session recordings:** Explore the customer journey for all visitor sessions. See exactly what users do when they visit your website.

- **A/B testing tool:** Create tests by device type and make changes using the Crazy Egg editor. Set a goal so you can see which variant is performing better.

YOUR TURN – TAKE ACTION NOW

- Install Crazy Egg and start recording your snapshot and user videos.

- Test your audience reactions and engagement level. Do some quick tips to see how responsive your audience is. Customer interaction is satisfying for both you and your audience. Don't hide away under your corporate brand; get your face out there and get networking!

- Post a poll on your social media feed.

- Promote and host a LIVE video Q&A on a social platform.

- Send an email campaign and ask for replies to spark conversation.

- Ask a question and ask your audience, perhaps for advice or feedback?

- Comment on 10 posts and see who replies.

- Post in several groups you are a member of and see which group is most interactive.

- Send a handwritten card or postcard to 10 of your most profitable customers to celebrate their success; or send an email or private message to congratulate them on their accolade that you saw on their social media or content marketing.

- Ask 10 of your connections for introductions.

- Request recommendations or reviews from 10 of your clients or invite them to participate in customer success stories. We invite our clients to showcase their success and then take them for lunch. Remember this gives your customers visibility too through including their brand, links to their websites and coverage across channels like social media and email.

Substance Step 3: The C.R.E.A.T.I.V.E. Content Communicator – Educate

Let's look at the best ways of engaging your customers and what types of content they are most likely to consume.

Consumers are in a very different mental state when they are consuming content that they are learning something from. If you can get someone into a state of **learning through educational content** then they will watch your video much longer. This type of content is often referred to as **added-value content.** You are not trying to sell through promotion but by building a relationship, this is called **social selling**.

Mental stimulation such as learning is part of keeping our brains healthy, young, and active.

- Our brains crave knowledge because we feel increased pleasure when we grasp a new concept.

- This means we will engage and consume more content when it is geared towards education and we see it as learning.

Development is an important part of the human psyche and research has found that learning has a positive impact on happiness and wellbeing.[8] Types of content that teach us something – such as 'how-to' tutorials – are very popular, as are any types of content that focus on making us more effective or efficient, for example:

1. Seven Steps to Social Media Success.

2. Four Things Never to Do on Social Media.

3. Eight Steps to Living a Happy and Contented Life.

TIP:

Next time you think about posting a promotional video, think about how much more engagement and sharing you would get if you created a quick tips video.

One of our most popular videos is our **weekly #TipsTuesday video** which appeals equally to both prospects and customers. We not only get the highest amount of view and shares, but when we share this in our weekly email digest we have the highest open rate and click through rate.

TAKE ACTION NOW

Kill writers block and use some **blog title idea generators.**
Get some ideas now and jot them down:

- **Inbound now:** https://www.inboundnow.com/apps/kill-writers-block/.

- **Husbspot:** https://www.hubspot.com/blog-topic-generator.

- **Title Generator:** https://www.title-generator.com/.

---

[8]*Source:* https://www.researchgate.net/publication/253807608_The_Impact_of_Lifelong_Learning_on_Happiness_and_Well-being.

Substance Step 4: The C.R.E.A.T.I.V.E. Content Communicator – Awareness

Getting brand awareness through content marketing can be achieved through the promotion of content across channels. You can also achieve this through the use of influencers – but you will need a clearly defined content strategy in place.

Types of content:

- blogs

- videos

- infographics

- case studies

- eBooks

- white papers

- checklists

- interviews

- testimonials

- social media posts

- gifs and memes.

Ideally, **PR (Public Relations) and content marketing should work hand in hand** as they are based on the same principles, such as figuring out what your ideal audience members want and telling a story in a way that is relevant to them.

Create content around unfulfilled needs

Maslow's Hierarchy of Needs (Figure 14.8) is particularly helpful when creating content for your audience, as we are all looking to fulfil our human needs.

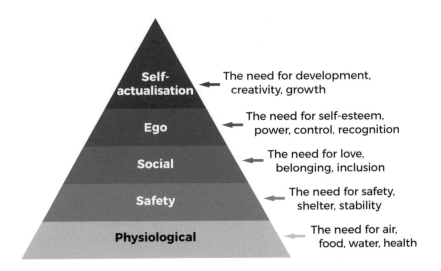

FIGURE 14.8 Maslow's Hierarchy of Needs.

There are many social communities built on this hierarchy and the idea allows marketers to achieve a balance and also purpose for the content they create.

To get brand awareness, we need to encourage recall through consistent and frequent content. According to Edgar Dale's Dale's Cone of Experience, we retain and recall:

- 10% of what we READ
- 20% of what we HEAR
- 30% of what we SEE
- 50% of what we SEE and HEAR
- 70% of what we SAY and WRITE
- 90% of what we DO.[9]

So, if we want the strongest brand recall, then opting for video is an obvious choice.

[9]*Source:* http://www.queensu.ca/teachingandlearning/modules/active/documents/ Dales_Cone_of_Experience_summary.pdf.

Developing your content marketing strategy

Before you can create a content marketing strategy, you need to answer these questions:

- **Your Vision:** How will your content highlight your company's values and how will it help you meet the organisation's goals?

- **Your Value:** What value are you bringing to your industry and to your customer?

- **Your Voice:** How do you want to be seen? Authoritative, friendly, customer-centric, or something else?

YOUR TURN – TAKE ACTION NOW

It's time to tell your brand story (Figure 14.9)!

FIGURE 14.9 Develop your brand story then position to gain brand awareness.

(continued)

Once upon a time...	He/she always...
But always had a problem...	He/she tried to solve it...
But he/she wished that...	Until one day...
Unlike his/her solution, this...	His/her wish came true: to...

FIGURE 14.10 Brand storyboard creation template.

- Align your customer journey and stages of their decision-making process and map these out on a piece of paper.

- Draw rectangle boxes for each stage of the journey and start to map out a rough **'storyboard'** of what content the customer may need at each stage.

- Each rectangle will be a picture to explain what is happening at each stage.

- Try and express emotions, body language, activities, pace, or paths; use captions to visualise your story.

(A good storyboarding tool is: **StoryBoardThat** – free and premium accounts available: https://www.storyboardthat.com/.)

TIPS:

1. Remember to look at customer personas and needs at each stage of the journey.

2. Research frequently asked questions and when these occur in the journey.

3. What obstacles do you encounter and how could you handle these in advance?

This process really helps visualise the steps a customer takes in their journey from becoming aware to purchase.

You should start to get a really good picture of what types of content you can create and this forms a great starting point for your strategy.

Five steps to create a content marketing strategy

1. **Plan:** for your audience: set your mission, goals, and KPIs (Figure 14.11).

2. **Audit:** assess activities and choose channels, budget, and decide on content types.

3. **Creation:** create and optimise content for SEO and establish your vision, value, and voice and your story.

4. **Performance:** processes in place for customer actions such as engagements, conversations, lead generation, nurture, and customer conversion.

5. **Distribution:** schedule and distribute content and measure ROI, optimisation, and testing.

A modern-day marketer spends the majority of their time on content marketing – not necessarily the creation of content.

- 55% content marketing such as creating, monitoring, and tracking;

- 20% on research and analysis, such as creating the plan, customer profiling (customer avatar/personas), and audience message;

Steps to an effective content strategy

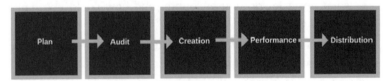

FIGURE 14.11   Effective content marketing strategy – the five-step process.

- 10% keyword and competitor research;

- 10% publishing and sharing content; 5% technical SEO on-page optimisation such as keywords, hyperlinking, etc.

YOUR TURN – TAKE ACTION NOW

Map out your content marketing strategy – this will be an ever-evolving document that you can add to and amend and should be dynamic, based on the performance and results of your content marketing campaigns. This is for your overall business and you will then break this down into individual campaigns and ideally a weekly planner.

Content marketing strategy template

Plan	
Audit	
Creation	
Performance	
Distribution	

Substance Step 5: The C.R.E.A.T.I.V.E. Content Communicator – Tips

It is easy to get into the habit of creating graphics for social media and quotes every day, but you need a mix of media.

Try and think about the types of content you create that could be visualised through multiple forms of media. For instance, a blog could be turned into social media snippets showcasing key points – you could create a live or animated video to story-tell the article. Or you could create a blog from a video transcription from a live video. You could create an infographic that highlights the main statistics and facts from your article. You could create an animated gif with shocking facts.

It is about being creative and presenting content to consumers through a variety of channels in a variety of formats. This will really help you test out which mediums and methods are gaining the best traction for reach, interaction, and engagement, lead and enquiry generation, and sales conversion (Figure 14.12).

Creating visible and engaging content

The quickest and easiest option is to look at what content has been underutilised in your business and make a plan to **re-purpose** it.

There will be content that just keeps on giving and performing well for your business and this type of content is referred to as **'evergreen'** – which basically means something that is timeless, that won't change and will stay relevant not just for a week but even years. Most businesses have an array of content that simply disappears into the archive but if you think it may be 'evergreen' content, then why not display it in a visible and

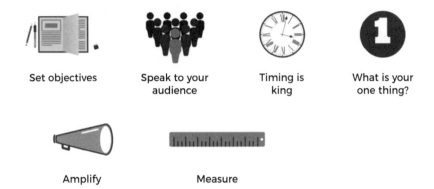

| Set objectives | Speak to your audience | Timing is king | What is your one thing? |

| Amplify | Measure |

FIGURE 14.12 Factors to consider when creating your content marketing strategy.

accessible way to keep re-purposing it by showcasing it as **'free resources'** on your website navigation?

It is quite possible that your **content could perform better for you in several months' time than it does the day you publish it.** This is due to the fact it will work its way through the search engine ranking, increasing visibility and, therefore, traffic.

Nobody ever wants to see content from 2010, but because Google always wants to show the newest most relevant content to its users, this creates an opportunity. You can look to plug that gap and create a brand new, up-to-date article and watch it climb through the ranks.

Psychology of colour

Colour will influence your consumer's behaviour and impacts on other senses too. When you look at branding, it's no accident that an organisation picks colours to represent their brand.

Here are what colours represent to help when creating your content marketing (Figure 14.13).

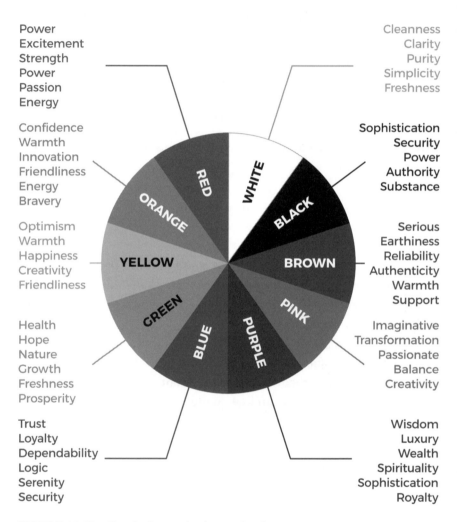

Power
Excitement
Strength
Power
Passion
Energy

Confidence
Warmth
Innovation
Friendliness
Energy
Bravery

Optimism
Warmth
Happiness
Creativity
Friendliness

Health
Hope
Nature
Growth
Freshness
Prosperity

Trust
Loyalty
Dependability
Logic
Serenity
Security

Cleanness
Clarity
Purity
Simplicity
Freshness

Sophistication
Security
Power
Authority
Substance

Serious
Earthiness
Reliability
Authenticity
Warmth
Support

Imaginative
Transformation
Passionate
Balance
Creativity

Wisdom
Luxury
Wealth
Spirituality
Sophistication
Royalty

FIGURE 14.13   Psychology of colour wheel.

YOUR TURN – TAKE ACTION NOW

Look at your own brand identity colour palette and what the colours represent and see how closely this aligns to your company mission, vision, and values.

YOUR TURN – TAKE ACTION NOW

Remember: we scan quickly, so we won't read every word in a headline. Keeping it short and simple is key: around 80 characters is a good target for headlines and text on social images.

Look at Figure 14.14 and time how many seconds it takes you to spot the mistake.

FIGURE 14.14   Find the mistake in the text above.

Get creative

If you already have graphic design experience, or are indeed a professional designer, you may already gave a design tool set you use, but here are our teams' favourite tools for creating engaging content for your audience.

1. **GIFMaker.me:** Create animated gifs, slideshows, and video animations with music online free https://gifmaker.me/ or an alternative is Giphy: https://giphy.com.

2. **Powtoons:** Create videos and presentations https://www.powtoon.com.

3. **Animoto:** Drag and drop video maker https://animoto.com/.

4. **Piktochart:** Create infographics https://piktochart.com/.

5. **Pixton:** Create Comics https://www.pixton.com.

6. **Designmantic:** Get some logo inspiration https://www.designmantic.com/.

7. **Canva:** Free graphic design tool https://www.canva.com/.

8. **Removebg:** Remove an image background in seconds https://www.remove.bg/.

9. **MailChimp:** Email marketing software with blog building drag and drop editor for mobile responsive emails https://mailchimp.com/.

10. **Click funnels:** Create marketing funnels https://www.clickfunnels.com/.

11. **Evergreen webinars:** create webinars and sign-up landing pages, with the whole process managed from reminders to follow-up emails and actual hosting of webinars and evergreen webinars that look live to visitors but are pre-recorded (includes interactive tools to create a live experience) https://www.webinarjam.com/.

YOUR TURN – TAKE ACTION NOW

So now it's your turn to get creative.

Make a list of every type of content that you would like to create and then find a matching tool and test it out.

Substance Step 6: The C.R.E.A.T.I.V.E. Content Communicator – Inspire

Reading blogs

As much as you will need to inspire your audience, you too will also need inspiration. And to encourage your creative juices to flow and let your writing and content flourish, you need to be engaging in content yourself. It is no good pushing content out without consuming content too. So, keep up to date with what matters to you and your industry and read and interact with blogs. Don't just expect others to comment like and share: you must lead by example.

Keep all the blogs you subscribe to in one easily accessible place: sign up to use **Feedly** https://feedly.com (free).

Consider using some **Blogger outreach tools** to find blogs to follow and potential influencers.

1. **Buzzstream:** https://www.buzzstream.com (free trial available).

2. **Buzzsumo:** https://buzzsumo.com/ (free trial available).

Writing blogs

The most common area of procrastination in marketing is content creation – especially when it comes to blog writing.

I think there's a misconception that it will take over your life – but we researched the number of blog articles required to keep your brand ahead of the competition, and for the majority of niches it is around three well-targeted articles a week.

Businesses who **blog tend to generate about 40% more traffic** due to appearing more times in search results and having more visibility in search engines.

Blogging or writing articles, as long as they are well-researched and have good volumes of demand, will result in more traffic because consumers want the content.

Your strategy

You need to dedicate time to:

- **creating and publish unique content** to your blog each month;

- **sharing reputable and helpful content** with your community on social networks;

- **engaging in conversations and discussions** on social networks;

- **empowering and promoting** others' content;

- **growing your network and community** by connecting and following;

- **analysing and reflecting** upon what's working and what can be improved upon.

It is feasible to spend only three hours a week on your system and realise success.

Substance Step 7: The C.R.E.A.T.I.V.E. Content Communicator – Visibility

Paid, earned, and owned media

Every business has the opportunity to influence customers through three types of media:

- **Paid** – Sponsorship and any form of paid advertising.

- **Earned** – PR, media, or blogger coverage, reviews, ratings, testimonials, word of mouth, viral content, social interactions.

YOUR TURN – TAKE ACTION NOW

If you **map out your plan** and make the commitment to marketing, you will **achieve results.**

Try a one-page spreadsheet or weekly planner like the one in Figure 14.15.

Weekly Digital Planner
Goals:

Time/period	Monday	Tuesday	Wednesday	Thursday	Friday

FIGURE 14.15   Example of a weekly digital planner.

TIP:

Here are a few tips to keep a mix of media for your content planner.

1. Aim to create at least one blog for a popular search term.

2. Upload a video on YouTube every week for SEO.

(Continued)

3. Use advertising to generate targeted traffic.

4. Build a lead and nurture funnel using landing pages and email campaigns.

5. Post daily on social media.

6. Create a piece of added-value premium content every month around a themed campaign, i.e. guides, etc.

7. Collect case studies and testimonials

Measure results daily and remember to always audit!

- **Owned** – Any of your corporate content such as websites, blog, brochures, social media platforms, etc.

Converged media is when paid, owned, and earned media are combined for form branded content which could also generate earned media. **Shared media** is shared content whereby there are multiple creators, such as word of mouth, referrals, community-driven content, and co-creation. Try and utilise these types of media across your business as much as possible.

Enhancing your visibility

1. Have a page dedicated to categories like webinars, case studies, white papers, and guides, etc.

2. Keep your content visible and keep driving traffic to your most successful content.

3. Create top content lists: Spotlight your most popular content and offer readers 'top 10 articles', 'most popular' on your blog to frontload content and consistently and frequently drive traffic to these pages.

4. Use advertising to support your content and sales process.

5. Involve influencers. Interview highly regarded experts in your field to help promote your content. If they're part of the content creation process, they're more likely to buy in to promoting your content.

YOUR TURN – TAKE ACTION NOW

Perform a content marketing performance audit

Did your content resonate? Did users engage?

There are **four key metrics** you will need to measure and analyse to assess how your content is performing;

1. consumption

2. sharing and engagement

3. leads

4. sales.

To get a feel for your content marketing performance, look at these two main categories to assess your content marketing: **buzz and impact.**

Buzz:

- likes

- shares.

Impact:

- comments

- downloads

- clicks

- views

(continued)

- backlinks to page

- backlinks to domain.

Check out your latest articles and blogs and social media posts to get a feel for what's buzzing and what is actually having an impact on your business.

Substance Step 8: The C.R.E.A.T.I.V.E. Content Communicator – Entertain

Creating entertaining content to capture and maintain consumer attention for prolonged periods of time is definitely a must when you consider that the amount of **video uploaded every minute on YouTube is over 300 hours!**[10]

As you can imagine, when viewers enjoy content, they view the integrated brands more favourably.

There is a vast amount of content available to consumers and the internet is flooded with new content each and every day. Given that the average attention span is between 10 and 20 minutes, why do some businesses find it difficult to get engagement online for short, quick consumption content?

The answer is simple: the content didn't capture our attention in the first place or it was boring.

Nielsen discovered that brand recall was 86% for branded content, and only 65% for regular ads.[11]

[10]*Source:* YouTube http://www.everysecond.io/youtube.
[11]*Source:* Nielson https://www.nielsen.com/us/en/insights/news/2016/quality-branded-content-outperforms-pre-roll-advertising.html.

Branded content doesn't promote products or services; but, for instance, if a company which made XYZ drink didn't market their drink but promoted recipes that could be made with that drink – that would be branded content. The content is created by the advertiser and consumers will recognise the brand although the content wouldn't be an out and out product or service promotion. For instance, a well-known fizzy drink company adopted a strategy of putting names on their bottles and cans and received a huge amount of mentions in social and news media.

Content can include articles, videos, podcasts, and even live elements that bring relevant value to the consumer.

TIP:

Try and take the dryness out of a topic and think of ways of explaining it through animation or comics.

YOUR TURN – TAKE ACTION NOW

Brainstorm five ideas for entertaining content. Research your competitors and look at innovative niches for your business. Look at key influencers online, not just in your market but across other niches too.

- podcast
- YouTube show
- live video
- animations
- comic strips.

Think about entertaining your audience and think about content you engage with and content that makes you smile.

Creating podcasts from video

Since video is one the most obvious and important content options, I want to share how to create podcasts utilising existing video.

You can take any video and quickly turn it into a podcast. An example of this is our **'Dynamic Digital Marketing Show'** on YouTube, which we turned into audio for our podcast which can be downloaded in iTunes.

Three easy steps to create and host your podcast:

1. Download your video from YouTube and convert the mp4 file into an audio file.

2. We then use a tool called Spreaker (podcast creation and hosting software) and upload each audio of the video as a podcast episode. You can also create podcasts straight from Spreaker if not using video. https://www.spreaker.com/.

3. Then, using iTunes Podcast Connect, we submit our podcast so it can be downloaded in iTunes. https://itunesconnect.apple.com.

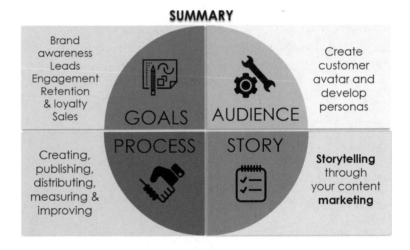

FIGURE 14.16   The C.R.E.A.T.I.V.E. Content Communicator.

SUBSTANCE: CHECKLIST

YouTube channel checklist.	
Video kit list, editing tools, apps, and screen recording.	
Video marketing strategy.	
Create video content marketing mission statement.	
Video planner and script activity.	
Ideas to stimulate conversation.	
Install Crazy Egg for website visit behaviour analysis and design recommendations.	
Test audience engagement level.	

Blog idea generator tools.	
Create brand story board.	
Content marketing strategy creation.	
Observe colour of psychology and impact on branding and marketing.	
Research creative design tools.	
Create weekly digital planner.	
Content marketing audit looking at buzz and impact metrics.	
Brainstorm five ideas for entertaining branded content.	

C.R.E.A.T.I.V.E Content Communicator

GOALS
Audit, goals, purpose & mission:
campaign, cost-savings & business-growth goals

AUDIENCE
Customer needs - What is the valuable content experience you will deliver at the particular stage of your customer's journey?

SUCCESS

STORY
Deliver value through building relationships that can be nurtured into thriving customer communities - **Story & distribution channels**

Conversation & measurement: Driving your audience to take a desired action. **Reach, Action, Conversion & Engagement:** Subscribers, leads, web traffic, SEO & online visibility

PROCESS

FIGURE 14.17   The C.R.E.A.T.I.V.E. Content Communicator Process.

Chapter 15

Sell – The Ultimate Reach and Retention Radar

The Ultimate **Reach & Retention Radar®**

> › **R**apport
> › **R**elationship
> › **R**epeat
> › **R**eferral
> › **R**eward

The
Ultimate
Reach & Retention®

FIGURE 15.1   The Ultimate Reach and Retention Radar.

We have looked into how to reach your audience through search and other digital channels, but the **Sell** element of the model addresses the idea of reaching your audience through other mediums – and perhaps even more traditional offline channels and methods.

Sell looks at how **relationship management, loyalty, referral, affiliate programmes, and partnerships** can be used to generate more profit for your business. It also covers ways of generating higher returns on investment through looking after existing customers.

The new marketing age

The internet and social media marketing have changed the way that businesses market for the better.

Over 20 years ago, as a marketer, if you wanted to do something like a direct mail campaign, you'd be looking at 21 days until you actually got a return on your investment. The cost investment was high and even production lead times were lengthy, never mind actually getting your message or offer in front of the customer. The call to action was generally either by phone or people could respond free of charge, again delaying the actual notification of interest to the business.

Imagine you saw an advert and responded to say you were interested and wanted more information: this could mean a further week or two until the consumer could even evaluate the offer. The sale cycle was much longer, plus the consumer could change their mind or even find alternatives in retail stores in the meantime.

The newer communication methods and channels, such as email marketing, mean you can send a campaign in a press of a button and literally start seeing results instantly – from people opening your email, clicking and visiting your website, to people buying and enquiring in a matter of minutes.

You can start a business and build a website in less than an hour and have instant online presence. You can start generating leads the same day and probably even make sales that day too. The fact that we have social platforms has opened up conversations between brands, their teams, and consumers and has been integral in the decision-making process.

Consider how **social selling has evolved this process** even further. We see emotionally connected consumers because of this relationship-focused marketing methodology.

What do I mean by social selling?

I mean building **relationships** with your audience by adding value at every stage of the customer journey to shorten the sale cycle and ultimately enhance the decision-making process (Figure 15.2).

The exciting aspect of social selling is that you actually never proactively 'sell' a product or a service. Instead, this method uses content that centres on solving the pain or problem of your audience.

FIGURE 15.2   Social selling quote by Dawn McGruer.

Sell Step 1: The Ultimate Reach and Retention Radar – Rapport

The first stage to establishing a brand in your consumers' consciousness is to build **rapport.**

Rapport shows that you value your prospects and customers and is essentially effective communication. It is about how you or your business actually interacts with prospects and customers to create a positive connection that enhances their experience with you.

In particular, we will be looking at an extremely powerful method of building rapport introduced above: **social selling**. This is how online marketing has changed the way we do business and interact throughout the customer journey, lifecycle, and decision-making process.

Consumers can research a vendor and take advice from peers or request recommendations for trusted suppliers. We often turn to our networks rather than searching on Google. This is a form of **social listening** which can reveal useful information for both parties to use in their own decision making and sales and purchase processes. Gone are the days of **'cold calling'** as people tend to have a more favourable impression of someone introduced through their professional network as opposed to contact from a complete stranger.

This **two-way mutually beneficial sales method** has revolutionised the way sales teams work and how consumers source products and services.

TIP:

Watch for pain points and requests for recommendations, both of which provide natural opportunities for you to provide a solution to a problem.

YOUR TURN – TAKE ACTION NOW

Search your name and business and check how easy you are to find on social platforms and perform some **on-platform research and social listening.**

(continued)

It is always useful to monitor what people are saying about:

- you;

- your company;

- your industry;

- and your competitors;

and this is true regardless of whether you are a consumer or vendor.

Make sure you are following any key brands, competitors, and topics too.

Sell Step 2: The Ultimate Reach and Retention Radar – Relationship

Why network?

The easiest way to build meaningful relationships is to **add value** where you can, be it through providing useful content or being an active networker who engages and interacts proactively. This whole approach is about getting you and your business on people's radar and keeping in front of people through online networking.

Simply being an active part of your community and being part of the conversation will really help in terms of establishing your professional brand and credibility as a recognised industry leader. Genuinely getting to know people and fact-finding strengthens your positioning and creates trust and in turn organic **lead generation** through networking.

Social networking platforms such as **LinkedIn** are extremely effective for social selling and research suggests that developing a more personal one-to-one relationship, rather than focusing on brand and business promotion, gives results that can far outweigh that of your competition by almost.

> *'Companies that use one to one relationships for social selling outperform competition 2.7x more often.'*
> Penny Price, marketing solutions LinkedIn

It is a completely different way of marketing a business when content is being shared from industry figureheads because they are positioned as the experts in their fields. Consumers want to be closer to the thought leaders and key personnel in a business.

It is far more likely that people will participate in a conversation with another person as opposed to a brand. For instance, creating an article on LinkedIn is again centred on the author and their own personal thought leadership and opinions within that industry. This triggers interaction in a more personal and human way, as comments and replies become two people talking rather than a person speaking to a faceless brand.

If you think about behaviour on social sites such as LinkedIn, it is far more likely that a user will connect with real people – even if they don't know them – than follow company pages of brands they are not yet familiar with. This is because people look at what people are saying and, if they like what they see, they are more likely to connect.

Individuals story-tell their lives and achievements through their news feeds and this ultimately helps their audience feel like they know them. The more you see a face, the faster your brain will recognise that person; and this idea works for brand recognition and association too. It is definitely more effective than trying to instill a brand identity first.

YOUR TURN – TAKE ACTION NOW

It is now your turn to find out what your relationship is like with your audience and how LinkedIn ranks you as a social networker.

LinkedIn uses a tool that you too can access: **The Social Selling Index (SSI).** This can be found on the LinkedIn Business Solutions site or by simply searching in Google for 'linkedin ssi index'.

Your Social Selling Index (SSI) measures how effective you are at the **four elements of social selling** and how you can aim to improve your score.

1. **Establishing your professional brand** – Complete your profile with the customer in mind. Become a thought leader by publishing meaningful posts.

2. **Finding the right people** – Identify better prospects in less time using efficient search and research tools.

3. **Engaging with insights** – Discover and share conversation-worthy updates to create and grow relationships.

4. **Building relationships** – Strengthen your network by connecting and establishing trust with decision makers.

TIP:

Remember your score will be updated daily based on your activity; so, to maintain or to improve a score, you should have daily social media interaction.

Where do you rank in your industry and against your peers? Get your score here (or Google LinkedIn Social Selling Index) https://business.linkedin.com/sales-solutions/social-selling/the-social-selling-index-ssi.

According to an internal study by LinkedIn, there is a strong correlation between achieving sales goals and sales reps with high SSI:

- 45% more sales opportunities;

- 51% more likely to hit quota; 78% of social sellers outsell peers who don't use social media.[1]

Sell Step 3: The Ultimate Reach and Retention Radar – Repeat

Unfortunately, in some businesses, once a customer has purchased they are quickly neglected in favour of attracting new business. Such a strategy ignores the fact that **retention is cheaper than acquisition.**

On average, customers spend approximately 33% more with a business they have bought from previously versus a first-time purchase.

So, without any further investment being required to target customers, marketing to stimulate repeat purchases will result in a higher ROI.

We know that customers tend to spend more with businesses they trust, so an additional benefit is that it's not only quicker to recognise revenue from purchases through a shorter sales cycle, but it's also easier to increase average order values and purchase frequencies. This can be done through opportunities to cross-sell or upsell to existing customers who have experienced your products and services previously. There is less to prove from the business's point of view, and less perceived risk from the customer's.

[1]*Source:* https://business.linkedin.com/sales-solutions/social-selling/what-is-social-selling.

According to Marketing Metrics, the success rate of selling to an existing customer is 60–70%, while the success rate of selling to a new customer is only 5–20%![2]

Tactics that encourage repeat business include keeping on your customers' radar, but another of the most successful strategies is to upsell and increase purchase frequency through case studies, testimonials, and reviews. If your audience can see the benefits and successes of others who have worked with you, then there is no better social proof (Figure 15.3).

FIGURE 15.3 Content designed for your audience's needs.

[2]*Source:* http://www.marketmetrics.com.

A common strategy used to encourage customers to purchase again is discounts, offers, and special customer-only VIP incentives.

Nielsen says 92% of consumers trust recommendations from people they know.[3]

YOUR TURN – TAKE ACTION NOW

Often, repeat purchases don't occur because the customer doesn't know about a particular product or service, you haven't been in touch and the relationship has dwindled, or they are perhaps dealing with your competitor. So, let's focus on the key strategies for repeat purchase. Think about how you could educate your customers about a new or additional product or service that would complement what they have already bought.

Approach your customers for:

- case studies

- reviews and ratings

- testimonials

- feedback by survey.

Aim for **at least 10 engagements,** if not more, to get an overview of why they chose you, how it impacted and benefited their business, and what amazing results they achieved as well as the ongoing success they are experiencing through continuing to work with you. It is important to balance these across channels, so look at Google reviews, social platforms, website, third-party review platforms, and providers.

[3]*Source:* Nielson http://www.nielsen.com/us/en/insights/reports/2012/global-trust-in-advertising-and-brand-messages.html.

Reviews and recommendations

Hosting reviews on your own channels is great; but having your reviews on channels not owned by yourself adds to social proof and trust.

For instance, a recommendation on LinkedIn links back to the reviewer's profile and the consumer can see it is their own words and not a cleverly written web editor's review.

Videos are especially compelling, but you need to ensure you have a storytelling approach that includes handling any frequently asked questions, sales objections, and obstacles to purchase.

Often, the easiest way of approaching this is to ask the questions directly to the customer to ensure they answer everything that the consumer needs to know.

TIP:

Use LinkedIn to request 'recommendations' as well as giving in exchange. On your LinkedIn profile just scroll down to the 'Recommendations' section and click on 'Ask for a recommendation'. Remember to customise the message to include key questions you would like them to answer in their review.

All of these reviews are great for persuading consumers to choose you over your competitors, but they are also good insight into consumer research. Your customer feedback will help you really clarify and construct very powerful and persuasive content marketing messages that address they reason your existing customers have converted.

Your customers can benefit from being part of your marketing through exposure for their brand or business. Using logos on your website and links back to your customers' websites will encourage participation as an added benefit.

Sell Step 4: The Ultimate Reach and Retention Radar – Referral

Empowering your biggest advocates in business, your customers, to pro-actively refer new business to you in exchange for an incentive is a highly effective strategy for a multitude of reasons.

Using referral marketing can enable a brand to engage audiences that are harder to reach or convert through a trusted peer in their network. The relevance of the product or service has already been established by your customer, who is in essence recommending you to fill the pre-existing need of their friend, colleague, or peer.

According to McKinsey, referrals influences up to 50% of ALL purchasing decisions and generate more than two times the sales of paid advertising.[4]

Incentivise your customers to refer – they will be your very own virtual sales team. As human beings we love to share positive experiences and want our peers to share that experience too. So, this is a very natural instinct and one easily adopted; we just need to give a gentle nudge to trigger this referral behaviour.

[4]*Source:* McKinsey http://www.mckinsey.com/insights/marketing_sales/a_new_way_to_measure_word-of-mouth_marketing.

If, for instance, at the point of sale you encourage your customer to share their latest purchase in social channels to their friends and network, then this acts as social proof and can generate interest from their peers. You can take it a stage further and send referral programme or scheme details via email, making it easy for them to refer friends and so worthwhile there is no reason they won't.

Even if only a small percentage of your customers refer new business to you, not only does this have a positive impact to your bottom line, it also causes a ripple effect because that person knows how the scheme works as they participated and this should encourage them to replicate this behaviour.

Don't forget it may not just be customers who want to refer to you; it could be a friend or colleague who sees a product or service and thinks 'that would be perfect for XYZ' and they too can suggest your products and services even if they haven't even used your business. This is why social proof is imperative to establish trust and showcase credentials.

If you have a good relationship with your customers, you can even ask them to set up reciprocal links their websites.

YOUR TURN – TAKE ACTION NOW

This is a simple activity – go to Google Search and type in 'referral scheme tools'.

Check out the free and paid tools and software that make it really easy for customers to refer.

This will not only help you get started, it will inspire you regarding developing or implementing referral programmes.

Sell Step 5: The Ultimate Reach and Retention Radar – Reward

Just as customers rate businesses and brands, the same is true in reverse. It is imperative for a business to know who their most profitable customers are as not every one will be your model customer that gives high returns and demands low levels of resource.

Does your business have a way of scoring customers to reward your most profitable?

Consider ranking your customers and clustering them into segments so you can focus on the ones you want. This helps you really identify their key characteristics.

- VIP customers

- high potential customers

- demanding customers

- rescued or abandoned cart customers.

Look at implementing a customer loyalty programme, which helps with repeat business and can also really increase average spends and purchase frequency.

Use tools like CRM (customer relationship management), which is a technology for managing all your company's relationships and interactions with customers and potential customers. Basically, a CRM is a central database of all your contacts hosted online instead of keeping business cards and endless spreadsheets. This allows you to hold profiles about each contact so you can search, segment, tag, communicate, and keep in touch with them easily. It allows you create tasks and reminders to efficiently manage the sale and after-sales process.

CRMs help customer retention because instead of sending generic newsletters or email promotions, you can really personalise communications based on their purchase history or where they rank in terms of your customer rating. For instance, you could invite all of your VIP customers to an exclusive event and ask them to bring a friend or colleague. This approach ticks all the boxes of the Sell – Reach and Retention Radar strategy from building rapport and relationships, to providing the opportunity for repeat or referral business; plus, you are rewarding them too.

According to Salesforce, using CRM tools improve retention as much as 27%.[5]

Benefits of CRM

- It can be used to not only find, connect with, understand, and nurture sales prospects, but also to maintain relationships with existing customers through the use of social media.

- It drives a positive digital and customer support experience, building relationships, attracting testimonials, and recommendations.

- It increases average order value and purchase frequency.

Referral tips

- Drive referrals at the time of purchase and onboarding.

- Identify opportunities for upselling and cross-selling.

- Keep on your customers' radar.

[5]*Source:* https://www.salesforce.com/hub/crm/benefits-of-crm/.

- Build rapport, relationships, and personalise offerings using CRM tools.

- Offer incentives such as referral, reward, and loyalty programmes.

- Use inbound marketing tools and software to automate the process. Use content such as blogs, events, SEO, social media, etc. to create brand awareness and attract new business.

Tag lines

Make it easy for your customers to tell others what you do and make referrals simple!

I urge you to focus on the benefit you offer and create a meaningful tag line about **what problem you solve and what your solution will give them.**

My tag line is not that I run a digital marketing agency and academy, but that **'I maximise digital marketing profits to scale and grow a business'.**

If you have a solid tag line, then people repeat it and use it to tell others what you do.

I have never met anyone who said they didn't want more profit or to scale or grow their business. Some organisations may not wish to grow their size, but growth can relate to increasing their customer base, average order value, or purchase frequency, not just hiring and employing more staff or expanding operations. It could be about scaling and growing their online presence and visibility. This is why **tag lines** are amazing as they can be manipulated to perfectly match the exact requirements of who you are talking to whilst being very clear in terms of your proposition.

YOUR TURN – TAKE ACTION NOW

Reach and retain campaign

Brainstorm ideas to get in front of your VIP customers virtually or face-to-face and come up with a referral campaign idea that aims to increase and improve rapport, relationships, repeat and referral business, as well as rewarding them too.

SELL: CHECKLIST

Get your LinkedIn Social Selling Index.	
Aim for at least 10 case studies, reviews, ratings, and testimonials.	
Research 'referral scheme tools'.	
Create a meaningful tag line about what problem you solve and what your solution will give them.	
Brainstorm referral 'Reach and Retain' campaign ideas that aim to improve or increase rapport, relationships, repeat and referral business, and reward customers too.	

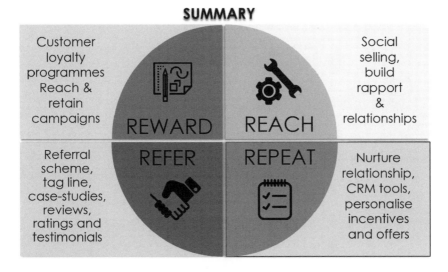

FIGURE 15.4 Summary of The Reach and Retention Radar.

FIGURE 15.5 The Reach and Retention Radar Process.

Chapter 16

Sponsor – The Brilliant Brand Booster

The Brilliant Brand Booster®

> **A**dverts
> **A**ffiliates
> **A**lliances

FIGURE 16.1 The Brilliant Brand Booster.

In this chapter we'll look at **Sponsor – The Brilliant Brand Booster,** a five-step formula to reach your audience, get them to engage and take action to ultimately generate leads and maximise your digital marketing spend and profits.

In particular, we will be covering online **advertising, affiliate schemes,** and **alliances** and how you can utilise the power of partnerships.

Brand boosting

If you want to really get your brand noticed, it's all about creating high-impact and memorable messages, and storytelling is paramount for boosting recognition, recall, and building relationships. These are all key elements in developing brand exposure.

A few ideas for brand boosting

- Strong branding and brand story board.
- Influencer marketing and high-profile partnerships.
- Strong online presence and channel marketing.

FIGURE 16.2 Amplification to reach more of your audience.

- Social networking and added-value content creation.

- Advocates who recommend and refer for commission.

- Amplification and reach to pull through new audiences (Figure 16.2).

Paid sponsorship and advertising

Social media advertising is increasingly popular because of its cost effectiveness and targeting potential.

All social platforms have advertising options, including LinkedIn and Twitter. Traditionally B2C was the main market for Facebook and Instagram adverts, but now even B2B works as well because of the amazing targeting options.

Advertising can provide a consistent and steady, as well as extremely good quality, stream of traffic to your landing pages from as little as 1p. Plus, it gives you the ability to re-market to people who might be interested, giving a 70% better conversion.

'A man who stops advertising to save money is like a man who stops a clock to save time.'

Henry Ford, Ford Motor Company founder

Sponsor Step 1: The Brilliant Brand Booster – Adverts

We will be exploring how consumers behave, as they will not always buy instantly after seeing an advert. And the reason adverts won't convert at this rate is because it may not be the right time or proposition for them; or they may have no idea who your brand or business is. For this reason, a common mistake when commissioning an ad is to focus only on 'closing the sale or conversion'.

A more effective strategy would be to build a relationship with your audience and nurture them and build a relationship with the brand or business.

Creating killer social media ads that convert

The first stage of an advertising campaign shouldn't ever just send traffic to your homepage, your offer, or your product/service. It's much better to drive your them to a blog or a landing page and focus on adding value and offer a 'lead magnet' (an irresistible bribe in exchange for their details, like name and email).

Once you have given them some free added-value in the initial advert (for instance as **video: '10 tips for better blogging'**) then you can move to stage two – which is to generate leads so you can continue to build and nurture the relationship and ultimately convert them into profitable customers. So, an example to follow the video could be a free guide: **'The Ultimate Guide to Blogging'**. It's far more likely that someone will part with their details and sign up for a free guide after you have already given them some valuable advice and tips in your video.

It would only be at the third advert that you would **'close the sale'** – once you have warmed them up and established some brand or business recognition. The example here could be an **'online blogging for business success course'** a high-value and low-cost item.

This is about two critical aspects of successful advertising:

- Getting them over the line to become a customer.

- Liquidating your advertising budget.

The ads in these campaigns are not spread out across days, weeks, or even hours: your audience are almost serendipitously seeing these adverts in their news feeds. **And this process can happen in a matter of minutes.**

Imagine: your adverts are not a cost but a revenue generator that can convert a percentage of your audience who are ready to buy or convert now. This covers your advertising cost that day and provides a level of **revenue and hopefully profit.**

Then, for those who don't convert, you can use a combination of re-marketing and lead nurturing through website and email marketing (Figure 16.3).

If you try and close sales using just one advert instead of a multi-step campaign, yes you will close some sales – and ultimately get some success – but your ROI will be lower.

It is important, though, that when you measure your **advertising ROI** it must encompass the true costs of the business – and not just the cost to reach and convert your audience deducted from straight revenue. The cost of the product or service needs to be included to get a true picture.

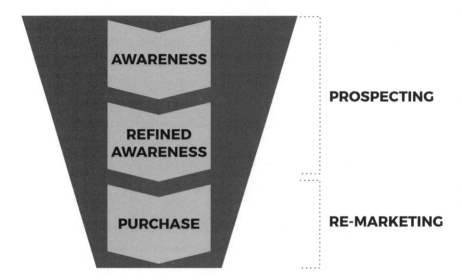

FIGURE 16.3   Re-marketing model.

The advertising profit calculation needs to go full circle from product and service costs such as:

- production
- marketing
- fulfilment.

Making your marketing a revenue generator

So many try social ads and don't get the ROI. Our adverts can generate **a lead every eight minutes** and our advertising costs us nothing: it's a main profit driver! If we can do this, where do others go wrong?

Pitfalls of social ad campaigns

1. No defined, documented strategy.
2. No defined personas for audience.

3. Choosing the wrong marketing objective.

4. Improper targeting.

5. Faceless corporation.

6. Selling too soon.

7. Not properly configuring your conversion tracking.

8. Neglecting to A/B test.

9. Lacking ad creative diversity.

Creating an advertising strategy

- Develop your advert goal; be specific and set SMART objectives for reach, acquisition, and conversion.

- Set your campaign budget and work out your target ROI (return on investment) and ensure you look at liquidating your advertising spend each day and consider the entire costs – not just to recruit the customer, but through to fulfilment.

- Identify your target audience and personas focusing on their needs and the problem you will present that your solution solves. It has to be a really appealing offering.

- Clarify campaign steps – what exactly you will use to engage, generate a lead, and close.

- Complete an advertising SWOT analysis to audit your current situation for benchmarking your starting point (if you haven't used advertising yet then look at competitors).

- Launch versions to test and run to get a good snapshot. Let adverts run for at least a few days to get a good audience reach; throughout this period the social platform will actually be optimising performance for you as it learns and analyses results. This should mean your advert will steadily get better results and provide accurate test results, presenting a clear winner.

- Analyse and re-launch the winner from the test and the cycle continues (Figure 16.4).

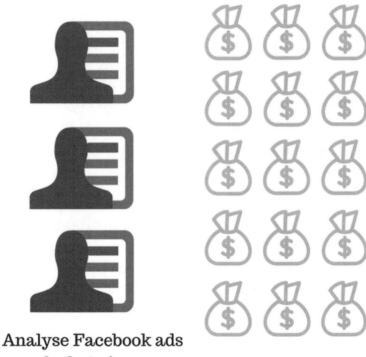

**Analyse Facebook ads
regularly to increase
conversion**

FIGURE 16.4   Analyse adverts to increase conversion.

Seven steps for social ad success

To avoid the common pitfalls, here are my advertising tips to keep you on track through seven steps for advertising campaign success.

1. **Targeting:** For your first campaign step, like a 'tips video', don't refine your audience – let them segment themselves. Choose a broad target.

2. **Advert objectives:** Always choose engagement or video views for the first stage. Choose conversion for the second and third.

3. **Pay for results:** If you have an option to pay for impression or engagement, always go for the latter; as impressions mean you pay

for the privilege of appearing on someone's news feed and they may not even see it, never mind interact or engage with your advert. On Facebook, don't boost adverts: use the Facebook Ad Manager as it has more options and is cheaper because you can choose to pay for results not impressions. Pay-per-click is better than impression as at least they are visiting your content and taking action.

4. **Create campaigns that close:** Never do one-off adverts unless it's just a brand awareness campaign showcasing an accolade or achievement. Always use free content for stages one and two; the conversion may happen offline, but always include conversion opportunities at every stage of the process. For instance, if someone watched the video and was ready to buy, they can click 'learn more' and go to a landing page. Thank you pages are great opportunities for upsells and conversions.

5. **Conversion tracking:** To track campaigns you must install a tracking pixel so that you can see accurate results and also build your remarketing audiences. Each social channel has a pixel code you can install – just visit the pixel tracking instructions on each network.

6. **Optimising adverts and A/B testing:** With each test, choose one of the following variables. I have provided example tests for each variable.

   • **Creative:** Ad with a video compared to ad with a single image.

   • **Audience:** Men aged 21–30, compared to men aged 31–40, compared to men aged 41–50.

   • **Optimisation:** Ad set optimised for conversions compared to ad set optimised for link clicks.

   • **Placements:** Mobile placements compared to desktop placements.

   • **Product set:** Product set with handbags from one brand compared to product set with handbags from a different brand compared to product set with handbags from another different brand.

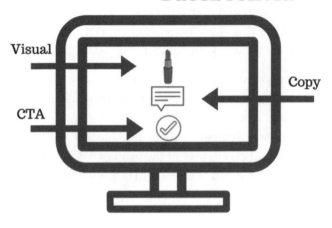

The Formula of a Facebook Ad

FIGURE 16.5 Facebook advert formula.

7. **Advert creatives and copy:** Use images that link to text, create different adverts for different audiences, test creatives, keep it short and simple with just one call to action and transparent – always include pricing (Figure 16.5). Make sure it clearly says:

- what you're offering
- how it benefits them
- what to do next.

YOUR TURN – TAKE ACTION NOW

Use each platform's own business websites, which all include case studies and helpful advice and insights to help you gear your social media advertising for better results.

Check out each of these platforms and look at opportunities based on past success stories for your industry.

- https://www.facebook.com/business

- https://business.twitter.com

- https://business.linkedin.com/

- https://business.instagram.com

- Search 'YouTube advertising success stories'.

Lead generation forms

Using lead generation forms for advertising saves time and money creating landing pages and keeps the user in the news feed and on-platform (Figure 16.6). Their information is auto-populated to save users time and effort too.

FIGURE 16.6 Example lead generation Facebook advert.

Case Study: Ad Success Story: Strategy – Leads Every Eight Minutes!

Here is an actual advertising campaign costing less than 1p with 30% conversion.

Step 1: Video with tips to get ahead in your career talking about digital salaries and showcasing a day in the life of a digital marketer, showcased to a broad audience. Call to action to landing page to learn more and get a free guide.

FIGURE 16.7 The 3As of advertising.

Step 2: Re-marketed to viewers with a 'Get Certified in Digital Guide' capturing their first name and email.

Step 3: Landing page with three calls to action: to sign-up for a guide, get in touch, or enrol. Any non-conversions were re-marketed to at each stage of the campaign too and this also builds an ongoing re-marketing list in Facebook to use for other adverts (Figures 16.7, 16.8, and 16.9).

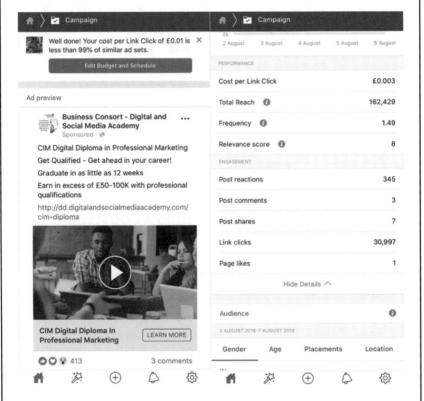

FIGURE 16.8   Example Facebook advert with campaign results.

(Continued)

FIGURE 16.9   Example landing page with dual call to action.

Results: Less than 1p per click; over 30% conversion on landing page.

Sponsor Step 2: The Brilliant Brand Booster – Affiliates

Don't confuse 'affiliate marketing' with 'referral marketing'. Yes, they are very similar; but think of referral marketing in terms of a customer or person who refers another person – perhaps as part of a referral scheme. In contrast, 'affiliate marketing' can be used to target larger audiences, as generally the 'affiliate member' markets the proposition of business not related to them to their audiences through email, websites, or social media etc.

An affiliate scheme is a marketing arrangement by which an online retailer pays commission to an external website for traffic or sales generated from its referrals.

Affiliate schemes require tools to manage them, much as referrals schemes do, to make it easy for both parties involved. Tools like 'affiliate pro' mean you can literally set up an affiliate scheme in minutes. The huge benefit of an affiliate scheme is that your affiliate members can self-manage their affiliate accounts and sign-up online and get started straight away.

If you actually provide marketing collateral and support, as well as good levels of commission, this will increase your success.

Each affiliate will be provided with a unique URL that tracks their audiences' visits to your website and upon conversion will record the sale and automatically calculate the commission. Using affiliate tools means you can set up specific rules and requirements for commission pay-outs, as well as setting up different affiliate commissions per member.

YOUR TURN – TAKE ACTION NOW

Check out affiliate scheme tools by searching Google and evaluating the options available.

TIP:

A good commission pay-out is 10–20%, depending on the value of the service; but based on our own scheme, this means average pay-outs per sale are around £150 to £300 – which is a good return for your affiliates as a passive income that adds to their current revenue streams.

I would suggest signing up for affiliate schemes so you can see how they work from a participant's point of view (Figure 16.10).

(continued)

FIGURE 16.10   Example affiliate scheme.

Sponsor Step 3: The Brilliant Brand Booster – Alliances

We've covered advertising and affiliate schemes, which provide great amplification and reach to pull through new audiences; now, we will look at alliances – such as powerful partnerships and influencer marketing.

Influencer marketing involves marketing products and services to those who have 'influence' over the things other people buy.

FIGURE 16.11 Example alliance – institutions, associations, and organisations.

Classic examples of powerful partnerships are when you form an alliance with an organisation, institution, or association. For instance, one of our academy's powerful partnerships is with the Chartered Institute of Marketing (Figure 16.11). We are listed on their website and vice versa. We send traffic to each other's websites and we are awarded commendations for achieving outstanding results as a CIM study centre of excellence. We work in partnership for joint gain and look to identify ongoing opportunities to continue the alliance. This provides joint PR opportunities and promotion and the relationship is mutually beneficial.

We have numerous relationships in place; but it is not just organisations that can be influencers: your own customers, suppliers, and employees can act as influencers to promote your business.

This is the simplest, yet hugely effective way, of quickly boosting your brand.

YOUR TURN – TAKE ACTION NOW

Identify **five influencer segments** for your business, looking at types or specific customers, suppliers, and employees.

Then, make a list of **10 organisations, institutions, and associations** that you could spark up alliances with.

Don't forget to look for **individual and brand influencers** that you don't yet have relationships with. These may be much harder to get in

(continued)

place or even get direct contact with. I would suggest you take steps to get yourself on their radar though interacting and engaging with their content, or there could be sponsorship opportunities to align yourself with influencers. Follow influencers, as it's unlikely that they will accept connection requests through LinkedIn.

Influencers in my field are people like Gary Vaynerchuk, and it is unlikely – however hard I try – that he will reach out to me; but I could do his mentor programme and build an alliance and relationship that way. Try and think outside the box, because if you work with an influencer it is impossible not to strike up some form of rapport, plus the investment will pay dividends in terms of just accessing their knowledge and expertise. Just getting a photo with them aligns you to them and is great for promotional use.

Consider getting experts and leaders in your industry on interviews, such as podcasts or YouTube shows. This is feasible and creates very engaging branded content.

SUMMARY

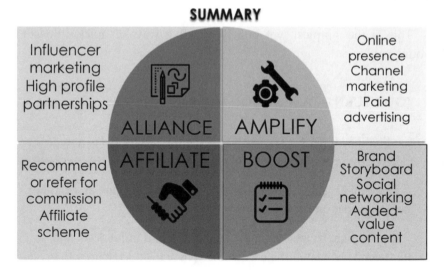

FIGURE 16.12   Summary of The Brilliant Brand Booster.

SPONSOR: CHECKLIST

Check out each social media platform and look at opportunities based on past success stories for your industry.	
Check out affiliate scheme tools by searching Google and evaluating options available.	
Identify alliance opportunities with: influencers such as customers, suppliers, employees, brands, high-profile individuals and leaders in your business and industry, organisations, institutions, and associations.	

Brilliant Brand **Booster**

SUCCESS

AMPLIFY
Strong online presence and channel marketing, amplification and reach to pull through new audiences

BOOST
Strong branding and **storyboard** and **social networking** and added-value **content creation**

AFFILIATE
Influencer marketing and high profile **partnerships**

ALLIANCE **Advocates** who recommend and refer for commission

FIGURE 16.13   The Brilliant Brand Booster Process.

Chapter 17

Strategy – The D.I.R.E.C.T. Digital Dynamo

The D.I.R.E.C.T. Digital Dynamo®

> **D**elve
> **I**nsights
> **R**esearch
> **E**valuate
> **C**reate
> **T**ools

FIGURE 17.1   The D.I.R.E.C.T. Digital Dynamo.

This chapter is about an important part of digital success but an area which is often neglected, with about 50% of businesses not having one. What am I talking about? I am referring to a **digital marketing strategy.**

One of the best ways to succeed in business is by setting out a plan for what you would like to achieve. Throughout this book we have looked at strategy for each of the channels and the actions and specific tactics to succeed for each of these areas. We will take these **communication disciplines** and combine them forming a powerful **integrated digital marketing strategy.**

The danger is that unless you break down actions from your overall strategy into a more manageable and actionable plan, then it will be difficult to implement, manage, and measure results. A strategy should always be broken down, not just into monthly but daily tasks.

We have broken down the elements you need to be able to collate the information required to complete your own digital marketing strategy using our own six-step system: **The D.I.R.E.C.T. Digital Dynamo.**

As part of this process, you will incorporate your strategy into an actual marketing plan which should draw from the overall business plan and goals and should be used as a vehicle to achieve these.

In this chapter, you will learn how to perform a real-world business online audit, carry out practical planning, and review customer behaviour trends using tools to benchmark where you are and the opportunities and threats to address. Our digital marketing strategy template and checklist will help you formulate this into an easy-to-follow plan so you can easily prioritise your daily actions.

'Strategy without tactics is the slowest route to victory.
Tactics without strategy is the noise before defeat.'
Sun Tzu, Chinese general

Strategy Step 1: The D.I.R.E.C.T. Digital Dynamo – Delve

In order to get a complete picture of where the business is, the first stage is an overall audit of all your communication channels and online visibility.

You need to really **delve** into your business's digital marketing effectiveness to get an accurate benchmark of where you are now and what needs to be done to achieve your digital marketing goals.

This activity will really help form the basis and content for your situational analysis when you create your plan.

Digital audits

There are a variety of audit templates that can be used. Some of the most popular are:

1. **SWOT analysis:** looks at the customer perspective of your brand or business (Figure 17.2).

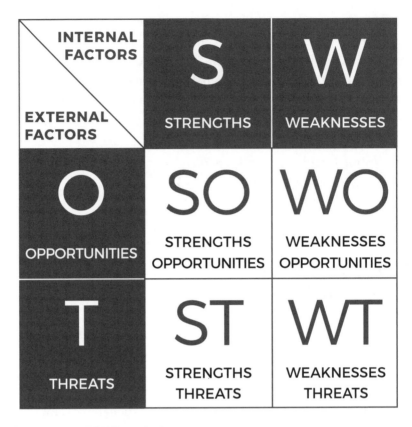

FIGURE 17.2   TOWS analysis.

2. **TOWS analysis:** the analysis of the SWOT for strategy creation.

3. **PESTEL:** market overview including economic factors (Figure 17.3).

4. **Marketing audit:** Internal factors assessing levels of internal communication, customer and prospect research, competitor analysis.

5. **7Ps model:** a critique of the business or brands marketing mix – can be used to set objectives, conduct a SWOT and competitive analysis.

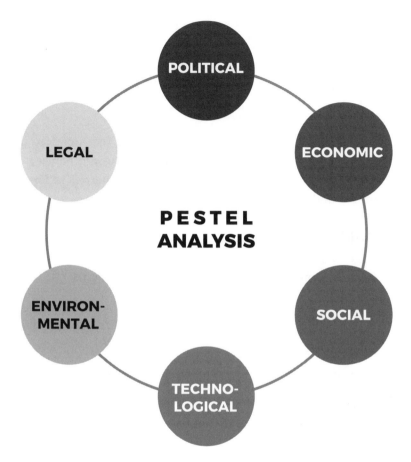

FIGURE 17.3 PESTEL analysis.

SWOT

SWOT is an acronym for:

- **S**trengths

- **W**eaknesses

- **O**pportunities

- **T**hreats.

SWOT was invented in the 1960s by a management consultant named Albert Humphrey and is used as a **situational analysis** for the strategy/business/project you are auditing and analysing.

TOWS

TOWS is a variant of SWOT and was developed by the American international business professor, Heinz Weirich. TOWS would be used after creating a SWOT. Strengths and weaknesses are internal factors; and opportunities and threats are external factors.

The four TOWS strategies:

- Strength/Opportunity (SO): use your strengths to exploit opportunities.

- Weakness/Opportunity (WO): to mitigate weaknesses, to exploit opportunities.

- Strength/Threat (ST): to exploit strengths to overcome any potential threats.

- Weakness/Threat (WT): to minimise any weaknesses to avoid possible threats.

PESTEL

The **PESTEL** model is very useful for identifying the economic factors that will affect the decisions of your company. PESTEL is an acronym for:

- Political factors – government policy, stability, corruption, foreign trade, tax policy, trade laws, or restrictions.

- Economic factors – economic growth, exchange, interest and inflation rates, income, and unemployment.

- Social factors – health, safety, population growth, age, cultural barriers, career, and lifestyle attitudes.

- Technological factors – automation, research and development activity, technology incentives, innovation, advancements, and awareness.

- Environmental factors – weather, climate, and climate change.

- Legal factors – discrimination, employment, consumer protection, copyright and patent, and health and safety laws.

Marketing audit

This is a marketing overview of your internal factors assessing levels of internal communication. There are six important areas your audit should cover:

- environment

- strategy

- organisation

- systems

- productivity

- function.

7Ps model: critique of the marketing mix

The 7Ps model was created by E. Jerome McCarthy in 1960 and published in his book *Basic Marketing. A Managerial Approach*. This model really helps evaluate and re-evaluate business activities (Figure 17.4).

Companies can use the 7Ps model to set objectives, conduct a SWOT analysis, and undertake competitive analysis.

FIGURE 17.4 7Ps marketing mix.

1. **Price:** looks at reduction of costs through improving manufacturing and efficiency, and increasing the perceived value of the benefits for the product or service.

2. **Place:** how products or services are provided to the user or consumer.

3. **Product:** the products or services that customers need that you will sell.

4. **Promotion:** the communications mix; such as, sales, advertising, sales promotion, public relations, direct marketing, online communications, and personal selling.

5. **Process:** the organisation personnel, service delivery of the product or service, and operating systems for the business.

6. **People:** customer experience, service, and support.

7. **Physical evidence:** the business buildings, equipment, signs and logos, annual accounts and business reports, brochures, your website, and business cards etc.

8. **Productivity:** the 7Ps is sometimes extended to 8 to adapt to more service-based businesses. This element encompasses performance and focuses on the ability to deliver to customers. Productivity combined with supplying the best quality.

YOUR TURN – TAKE ACTION NOW

Conduct a 7 or 8P audit for your business activities and record your observations.

Price	
Place	
Product	
Promotion	
Process	
People	
Physical evidence	
Productivity	

Strategy Step 2: The D.I.R.E.C.T. Digital Dynamo – Insights

When faced with metrics and large chunks of data, it is easy to get overwhelmed by what, when, and how to measure – never mind actually drawing tangible insights from your reports.

Customer insight tools

- **In-platform and website analytics:** Tools such as Google Analytics, social media platforms, email marketing dashboards, etc.

- **SEO tools:** Google Search Console and SEO tools for research and monitoring.

- **Google Trends:** See what's hot and trending on the internet and predictions for the future.

- **Google Think Insights:** The latest marketing research and digital trends from Google.

- **Predictive search:** Use Google Search to see the most popular searches.

- **Shopping insights:** See trends across the internet for shopping behaviour.

- **Google Surveys:** Google's market research tool to survey internet users, target your audience, create your questions, and pay for responses.

Your research will need to include **external insights (competitor research)** as well as using **internal data sources,** such as reviewing insights from internal reporting for customer and prospect research.

The process of understanding your market will involve you drawing on both **primary research** (data that has not been collected before) and **secondary research** (existing data that has already been produced).

There are two methods of research that you can use for collecting new data for your primary research:

- **Qualitative research,** which is used for gaining an understanding of underlying reasons, opinions, and motivations – typically from a smaller sample. **Examples:** focus groups (group discussions), individual interviews, and participation/observations, etc.

- **Quantitative research,** which is used to quantify attitudes, opinions, and behaviour from a larger sample. **Examples:** surveys, face-to-face and telephone interviews, online polls, etc.

YOUR TURN – TAKE ACTION NOW

Test out the customer insight tools and record your results, which will help you make accurate predictions about customer needs and preferences; you need to collect consumer data at various points throughout the sales cycle.

These insights, observations, and research are all useful when profiling your ideal customer and mapping your customer journey.

Customer insights should unveil some important trends and opportunities that you will use to develop your digital strategy.

You can add all of your audit findings into your SWOT (use Figure 17.5 as a template), which can then be used to set the scene of where your business is and develop your digital strategy.

- **Strengths example:** Good online presence in Google for key products, services, brands.

- **Weaknesses example:** Flagship products or services don't present in Google under searches.

- **Opportunities example:** Create online video, do live video through social media channels.

- **Threats example:** Competitor is dominating digital channels.

(continued)

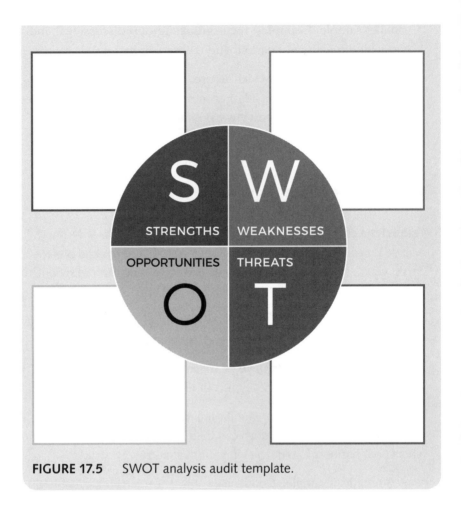

FIGURE 17.5　SWOT analysis audit template.

Strategy Step 3: The D.I.R.E.C.T. Digital Dynamo – Research

After you have performed an audit, it is important to review your findings and continue to research the broader picture outside your business as well as competition – including consumer trends, insights, new technologies, and tools – that may impact on your business or that you may wish to implement in the business.

This is the deeper research that needs to be undertaken from your SWOT analysis findings.

Use the following information to evaluate your positioning within the market:

1. case studies and success stories;

2. digital marketing best practices;

3. areas that require change;

4. analysis of financial data from past years;

5. factors directly affecting profit;

6. research growth opportunities.

Record your research against each of your strengths, weaknesses, opportunities, and threats to add more detail to your SWOT analysis.

It is now time to start thinking about your digital strategy and the **RACE Digital Marketing Planning Framework** (Figure 17.6) was developed by SmartInsights to help you analyse the full customer lifecycle or marketing funnel.

This is a strategic planning process and RACE is an acronym formed of the four stages that define this model (Reach, Act, Convert, Engage).

- **Reach** – Building awareness using online marketing techniques which will drive visits to your site.

- **Act** – Encouraging interactions on your website or social media to help you generate leads.

- **Convert** – Re-targeting and nurturing leads to convert into profitable customers.

- **Engage** – Increasing sales from existing customers.

RACE Planning Framework

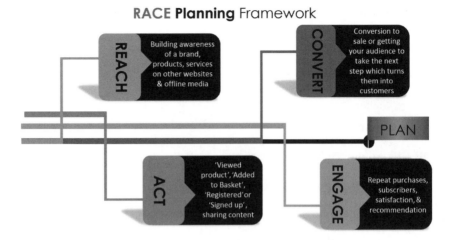

FIGURE 17.6   RACE Digital Marketing Planning Framework.

Use key performance indicators (KPIs) at each of the four touchpoints to evaluate your marketing, which will help create the specific tactics for your digital marketing plan.

YOUR TURN – TAKE ACTION NOW

Perform a **digital marketing audit** paying particular attention to the **RACE Planning Framework.** Look at how well you are using each channel to reach your audience, generate leads, convert customers, and engage existing customers. Figure 17.7 shows an example.

TIP:

Look at all digital marketing channels and compare against competitors.

Digital Marketing Audit
Record Strengths, Weaknesses, Opportunities & Threats every week, month, quarter & year

Search Engine Optimisation / Keyword Research	Blogging / News / Online PR
S	S
W	W
O	O
T	T
Content Creation: Video / Guides / Templates etc	**Social Media**
S	S
W	W
O	O
T	T
Advertising: Third Party, Social, Google	**Website / Mobile**
S	S
W	W
O	O
T	T
Email Marketing	**Notes / Results**
S	
W	Volume - Traffic
O	Quality - Leads
T	Value - Conversion

FIGURE 17.7 Example of a digital marketing audit.

Strategy Step 4: The D.I.R.E.C.T. Digital Dynamo – Evaluate

Evaluate your entire audit's findings. Before creating your digital marketing plan, you will need to be clear on the following elements.

- Establish digital marketing goals.

- Determine your customer base (avatar and personas).

- Understand customer pain points.

- Craft a value proposition.

- Determine how much business you want to generate.

- Align your internal growth strategy with your lead strategy.

- Evaluate SEO, email, affiliate marketing, inbound marketing, and online advertising.

- Review required resources and training.

- Set your budget.

YOUR TURN – TAKE ACTION NOW

Once you have a clear evaluation of your current position then the next step is to start looking at your overall business goals and the current gap in achieving them. This will form the basis of your strategy for your digital marketing plan.

If you have a team, then present your findings and the opportunities you believe exist.

Strategy Step 5: The D.I.R.E.C.T. Digital Dynamo – Create

Once you've defined each element in Figure 17.8, you have all the information you need to create your **digital marketing plan.**

A goal without a plan is just a wish!

A digital marketing plan will include information such as:

- Short-, medium-, and long-term business goals.

- Strategies to achieve the goals.

- Channels to use.

- Action plans.

FIGURE 17.8 Defining goals, objectives, and critical success factors.

- Investment and budget.

- Timing and roadmap.

In marketing, a popular framework used to assist with marketing planning is the **SOSTAC®** marketing model, created by P.R. Smith, originally developed in the 1990s.

SOSTAC® stands for:

- **Situation** – where are we now?

- **Objectives** – where do we want to be?

- **Strategy** – how do we get there?

- **Tactics** – how exactly do we get there?

- **Action** – what is our plan?

- **Control** – did we get there?

SOSTAC® digital marketing plan

Situation analysis

This utilises the findings from your **audit** – looking at where your business is now. This will consider customer reviews, brand perception, the platform/s used, customer personas and insights, SWOT analysis, competitor analysis, internal and external capabilities, and the digital marketing channels landscape.

Objectives

Use SMART objectives (specific, measurable, attainable, relevant, and time-based goals).

Goal setting: P.R. Smith developed the 5Ss of digital marketing around 2000, to assist in setting goals. Use these checkpoints to ensure your goals, and then objectives, have a meaningful business outcome that doesn't just relate to sales but the whole organisation.

1. **Sell:** grow sales.

2. **Speak:** get closer to customers through dialogue and participation.

3. **Serve:** add value.

4. **Save:** save costs.

5. **Sizzle:** positive brand experience.

Strategy

This looks at how you get there, in terms of fulfilling your objectives, and will include:

- **Segmenting your target audience:** profile of audiences the company should target.

- **Positioning:** what positioning the business and its products or services should take in the marketplace including **OVP (online value proposition);** what online experiences and content your brand offers.

- **The 7 (or 8) Ps marketing mix to focus on your objectives:** how can they be used to gain competitive advantage.

  o How could products or services be developed?

  o Review pricing and possible competitive strategies.

  o Where are you and where could you be selling your products or services?

  o Physical evidence – the experience your customers have of your brand and your service and how this could be improved.

  o Do the people who represent your brand or service need extra support or training?

  o How can you adapt processes to increase sales and maintain customer relationships?

  o What are the marketing promotion and marketing communications tactics you will need to implement to meet your objectives?

Tactics

Here you need details of strategy tactics for individual marketing communication channels, e.g. SEO, Ad Words, email, etc. (Figure 17.9).

Using marketing tactics without a marketing strategy is pointless

Strategy example

Tactic 1: SEO

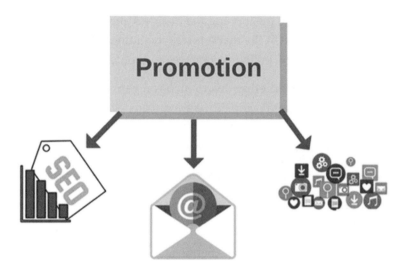

FIGURE 17.9 Develop a strategy to promote your business across online channels.

Actions: details of tactics – who does what and when considering internal and external resources and skills, processes and systems (often displayed in a Gantt chart – Figure 17.10).

Actions for Tactic 1: SEO

keyword analysis

on-page optimisation and content

link building.

Control

Measuring results and KPIs so you know whether you are moving towards achieving your objectives. **Create KPIs for each tactic** that link back to objectives, and then use monitoring dashboards to track progress and performance.

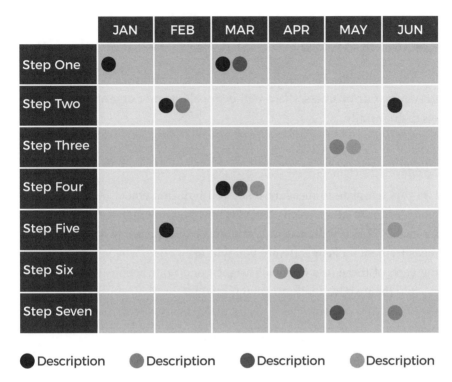

	JAN	FEB	MAR	APR	MAY	JUN
Step One	●		●●			
Step Two		●●				●
Step Three					●●	
Step Four			●●●			
Step Five		●				●
Step Six				●●		
Step Seven					●	●

● Description   ● Description   ● Description   ● Description

FIGURE 17.10   Use a Gantt chart to plan actions and timelines.

Resources

Add the **3Ms** – this incorporates the men and women (do we have the expertise and abilities?), money (do we have the budget?), and minutes (do we have enough time: timescales, schedule, and deadline?).

Budgeting

1. As a general rule of thumb, companies should spend around **5%** of their total revenue on marketing to maintain their current position.

2. Companies looking to grow or gain greater market share should budget a higher percentage – usually around **10%**. This percentage, of course, will vary by company and industry

ROI (return on investment) calculation

Sales Growth – Marketing Cost / Marketing Cost = Return On Investment

Although your marketing efforts will have an impact on scaling and growing your business, there will be an element of organic growth that occurs naturally.

Digital measurement template

Use this template to measure what you will implement (A KPI for each tactic, which relates to each objective) how you will manage (what metrics for each KPI you will measure), and you will measure (what analytics or measurement tools or software you will use). Then, why you are measuring each of these (the tangible insights) and your actions (how you will react to the insights to improve your results).

	Implement	Manage	Measure
What			
How			
Why			

YOUR TURN – TAKE ACTION NOW

Map out your entire digital marketing plan.

Situational Analysis				
Objectives				
Strategy				
Actions				
Control		Implement	Manage	Measure
	What			
	How			
	Why			

Strategy Step 6: The D.I.R.E.C.T. Digital Dynamo – Tools

In this book we cover eight powerful ways to market your business; but it is important that for each strategy you understand each of these in its entirety.

So, here is a quick overview of costs and a glossary of terms.

Digital marketing tools by strategy

- Organic SEO or social media – free – just the resource involved internally or externally.

- Paid advertising and PPC – paid advertising and pay-per-click.

- Email marketing – free, but email marketing platform may have a cost.

- Display retargeting – paid advertising for re-marketing.

- Programmatic advertising – use of software to buy digital advertising.

- Website testing – again, use of software and testing tools may incur a fee.

- Video hosting – free using YouTube.

- Content creation – again, free if creating in-house – just resource cost; but you may choose to use an external agency.

- Content curation – process of gathering information relevant to a particular topic or area of interest; if done in-house – free; or there are paid options available.

- Website analytics – free Google Analytics; but Kissmetrics is a paid option.

- Customer service – software for 'live chat' or messenger marketing chatbots incur fees.

- Search engine optimisation – free, but again SEO tools may incur a fee.

- Affiliate marketing – software tools may incur a fee like 'affiliate pro' and the commission payable for successfully converted affiliate referrals.

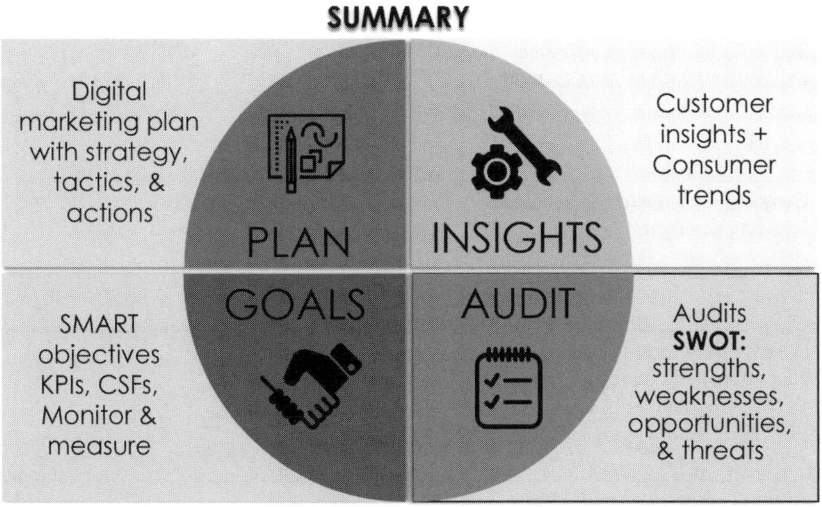

SUMMARY

Digital marketing plan with strategy, tactics, & actions	PLAN	INSIGHTS	Customer insights + Consumer trends
SMART objectives KPIs, CSFs, Monitor & measure	GOALS	AUDIT	Audits **SWOT:** strengths, weaknesses, opportunities, & threats

FIGURE 17.11   Summary of The D.I.R.E.C.T. Digital Dynamo.

STRATEGY: CHECKLIST

Conduct a 7 or 8P audit for your business activities and record your observations.	
Gain customer insights.	
Perform a SWOT analysis.	
Evaluate and research SWOT findings and record against your strengths, weakness, opportunities, and threats.	

RACE Framework – assess your reach, lead generation, sales conversion, and engagement with existing customers.	
Carry out a full digital marketing audit including competitor research.	
Evaluate and create a report containing your entire audit findings.	
Present findings to team for strategy development.	
Collate the information for each element of your digital marketing plan.	
Create KPIs for each tactic.	
Identify metrics for each KPI.	
Review resources – 3Ms, expertise and resource, budgets and timescales.	

Ensure you are recording the information required to calculate your ROI.	
Map out your entire digital marketing plan.	

D.I.R.E.C.T Digital Marketing Dynamo

INSIGHTS
Collect customer insights and look at consumer behaviour trends

AUDIT
Perform an audit such as a SWOT findings and record strengths, weakness, opportunities, and threats

SUCCESS

GOALS
Set overall goals and create SMART objectives and KPIs for each tactic to measure performance and progress

STRATEGY **Create strategy** in digital marketing plan to reach your audience, generate leads, convert sales, and promote engagement with existing customers

FIGURE 17.12   The D.I.R.E.C.T. Digital Dynamo Process.

Chapter 18

Score – The Radical Results Reaper

The Radical Results Reaper®

> **M**etrics
> **M**easure
> **M**onitor
> **M**eaning
> **M**anipulate
> **M**oney

FIGURE 18.1 The Radical Results Reaper.

This final area of digital marketing is about having the right tools, resources, and skills in place to measure and monitor campaign success – to not only achieve goals, but ultimately gain profit too.

I am yet to meet any business that has set up its Google Analytics Account correctly. I see many trying to decipher a monthly report of 20-odd pages versus using daily stats to draw tangible insights to improve marketing campaigns. The main focus when looking at measuring campaign success is asking how does your business **score.**

The questions we are looking at analytics to answer at a high level are:

- Does every digital marketing action we take result in revenue?

- How could we improve and maximise ROI (return on investment)?

- Is our business sustainable and profitable?

Our **Radical Results Reaper** is made up of our six Ms – Metrics, Measure, Monitor, Meaning, Manipulate, Money – and covers:

- What are the key terms relating to measuring campaigns?

- What to measure – why and when?

- What tools can you use to measure?

- Taking data and turning it into marketing actions.

- Testing and improving campaigns.

- Measuring ROI – return on investment.

- How to identify which channel returns the best leads and conversions.

- How to use analytics to ensure you don't go throwing money at channels when you could be optimising current traffic.

Score Step 1: The Radical Results Reaper – Metrics

First, let's look at the key terms relating to measuring campaigns. We are going to cover the essentials terms required in measuring campaign success.

Every campaign must have a **goal** which has a broad outcome: the overall **'what'** you want to achieve.

Here are 10 typical business goals:

1. Increase sales.

2. Build brand awareness.

3. Grow market share.

4. Launch new products or services.

5. Target new customers.

6. Enter new markets internationally or locally.

7. Improve stakeholder relations.

8. Enhance customer relationships.

9. Improve internal communications

10. Increase profit.

FIGURE 18.2 Examples of key performance indicators.

Marketing KPIs will be an essential part of tracking your **marketing** investment. A **key performance indicator** is used to measure performance and success. A KPI needs to be intimately connected with a key business objective (see Figure 18.2 for examples).

A **metric** is just a number within a KPI that helps track performance and progress. So, for each KPI you would measure specific metrics.

Critical success factors (CSFs) are elements that are vital for a strategy or business to be successful. They are indicators for opportunities, activities, or conditions required to achieve an **objective** within a project or mission.

Example:

CSF = what you need to do to be successful
KPI = measure whether you are successful or not.

Typical marketing KPI examples for marketing campaigns:

- sales revenue;

- cost per lead;

- customer acquisition cost (CAC);

- marketing qualified leads (MQL);

- sales qualified leads (SQL);

- customer lifetime value (LTV);

- marketing spend per customer;

- marketing ROI – return on investment;

- traffic-to-lead ratio (new contact rate);

- lead-to-customer ratio;

- landing page conversion rates;

- organic traffic;

- customer engagement and customer retention;

- social media traffic (engagement and conversion rates);

- mobile traffic, leads and engagement, and conversion rates.

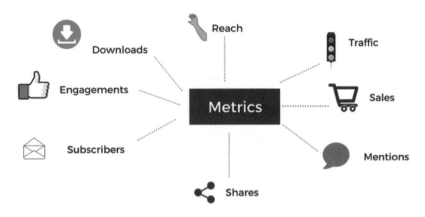

FIGURE 18.3 Examples of metrics.

So, for instance, to calculate **customer lifetime value** you would need to use the following numerical **metrics** (see Figure 18.3 for other examples of metrics to measure) and the equation:

(Average sale per customer) × (Average number of times a customer buys per year) × (Average retention time in months or years for a typical customer)

Vanity metrics are things you can measure that aren't necessarily crucial, and are better combined with other metrics.

EXAMPLE:

The open rate of emails is a vanity metric because it could mean that every time someone clicked on an email in Outlook's viewing panel it marked it open in your email marketing platform analytics. So, looking at the open rate **and click-through rate** would provide a more balanced view.

Objectives and KPIs

Once you have an **overall goal** in mind you will need to develop a strategy to achieve that goal and objectives to achieve the strategy.

The objectives are really the **'how'** you will do it bit.

The **objectives** (not usually more than four) for your business goals must be **measurable**. Using the **S.M.A.R.T. system** will ensure you create effective goals.

S.M.A.R.T. is an acronym for:

1. **Specific** – Create a clear and precise but not ambiguous goal with a specific outcome.

2. **Measurable** – Include a tangible measurement to work towards that indicates success.

3. **Achievable** – Set a milestone that will be challenging but not unrealistic.

4. **Relevant** – Ensure that your goal has a purpose that will be beneficial to the business.

5. **Time-Based** – Specify a period of timeframe you aim to achieve this goal by.

For example, a S.M.A.R.T. objective for the goal 'grow market share' would be:

'Grow market share by 10%, in the UK, for product line XYZ, by the end of the fiscal year.'

So **KPIs** should be focused on **S.M.A.R.T. objectives,** namely **goals** that are specific, measurable, attainable, realistic, and time-based.

Using KPIs as part of writing a S.M.A.R.T. goal helps improve the measurement aspect of the goal, as KPIs are the individual tasks which need to be completed in order to reach your objective. So, for each of your **S.M.A.R.T. objectives** you will need a set of KPIs (three to five) to be able to track your progress and know what is working and what is not.

EXAMPLE

Objective: Decrease employee turnover rate by 25% over the next quarter.

KPI 1: Increase training hours per annum/per employee by 10%.

KPI 2: Increase number of employees who can communicate organisational values to 85%.

KPI 3: Reduce time to respond to an internal complaint to 24 hours.

YOUR TURN – TAKE ACTION NOW

So, let's look at market share, which is one of the most popular KPIs that marketers can use in order to judge the effectiveness of marketing campaigns.

You would require the following metrics to calculate market share:

1. Total sales or revenue for the company over a fiscal period for the UK.

2. Total sales or revenue for the industry over a fiscal period for the UK.

Calculate your market share: You can determine a company's market share by dividing its total sales or revenues by the industry's total sales over a fiscal period.

Score Step 2: The Radical Results Reaper – Measure

Now let's look at what to measure – the why and when.

For any marketing campaign you will need tools or software in place – often referred to as analytics – to measure the metrics for your KPIs.

Marketing analytics is the practice of collecting, measuring, managing, and analysing marketing performance to maximise its effectiveness and optimise return on investment (ROI).

Basically, analytics tools do the heavy lifting for you when analysing data and metrics, which allows you to manipulate data to view certain segments and also helps identify any trends or patterns.

Measuring will help you:

- see if you are on the right track to achieving your goals;
- see if what you are doing is working;
- know when to adjust your strategy and how;
- know when you have achieved your goal;
- justify your budget;
- justify your investment.

I have seen businesses literally run a campaign over a month and assess the results at the end; but this is quite possibly one of the worst strategies for monitoring that you could ever apply or use in your business. It is important to be dynamic and responsive to the campaign's results and recognise if you are en route to success. For this reason, I would always suggest monitoring results every 24 hours so you can

THE DYNAMIC DIGITAL MARKETING MODEL

easily see the impact specific actions and marketing activities are having on your desired outcomes.

YOUR TURN – TAKE ACTION NOW

Make a list of all the software and platforms used in the business and access the analytics dashboard. Start looking at recording metrics for each channel, such as using your email marketing analytics dashboard so you have a benchmark of where you are now for metrics like open rate, click-through, etc.

Examples of analytics dashboards:

- website analytics;

- email analytics;

- CRM analytics/sales or proposal pipeline analytics;

- marketing funnel analytics;

- landing page analytics;

- Google Search ranking analytics;

- social media analytics.

Score Step 3: The Radical Results Reaper – Monitor

Now let's look at **what tools** you can use to measure your success.

Once you have implemented your campaign and it is running, the ongoing management will include monitoring the results. Effective monitoring of your campaign success should be done through a **marketing dashboard** which is a reporting tool that displays marketing analytics, KPIs, and metrics and consolidates data and displays it in a meaningful way (Figure 18.4).

FIGURE 18.4   Measure data to provide insights.

A marketing dashboard should do the following:

- Show KPIs (key performance indicators).

- Integrate data from various sources and present a consolidated view.

- Provide a way to measure the overall results and investments of your marketing campaigns.

- Provide the ability to measure these metrics and make decisions based on this information.

Google Analytics tends to be the most popular tool: https://analytics. google.com. There are other analytics tools on the market, such as Kissmetrics, but these come at a cost.

Google Analytics ABCs: The most important KPIs:

- **A**cquisition (amount of traffic to your website).

- **B**ehaviour (level of engagement on your website).

- **C**onversions (effectiveness of your website in converting visitors to customers or leads).

YOUR TURN – TAKE ACTION NOW

If you already have Google Analytics, then you can skip the next steps. Otherwise set up Google Analytics to **start analysing acquisition, behaviour, and conversion**.

Google Analytics Quick Set-Up

1. Create an account.

2. Add the name, URL, and industry of your website.

3. Get your custom tracking code which will allow Google Analytics to monitor your website.

TIPS:

Here are five quick tips to help you get the best from Google Analytics.

1. **Set-Up Dashboards:** Create easy-to-follow reports and dash-boards. Go to 'Home Page' > Click on 'Discover' bottom left on desktop > Data Studio > Data Sources > Click Blue + Button Bottom Right to Add a New Source > Select Google Analytics. This uses the same data and just allows you to create custom reports. The Gallery means you can see what others have created and use their templates.

2. **Use 'Google Search Console' Reports:** These are located in **Acquisition > Search Console;** you must turn on data sharing:

Admin > Product Linking > All Products > Make sure Search Console is connected.

3. **Filter traffic from your own business and employees to stop this being included in your date and skewing analytics:** Admin > Filters > Create New > Enter Filter Name (IP) > Exclude Traffic > From IP Address > Enter IP Addresses.

4. **To track Conversion, you must set up Goals:** Admin > Goal > + New Goal > Goal set-up > Select a template to start with a pre-filled configuration from the list:

   • revenue

   • acquisition

   • enquiry

   • engagement.

   Add Goal Description and type and then details such as URL destination or the funnel steps you want the user to complete.

5. **Insights:** Top right: Use this area to see Analytics Intelligence, such as trends and changes or spikes in traffic.

Score Step 4: The Radical Results Reaper – Meaning

This section is about identifying **which channel** returns the best leads and conversions, and turns data into marketing actions.

According to a report by Forrester, 74% of firms say they want to be data-driven; however, just 29% are successfully transforming analytics data into business actions.

YOUR TURN – TAKE ACTION NOW

Sometimes looking at data is quite daunting, and it can be difficult to then draw any tangible meaning from the reports. Try these tips to visualise your data in order to draw meaningful insights and trends.

1. If you are using Google Analytics, the **'Data Studio'** will help visualise data for analysis and not just reporting.

2. On your **'Home'** page navigate to **Discover** > Check out the **Google Analytics Academy** to master analytics in more detail.

3. **Setting up goals to see the full customer journey** from acquisition to conversion will also provide a good view of what is working and what isn't on your site. Once your goals are set, track them under **Conversion** > **Goals** > **Overview.**

4. The **insights** area will help you see trends and break down your data into more meaningful and tangible insights that you can turn into actions.

5. To see which channel returns the best leads and conversions, you can navigate to **Conversions** > **Multi-Channel Funnels** > **Top Conversion Paths.**

6. To see where your website visitors are coming from, how they navigate through your site and where they exit your website, navigate to **Audience** > **Users Flow** to visualise your users' path through your site. In other words, it shows you the exact steps users took to accomplish a task on your site.

7. If you **set clear objectives and KPIs** you should know what metrics you are looking for; and then it is just a case of looking at where you were and where you are now and how you have improved (or not as the case may be). Then it will come down to testing to try and improve your results.

Score Step 5: The Radical Results Reaper – Manipulate

Now you need to start testing and improving campaigns based on your findings. You wouldn't want to get to the end of a campaign and realise you could have changed and shaped the results for better returns on investments or reaped better results in terms of achieving your goals and objectives.

There may be trends that start to appear or spikes of activities that can be clearly seen by viewing small increments of data and metrics.

Once you are tracking goal conversion, a great way to use the data is to look at conversion rate percentage, then optimise and promote your high converting pages.

- **Conversion rate calculation:** All you have to do is divide the number of conversions you get in a given timeframe by the total number of people who visited your site or landing page and multiply it by 100%.

- **A/B testing**: for instance, testing performance on desktop versus mobile. We covered A/B testing in Chapter 11, but this means testing how specific webpages or landing pages convert. For example, if someone lands on a page, how effective is the content in getting them to complete the goal of that page?

Many businesses use data to support their decisions instead of driving their actions, but data is only valuable if you can translate it into actionable insights.

You need to figure out what you want from your data so you can take action. Once you have your data presented visually it is much easier to

FIGURE 18.5 Measure data and visualise information to gain insights.

translate, but you need to remember to relate it back to the bigger goal and objective (Figure 18.5).

- **Data:** raw and unprocessed facts. Data can be quantitative (measured) or qualitative (observed).

- **Information:** visualisation in the form of reports and dashboards.

- **Insights:** analysing and forming conclusions. Insights that can then influence decisions and drive change.

If, for example, you collected data about your sleep and saw a report over a week that said you slept on average 6 hours – and you know the average or target sleep per night is 8 hours – then you can conclude you need more sleep. The action would then be to try methods to increase the amount of sleep.

'Measurement is fabulous. Unless you're busy measuring what's easy to measure as opposed to what's important.'
Seth Godin, author and entrepreneur

YOUR TURN – TAKE ACTION NOW

Get to grips with data, information, insights, and actions

Step 1: Access your analytics dashboard and identify data you want to analyse – this could be an email marketing dashboard and an email campaign.

Step 2: Pull a report and view this information – such as an email campaign report.

Step 3: Analyse the information and draw a conclusion considering the goal and benchmarks, etc. It might be that you had an open rate target of 20% and you reached 15%, in which case your actions would be around improving this through testing etc.

Score Step 6: The Radical Results Reaper – Money

Analytics will make sure you don't throw money at new channels when you could be optimising your current successful channels or web traffic. You can see exactly which channels feed your conversion and you can look to optimise and improve these channels.

Acquisition > Behaviour > Conversion

Rather than just focusing on what you will spend and looking at budgets, you should also be constantly striving to improve return on investment. An important factor here is saving money and reducing costs.

Five ways to cut marketing costs without losing business

- **Repurpose** content and campaigns.

- **Customer insight** to target the right customers and re-marketing – which gets on average 70% better conversion and is much cheaper when looking at advertising spend.

- **Advertise online** and leverage publicity opportunities online.

- **Nurture** what you've got and increase conversion, as it's not just about increasing inbound leads or traffic – you need to optimise conversion of existing traffic.

YOUR TURN – TAKE ACTION NOW

A quick money saving exercise: Use analytics to identify your top performing channels for conversion.

- Look at how you are getting that traffic; for instance, is it free (organic) or paid (advertising)?

- Identify the average cost per conversion across all channels and aim to reduce all channels to that price point.

- Also, find the top performing paid channel and, if it is advertising, implement an A/B test to see if you can optimise spend.

- Then, look at the top performing free traffic channel and look at incorporating what you are doing there across paid channels to compensate spend – and ultimately look to reduce paid spend as you may increase free traffic from that channel.

- Last, review the five ways to reduce costs and look at ways you can adopt these into your business.

- **Proven strategies** – because self-taught is fine, but productivity equals profit and using the right tools and techniques from the start will save time, money, and effort. Utilise trends to gain competitor advantage.

SUMMARY

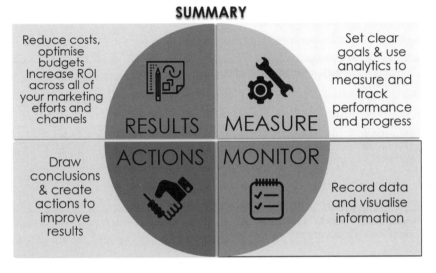

FIGURE 18.6   Summary of The Radical Results Reaper.

SCORE: CHECKLIST

Try and calculate your market share.	
Make a list of all the software and platforms used in the business and access the analytics dashboard and start looking at recording metrics for each channel.	

Set up Google Analytics and ensure settings are pulling the information you need into view.	
Take your data and turn your information into visual reports and dashboards.	
Get to grips with data, information, insights, and actions.	
Use analytics to identify your top performing channels for conversion.	
Review the five ways to reduce costs and look at ways you can adopt these into your business.	

Radical Results **Reaper**

MEASURE
Clear metrics per KPI per tactic for the strategy that you have in place to achieve your goals and objectives

MONITOR
Use analytics to measure and track results and optimise results for digital campaigns

SUCCESS

MANIPULATE
Use data, information, and insights to develop tangible actions to improve performance

MONEY
Reduce costs and optimise budget to get the best return on investment across all of your marketing efforts and channels

FIGURE 18.7 The Radical Results Reaper Process.

Chapter 19

The Digital Challenge

We practise what we preach, and there is no better way to show you the sort of results you can expect to achieve through implementing our proven strategies that we cover in this book than by showing you the exact campaign, step-by-step, that we used to increase our customer base by over 10% in just 30 days.

What makes this strategy even better is the simplicity of it. A beginner or professional marketer could implement the campaign in a matter of days and achieve amazing results.

Case Study: How Business Consort got an 11% increase in customer base in just 30 days

I'd like to share our '30-Day Digital Challenge' campaign, which was a campaign in which we hosted 10-minute live video tips every day for a month through Facebook, then shared the content across an array of platforms, and gained an 11% increase in customer base and more.

You can see the content live online in Google Search and engage with the content on our site and channels. You'll not only get a flavour for the

30 DAY
DIGITAL CHALLENGE
Get 30 free daily digital tips

Dawn McGruer MCIM FRSA
Digital Marketing Speaker,
Author and Trainer

Take the
challenge

FIGURE 19.1   Example of The Digital Challenge branding.

campaign content, but can also take the challenge and learn from the 30 days of tips to reap similar results (Figure 19.1).

I am going to share every step of what we did and how we did it, from developing the initial concept and idea for the digital marketing campaign through to completion.

So, we always start a campaign with a brainstorming session, and we use a pretty simple template to get the idea going.

We use the five Ws to start the process of campaign planning.

1. Who
2. What
3. Why
4. When
5. Where.

WHO is the campaign audience?

- So, for this campaign, we were looking at our persona **'Marie the Marketing Manager'** who is responsible for creating, managing, and measuring marketing campaigns.

- She needs to ensure her strategic efforts are getting a return on investment and her team or agency are getting the best results for her budget.

- She needs to make sure the campaign helps her achieve her goals and objectives and increases her organisation's online visibility.

- Then she takes those ideas away and researches to get clarity on what the best opportunities are based on her customer needs and current trends.

- Her biggest challenge is knowing the best strategy that guarantees fast, effective, and cost-efficient results.

WHAT were we going to do and what was the campaign's purpose?

- The reason we were creating this campaign was that we were launching our new online fast-track course, but we didn't want to just take the traditional route of announcing and unveiling our course.

- We knew that would work and we'd get sales – after all we are established, have a good online presence, and have a customer base of over 25 000 as well as 5 million subscribers.

- But we didn't just want a boost; we wanted a massive buzz that was so big it got big results. We really wanted something that would last and wasn't forgotten about after a few days or weeks.

- We wanted a hard-hitting campaign that everyone would be talking about and getting involved with.

- So, we formed our **campaign objectives** – which were to reach more of our audience, get them to take action, as well as engaging our existing customers. Which meant we had to think of an idea that would promote audience participation.

So, how could we get this with a launch?

Well the concept we know works amazingly well is always social selling. We wanted to create content that combined inbound and outbound marketing but never sold or spoke about our launch.

The reason behind this was the fact that we knew that for all of our online courses, when someone sees the content or experiences training from us – either online through webinars or taster content or face-to-face at courses or events – we have a really high conversion and repeat and referral business rate.

So, we decided to **create a challenge to empower our audience** to get involved and use the tips we would be giving throughout the challenge to generate real results for their business covering all aspects of digital marketing.

How could we replicate current conversion strategies through an online campaign?

We decided the best way to do this was through bite-size, easy to consume and implement, live learning.

We'd focus on lunchtime learning to capture people's attention during lunch breaks; but also record the content for those who couldn't make it.

We'd share this content across all of our channels and we'd give our subscribers and group members more value through providing the recordings which they could access anywhere and anytime.

Then we started to think bigger: we wanted multiple campaign success factors. We started to think about the stages of the campaign and what people could do during and after.

How did we decide what the videos would be about for the campaign?

Regarding the topics for the videos, we first decided on the main categories for our industry, such as social media, email marketing, content marketing, etc.

We then heavily researched **demand** and what specific questions our audience were searching for using Google Search suggestions and key-word planner tools.

We came up with lots of topics and turned these into crunchy headlines.

WHY were we doing the campaign? Who were our audience and what were our desired outcomes?

We needed to think about what we ultimately wanted the campaign to achieve; why the audience would care; what they would get out of it; and why it would ultimately give us a return on investment and make us money.

The campaign could have multiple outcomes:

- reach more of our audience through video views and web traffic;

- generate leads and grow our Facebook Group;

- convert customers and get repeat business;

- engage and reward our current audience, customers, and subscribers.

But when we were creating our campaign, we needed a really compelling and current reason that involved not only helping our audience but contributing to a higher cause. And this is where campaign success will primarily stem from. This is what makes your campaign press-worthy and is the critical success factor for gaining reach through influencers and news outlets.

This is where many campaigns fail, because a business sets out to market their business for the sole purpose of selling. And this is also where you can make your campaign really stand out from the crowd and gather momentum.

You need to find a back story, something that is happening in your niche or industry that is impacting on the masses, such as the economy, etc. At the time we were researching, Damien Hinds, the then Education Secretary, had announced that we were facing a huge digital skills gap and that hundreds of thousands of jobs would go unfilled if we didn't address the issue and upskill the youth of today.

This was a perfect lead in to find statistics to support this and then base our entire campaign around this story. So, our campaign would help bridge this gap through developing digital skills in business for all age ranges and levels of expertise.

Never skip this step because, as you know, storytelling is memorable and powerful. As you aren't promoting or selling anything, there is no reason people wouldn't advocate the campaign and share it or cover it in their publications.

WHEN would we run the campaign? And how long would the campaign run for?

We planned around holidays and decided on March – which is my birthday month and meant we could celebrate this in one of our campaign videos too.

We took the decision to run it for 30 days, because we literally had so many ideas. And we set some quite high targets with a view that the content could be repurposed for months to come.

We started a week in advance talking about the 'challenge with digital' – as keeping people's interest for any longer than this tends to be too much – and announced it through a press release and live video across all channels.

About a week in advance of this, we launched to influencers to gain momentum and buy-in to help us with reach.

Then, at the campaign start, every day at 1 p.m. I went live for 10 minutes through Facebook using BeLive TV to schedule and manage the broadcast.

WHERE would we run the campaign?

Marie our Marketing Manager persona was a 'business professional' – so wouldn't LinkedIn be the best platform?

Many would think so; but we wanted to prove something to the many people who still believe Facebook isn't for business audiences.

We wanted to show that as a B2B organisation (we are also B2C but for this persona our focus was business-to-business) we could reach our target business. Remember that business people are also consumers and have a personal life too; and that outside their job they may engage in consumer activities.

So, did Marie hang out on Facebook?

Well, bearing in mind our age range was 25–55 for this persona – and that's Facebook's main demographic – we just needed to find out if we could reach her through targeting. Was there an audience that matched Marie's interests on Facebook?

The answer was a resounding yes.

We used our Facebook page to determine how we could reach this audience and what its potential size was. We searched for all the sites, interests, books, associations, institutes, organisations, etc. that we knew Marie our Marketing Manager persona used as sources of information.

And then we decided to challenge the common misconception on reaching business consumers and use Facebook as opposed to the more obvious LinkedIn.

I can honestly say that the decision was the best we made as we were then able to use it as a business case to educate the non-converted.

WHAT were the processes to manage the campaign?

- We used my Facebook profile and our company page as well as Facebook advertising.

- We would also take the video once the live feed had finished, save it, and download it.

- We then uploaded it to YouTube, optimised it for Google Search, and used **YouTube** auto-transcribe so our viewers had subtitles and didn't need to have volume when watching.

- We set up a YouTube playlist for the challenge so people could watch in order.

- We embedded it on our blog and used the transcription for the article text.

- We set up Google alerts for each blog so we knew when it appeared in Google Search engine results and we tracked ranking. We linked each article to the next.

- We downloaded the srt.file from YouTube and went back to Facebook where our video was and edited it so we could add the subtitles. We then uploaded the video onto our Facebook Page and shared it.

- Then we uploaded it natively to all social platforms and shared it.

- For all of our group members, we added the recordings.

- We encouraged everyone to join the group on our videos, as well as engaging, liking, sharing, and commenting, subscribing to social and YouTube channels and our blog, and signing-up through landing pages with the added incentive of getting a free guide for the entire 30 days of tips. These multiple calls to action allowed us to easily see what people were engaging in.

- We emailed all challenge subscribers to motivate them to tell us how they were doing by replying to emails and to remind them to join.

- We also encouraged people to tell us their problems and ask for content they wanted so we could be dynamic and include personalised content for our audience.

- We scheduled live streaming video using BeLive TV to ensure people were notified in advance and all the way up to the live video.

And it wasn't until day 30 that we announced the launch of our new programme in one sentence at the end of the video, simply saying 'if you have enjoyed the 30 days of tips then why not join our new fast track programme'.

Daily we measured (just using an Excel spreadsheet):

views, live and recorded, on Facebook;

YouTube views and channel subscribers;

engagement: comments, likes, shares;

email subscribers through the 'join the Challenge' landing page (incentive of free guide and entire 30 days of tips videos);

new blog subscribers;

new Facebook group members.

We could easily see day by day the increases and take those metrics and turn them into tangible insights to adapt to any trends that were impacting on results.

Campaign template

- **Name:** 30 Day Digital Challenge.

- **Theme:** 30 days of digital marketing tips.

- **Back story:** Damien Hinds, Education Secretary (skills gap) National Stats office 750K jobs unfilled by 2020.

- **What:** 30 days of live video, YouTube, Blog, social snippets, ads.

- **How:** Reach, act: group, comment, like, share, watch, download pdf guide, join challenge, podcast, traffic; convert: sales; engage: customers.

- **Why:** Targets – 1 million video views, 10% increase in traffic, 10% increase of social network audience and engagement, 10% increase in daily leads and sales. Repeat business increase of 10%.

Results: proven campaign tactics

Let's look at the exact results at each stage of the campaign and detail what tactics were critical to the success of the campaign.

1. **REACH:** The objective was 1 million video views – this is still GROWING – and increased web traffic by 27% within a week. Massive brand awareness.

2. **ACT:** We doubled our engagement (comment, like, share, follow) on the first day and this sky-rocketed to over 1000%; doubled group members; tripled our blog and email subscribers; and we were getting over 250 leads a day into our nurture series direct to the team.

3. **CONVERT:** Customer base increase of 11% (over 2500 new customers) and we never mentioned selling throughout the campaign! Launched our NEW Online Fast Track Course – 100 conversions within 60 minutes of its first mention!

4. **ENGAGE:** Built relationships with current customers – we also increased referrals and recommendations and repeat business by 10%.

Content

- **30 Days LIVE on Facebook** – Market research topics trending to match demand.

- **Digital assets:** Five hours of video made into 'Digital Marketing Made Easy – Podcast' and course content.

- **Digital presence** in Google – Blogs with Video, Facebook Group content, and still capturing sign-ups for the Challenge content PDF guide; increase of social media audience and YouTube audience.

YOUR TURN – TAKE ACTION NOW

Ready to revolutionise your digital marketing? . . . Then why don't you take our 30-Day Digital Challenge?

* **Just Google 'Business Consort Digital Challenge' to join.**

Using our campaign template and brief, it is time for you to create your campaign. Creating a digital marketing plan covers any period from now to 12 months, but campaigns will normally be drawn every month from the overall plan to achieve the goals and objectives for the strategy.

Campaign Brief

* Name:

* Theme:

* Back story:

* What:

* How:

* Why:

Chapter 20

Digital marketing success stories

FIGURE 20.1 Business Consort Academy has trained and certified over 25 000 students.

Sarah McDermott: Property investor, portfolio builder, entrepreneur.

'Dawn is exceptionally knowledgeable in this field. What she doesn't know really isn't worth knowing. She's also a **wonderfully engaging speaker** and teacher.

We are now implementing the insider tricks and systems that we learnt on the course, and have already had **successful results in just a couple of weeks**.

I would highly recommend Dawn's courses for the relatively low cost of the course, **the value for money was outstanding for the content,** the after support, the high level of speaker. I left feeling empowered and like we had entered a whole new world of digital.

If you're thinking of booking one of **Business Consort Digital & Social Media Academy** courses just do it, you won't regret it!!!'

Barbara Dowell: Marketing Communications Manager at Hitachi Medical Systems UK.

'Digital strategy from the ground roots upwards. But simplified! Easy numerical steps to follow, pain points identified to focus the mind, and solutions that work. Fascinating tips n' tricks and takeaways that perform. Highly motivating and stimulating – Testimony to Dawn's experience, skill, and expertise.'

Jack Biggs: Administrator at The Qualifications Platform Ltd.

'The way Dawn taught the strategy and presented all of the information was excellent. The course was intense in parts but the way she taught it ensured everything was retained. It's almost as if she's presenting you with an arsenal of digital marketing tools and she shows you how you can apply them to work for you. I couldn't recommend Dawn and the courses she provides enough, they're excellent!'

Darius J Ward: Serial Startups.

'After hundreds of hours and thousands of pounds spent on courses, books, manuals & how to guides I was no further forward on knowing the HOW of digital marketing. Whilst I'd learned a lot I still had no clue where to start or WHAT to do. Until I met Dawn that is, absolute clarity, an exact plan of action from 1st step to completion and a clear and concise vision of what I can do, what I need to do and am now going to do with my Digital Marketing path. Just brilliant.' **"Dawn combined the what and how of**

Digital Marketing in perfect symphony. As a result of her guidance and class training, I've become a Certified Digital Professional and secured my first 6-figure contract with a major International company."

Graham Rae: Programme Manager at Warranty Direct at BNP Paribas.

'Great insight from Dawn into the latest Digital Marketing techniques, tools and tips via the Business Consort Digital Marketing course. Informative, engaging and practical. SEO, social media, e-mail, content, ad campaigns, digital strategy, revenue generation in a nutshell. Recommended!'

Neil Walker: Award-winning EMEA channel and partner marketing leader.

'Dawn is an engaging presenter and her insights helped simplify the complexity of "Digital". Dawn's expertise with social media marketing was woven throughout the course and, as a practising marketer, I am looking forward to trying out some of the tools and best practices which Dawn shared.'

Simon Perriton: CEO Just IT Training, Chairman JITR, CEO Skills Team, Joint MD Central Careers Hub.

'Dawn has worked with Just IT for the last 6 months and added great value to the Digital Marketing pathway that we run. She is passionate about her sector and incredibly knowledgeable about all things digital. She has brought people together to facilitate change and Dawn has worked well as a collaborator to innovate with new services which have benefited both candidates and employers.'

Caitlin Holmes: Marketing Coordinator at Connect Childcare.

'I have learned the best ways to use content to engage web visitors and get them on my email list. Dawn shared a brilliant campaign idea with us which I have already added to our digital marketing plan for when we launch. Dawn recommended lots of simple to use tools which will help with anything from metrics tracking, creating videos and even creating graphics for the web, all of which I have already started to use within our business. Not only was the course both fun and challenging but Dawns direct feedback for improving our Digital Marketing Strategy was invaluable. She has a logical method of teaching that really got us all engaged. I can't speak highly enough of this course.'

Fiona Challis: Multi-award-winning speaker, author, channel enablement and sales expert.

'Dawn is truly outstanding to work with! Not only was Dawn a dynamic speaker with excellent presentation skills, she has extensive knowledge and is a true expert in digital marketing and how to drive new lead generation and build lasting relationships with your prospects online. She completely 'wowed' us with the number of online tools and tricks that we can use immediately to grow. However, most importantly she practices what she preaches, hence being ranked number 1 on LinkedIn in her market. This is great social proof that everything Dawn teaches delivers results! She really is a great attribute to any company she works with!'

Helen McCarthy: PR Manager at Sweet Squared.

'I would highly recommend Dawn and her business consort training courses to anybody looking to develop their digital marketing skills, or to train their team to fill in any skills gaps. Dawn is an excellent trainer as her knowledge is extensive and she is a passionate Digital Marketer herself. She also has vast experience of working with a variety of businesses, which means she can guide you through the process of implementing a digital strategy that actually works and will help to grow your business. Having studied part time in the past with a solely academic institution, I chose Business Consort as I wanted a provider with a more commercial and practical approach. I knew Dawn would be able to teach me the skills I needed to generate leads and engage my customers as I could see her using those same techniques as she marketed to me. Having completed 3 face-to-face intensive courses covering digital marketing, email and social media my skills have already vastly improved. I am now studying for the Level 6 CIM Diploma in Digital Marketing with the help of Dawn and the online training portal, which is excellent and easy to use. In the meantime, I have already mastered a range of tools that are helping me to deliver better results for my employer every day.'

Catherine Meardon: Strategic marketing consultant specialising in global brand strategy, digital marketing, and new product development.

'I have also been on four intense digital marketing days with Dawn. All the courses have been really engaging. Dawn is so knowledgeable and experienced in digital marketing techniques and strategies, it is amazing that she shares all this with her candidates. Her courses are really engaging and informative, so I have enjoyed the time in the classroom as well as learning through the online course. The tips that she has shared have really helped my business grow. She is also extremely helpful while you are covering the coursework. I really recommend Dawn's courses and working with her to develop your digital marketing skills.'

Lucy Middleton: Digital marketing and social media marketing consultant.

'Dawn generously shared her social media expertise and passion with me and opened my eyes wide open to some of the best tools and insights across all of the major platforms. I found her training style and content compelling and was gripped for the entire day. I have come away feeling excited to use the knowledge I have gained. I cannot recommend this course highly enough. Thank you for a greedy day of mind-food which I shall be feasting upon within my business!'

Mark Frost: Founder and Director at Gateway Financial Planning Limited.

'Dawn's social media courses are first class. Dawn is up to date on the latest in social media tools and an expert in how businesses can use these tools to improve their business. When you attend a course with Dawn she will focus on how attendees can apply these tools to their own business. Dawn's courses are always a worthwhile investment of time & money.'

FURTHER RESOURCES

What next? Become a digital marketing success story!

YOUR TURN – TAKE ACTION NOW

Get the tools, insights, and inspiration you need to take your marketing to the next level.

Get certified in digital marketing

Complete Business Consort's CIM accredited and certified **Online Fast Track Academy Course.**
Guaranteed to be packed full of tips, trends, and techniques that you can implement straight away!

Develop your digital skills to further maximise your digital marketing profits to scale and grow your business!

Choose to upgrade and add the prestigious **CIM Digital Diploma in Professional Marketing and get ahead in your career. One of the most in-demand qualifications by employers.**

Graduate in as little as 12 weeks with a worldwide recognised professional qualification.

Learn More: https://courses.digitalandsocialmediaacademy.com/ courses/fast-track-digital-marketing

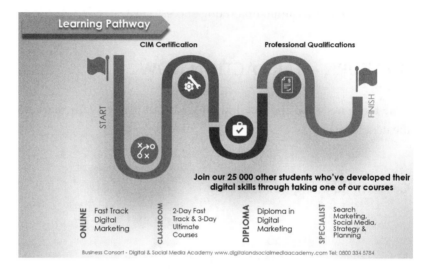

You don't have to do it alone

Connect with me and my academy – Business Consort –I would love to get to know you!

dawn / mcgruer

Dawn McGruer (Author) Website and Social Media Accounts

- Website: www.dawnmcgruer.com

- Email: info@dawnmcgruer.com

- Facebook: https://www.facebook.com/businessconsort

- Twitter: https://twitter.com/dawnmcgruer

- LinkedIn: https://www.linkedin.com/in/businessconsort/

- YouTube: Search 'Dawn McGruer'

- Instagram: https://www.instagram.com/dawnmcgruer/

- Podcast: Dynamic Digital Marketing Show (Available to download in iTunes)

Business Consort (Digital & Social Media Academy) Website and Social Media Accounts

(continued)

- Website: https://www.digitalandsocialmediaacademy.com

- Email: info@digitalandsocialmediaacademy.com

- Facebook: https://business.facebook.com/businessconsortacademy

- Join like-minded professionals in our Facebook Group: Business Consort Brain, Body & Business! https://www.facebook.com/groups/businessconsort/

- Twitter https://twitter.com/businessconsort

- LinkedIn https://www.linkedin.com/school/business-consort-networking-events/

- YouTube: Search 'Business Consort'

- Instagram https://www.instagram.com/businessconsort/

- FREE Stuff: https://www.digitalandsocialmediaacademy.com/free-digital-marketing-guides/

- Podcast: Digital Marketing Made Easy (Available to download in iTunes)

INDEX